C++ For Dummies, 5th Edition

W9-BMD-124

Cheat Sheet

Declarations

Declarations use both intrinsic and user defined types. The intrinsic types are

```
[<signed | unsigned >]char
[<signed | unsigned>] [<short | long>] int
float
double
long double
```

Declarations have one of the following forms:

```
// declaration of a simple variable
[const] type objName [ = expression];
// declaration of a class object
[const] type objName[(argument list)];
// declaration of a function
type fnName([argument list]);
```

Users may also define their own types using the class or struct keywords:

```
    <struct | class> ClassName [ : [public] BaseClass]
{

    public:
      // public data members
      type dataMemberName;
      // public member functions
      type memberFunctionName([arg list]) [{...}]
      // const member function
      type memberFunctionName([arg list]) const [{...}]
      // virtual member functions
      virtual type memberFunctionName([arg list]) [{...}];
      // pure virtual member functions
      virtual type memberFunctionName([arg list]) = 0;
  protected:
    // repeat for any protected members};
};
```

Template declarations have a slightly different format:

```
// type T is provided by the programmer at use
template <class T, {...}> type FunctionName([arg list])
template <class T, {...}> class ClassName { {...} };
```

For Dummies: Bestselling Book Series for Beginners

C++ For Dummies, 5th Edition

Cheat Sheet

Expressions

Expressions have both a value and a type. Expressions take one of the following forms:

```
objName                    // for a simple object
operator expression        // for unary operators
expr1 operator expr2       // for binary operators
expr1 ? expr2 : expr3      // for the ternary operator
funcName([argument list]); // for function calls
```

Operators

	Operator	Cardinality	Associativity
Highest precedence	() [] -> .		left to right
	! ~ + - ++ —— & * (cast) sizeof	unary	left to right
	* / %	binary	left to right
	+ -	binary	left to right
	<< >>	binary	left to right
	< <= > >=	binary	left to right
	== !=	binary	left to right
	&	binary	left to right
	^	binary	left to right
	|	binary	left to right
	&&	binary	left to right
	||	binary	left to right
	?:	ternary	right to left
	= *= /= %= += -= &= ^= |= <<= >>=	binary	right to left
Lowest precedence	,	binary	left to right

For Dummies: Bestselling Book Series for Beginners

by Stephen Randy Davis

WILEY

Wiley Publishing, Inc.

C++ For Dummies®, 5th Edition

Published by
Wiley Publishing, Inc.
111 River Street
Hoboken, NJ 07030-5774

Copyright © 2004 by Wiley Publishing, Inc., Indianapolis, Indiana

Published by Wiley Publishing, Inc., Indianapolis, Indiana

Published simultaneously in Canada

For general information on our other products and services or to obtain technical support, please contact our Customer Care Department within the U.S. at 800-762-2974, outside the U.S. at 317-572-3993, or fax 317-572-4002.

Wiley also publishes its books in a variety of electronic formats. Some content that appears in print may not be available in electronic books.

Library of Congress Control Number: 2004102365

ISBN: 0-7645-6852-3

Manufactured in the United States of America

10 9 8 7 6 5 4 3 2 1

5B/SW/QU/QU/IN

WILEY

About the Author

Stephen R. Davis lives with his wife and son near Dallas, Texas. He and his family have written numerous books including *C++ For Dummies* and *C++ Weekend Crash Course*. Stephen works for L-3 Communications.

Dedication

To my friends and family, who help me be the best Dummy I can be.

Author's Acknowledgments

I find it very strange that only a single name appears on the cover of any book, but especially a book like this. In reality, many people contribute to the creation of a *For Dummies* book. From the beginning, editorial director Mary Corder and my agent, Claudette Moore, were involved in guiding and molding the book's content. During the development of the five editions of this book, I found myself hip-deep in edits, corrections, and suggestions from a group of project editors, copyeditors, and technical reviewers — this book would have been a poorer work but for their involvement. And nothing would have made it into print without the aid of the person who coordinated the first and second editions of the project, Suzanne Thomas. Nevertheless, one name does appear on the cover and that name must take responsibility for any inaccuracies in the text.

I also have to thank my wife, Jenny, and son, Kinsey, for their patience and devotion. I hope we manage to strike a reasonable balance.

Finally, a summary of the animal activity around my house. For those of you who have not read any of my other books, I should warn you that this has become a regular feature of my *For Dummies* books.

My two dogs, Scooter and Trude, continue to do well, although Trude is all but blind now. Our two mini-Rex rabbits, Beavis and Butt-head, passed on to the big meadow in the sky after living in our front yard for almost a year and a half.

If you would like to contact me concerning C++ programming, semi-blind dogs, or free-roaming rabbits, feel free to drop me a line at `srdavis@acm.org`.

Publisher's Acknowledgments

We're proud of this book; please send us your comments through our online registration form located at www.dummies.com/register/.

Some of the people who helped bring this book to market include the following:

Acquisitions, Editorial, and Media Development

Project Editor: Linda Morris

Acquisitions Editor: Katie Feltman

Copy Editor: Melba Hopper

Technical Editor: Wiley-Dreamtech India Pvt Ltd

Editorial Manager: Leah Cameron

Permissions Editor: Laura Moss

Media Development Specialist: Travis Silvers

Media Development Manager: Laura VanWinkle

Media Development Supervisor: Richard Graves

Editorial Assistant: Amanda Foxworth

Cartoons: Rich Tennant, www.the5thwave.com

Production

Project Coordinator: Adrienne Martinez

Layout and Graphics: Amanda Carter, Andrea Dahl, Denny Hager, Michael Kruzil, Lynsey Osborn, Jacque Schneider

Proofreaders: Andy Hollandbeck, Carl Pierce, Dwight Ramsey, TECHBOOKS Production Services

Indexer: TECHBOOKS Production Services

Special Help: Barry Childs-Helton

Publishing and Editorial for Technology Dummies

Richard Swadley, Vice President and Executive Group Publisher

Andy Cummings, Vice President and Publisher

Mary C. Corder, Editorial Director

Publishing for Consumer Dummies

Diane Graves Steele, Vice President and Publisher

Joyce Pepple, Acquisitions Director

Composition Services

Gerry Fahey, Vice President of Production Services

Debbie Stailey, Director of Composition Services

Table of Contents

Introduction

● ●

*W*elcome to *C++ For Dummies,* 5th Edition. Think of this book as C++: *Reader's Digest Edition,* bringing you everything you need to know without the boring stuff.

What's in This Book

C++ For Dummies is an introduction to the C++ language. *C++ For Dummies* starts from the beginning (where else?) and works its way from early concepts and through more sophisticated techniques. It doesn't assume that you have any prior knowledge, at least, not of programming.

C++ For Dummies is rife with examples. Every concept is documented in numerous snippets and several complete programs.

Unlike other C++ programming books, *C++ For Dummies* considers the "why" just as important as the "how." The features of C++ are like pieces of a jigsaw puzzle. Rather than just present the features, I think it's important that you understand how they fit together.

If you don't understand why a particular feature is in the language, you won't truly understand how it works. After you finish this book, you'll be able to write a reasonable C++ program, and, just as important, you'll understand why and how it works.

C++ For Dummies can also be used as a reference: If you want to understand what's going on with all the template stuff, just flip to Chapter 27, and you're there. Each chapter contains necessary references to other earlier chapters in case you don't read the chapters in sequence.

C++ For Dummies is not operating- or system-specific. It is just as useful to Unix or Linux programmers as it is to Windows-based developers. *C++ For Dummies* doesn't cover Windows or .NET programming. You have to master C++ before you can move on to Windows and .NET programming.

What's on the CD

The CD-ROM included with *C++ For Dummies* contains the source code for the examples in this book. This can spare you considerable typing.

Your computer can't execute these or any other C++ program directly. You have to run your C++ programs through a C++ development environment, which spits out an executable program. (Don't worry, this procedure is explained in Chapter 1.)

The programs in *C++ For Dummies* are compatible with any standard C++ environment, but don't worry if you don't already own one. A full-featured C++ environment known as Dev-C++ is contained on the enclosed CD-ROM. You can use this tool to write your own C++ programs as well as explore the programs from the book.

No worries if you already own Visual Studio.NET. Some people need an introduction to C++ before going into the many features offered by .NET. *C++ For Dummies* is just as happy with Visual Studio as it is with its own Dev-C++. *C++ For Dummies* does not contain Visual Studio.NET. However, the programs in the book have been tested for compatibility with the industry standard "unmanaged C++" portion of Visual Studio.NET.

What Is C++?

C++ is an object-oriented, low-level ANSI and ISO standard programming language. As a low-level language similar to and compatible with its predecessor C, C++ can generate very efficient, very fast programs.

As an object-oriented language, C++ has the power and extensibility to write large-scale programs. C++ is one of the most popular programming languages for all types of programs. Most of the programs you use on your PC every day are written in C++.

C++ has been certified as a 99.9 percent pure standard. This makes it a portable language. There is a C++ compiler for every major operating system, and they all support the same C++ language. (Some operating systems support extensions to the basic language, but all support the C++ core.)

Conventions Used in This Book

When I describe a message or information that you see onscreen, it appears like this:

```
Hi mom!
```

In addition, code listings appear as follows:

```
// some program
void main()
{
    ...
}
```

If you are entering these programs by hand, you must enter the text exactly as shown with one exception: The number of spaces is not critical, so don't worry if you enter one too many or one too few spaces.

C++ words are usually based on English words with similar meanings. This can make reading a sentence containing both English and C++ difficult to make out without a little help. To help out, C++ commands and function names appear in a different font `like this`. In addition, function names are always followed by an open and closed parenthesis like `myFavoriteFunction()`. The arguments to the function are left off except when there's a specific need to make them easier to read. It's a lot easier to say: "this is `myFavoriteFunction()`" than "this is `myFavoriteFunction(int, float)`."

Sometimes, the book directs you to use specific keyboard commands. For example, when the text instructs you to press Ctrl+C, it means that you should hold down the Ctrl key while pressing the C key and then release both together. Don't type the plus sign.

Sometimes, I'll tell you to use menu commands, such as File➪Open. This notation means to use the keyboard or mouse to open the File menu and then choose the Open option. Finally, both Dev-C++ and Visual Studio.NET define function keys for certain common operations — unfortunately, they don't use the same function keys. To avoid confusion, I rarely use function keys in the book — I couldn't have kept the two straight anyway.

How This Book Is Organized

Each new feature is introduced by answering the following three questions:

✔ *What* is this new feature?

✔ *Why* was it introduced into the language?

✔ *How* does it work?

Small pieces of code are sprinkled liberally throughout the chapters. Each demonstrates some newly introduced feature or highlights some brilliant point I'm making. These snippets may not be complete and certainly don't do anything meaningful. However, every concept is demonstrated in at least one functional program.

Note: A good programmer doesn't let lines of code extend too far because it makes them hard to read. I have inserted newlines appropriately to limit my programs to the width of the book page.

And There's More

A real-world program can take up lots of pages. However, seeing such a program is an important didactic tool for any reader. I have included a series of programs along with an explanation of how these programs work on the enclosed CD-ROM.

I use one simple example program that I call BUDGET. This program starts life as a simple, functionally-oriented BUDGET1. This program maintains a set of simple checking and savings accounts. The reader is encouraged to review this program at the end of Part II. The subsequent version, BUDGET2, adds the object-oriented concepts presented in Part III. The examples work their way using ever more features of the language, culminating with BUDGET5, which you should review after you master all the chapters in the book. The BUDGET programs can be found on the book's CD-ROM. For a complete overview of the CD-ROM's contents, see this book's Appendix.

Part 1: Introduction to C++ Programming

Part I starts you on your journey. You begin by examining what it means to write a computer program. From there, you step through the syntax of the language (the meaning of the C++ commands).

Part II: Becoming a Functional C++ Programmer

In this part, you expand upon your newly gained knowledge of the basic commands of C++ by adding the capability to bundle sections of C++ code into modules and reusing these modules in programs.

In this section, I also introduce that most dreaded of all topics, the C++ pointer. If you don't know what that means, don't worry — you'll find out soon enough.

Part III: Introduction to Classes

The plot thickens in this part. Part III begins the discussion of object-oriented programming. Object-oriented programming is really the reason for the existence of C++. Take the OO features out of C++, and you're left with its predecessor language, C. I discuss things such as classes, constructors, destructors, and making nachos (I'm not kidding, by the way). Don't worry if you don't know what these concepts are (except for nachos — if you don't know what nachos are, we're in big trouble).

Part IV: Inheritance

Inheritance is where object-oriented programming really comes into its own. Understanding this most important concept is the key to effective C++ programming and the goal of Part IV. There's no going back now — after you've completed this part, you can call yourself an Object-Oriented Programmer, First Class.

Part V: Optional Features

By the time you get to Part V, you know all you need to program effectively in C++. I touch on the remaining features of the language. Features such as file input/output, error-handling constructs, and templates are left to this part.

Part VI: The Part of Tens

What *For Dummies* book would be complete without The Part of Tens? Chapter 29 shows you the top ten best ways to avoid introducing bugs into your programs, bugs that you would otherwise have to ferret out on your own.

Chapter 30 takes you through the most important tools and options in the Dev-C++ environment. Although Dev-C++ is not part of the C++ language, understanding these options enhances your programming experience.

Icons Used in This Book

 This is technical stuff that you can skip on the first reading.

 Tips highlight a point that can save you a lot of time and effort.

 This icon alerts you to examples and software that appear on this book's CD-ROM.

 Remember this. It's important.

 Remember this, too. This one can sneak up on you when you least expect it and generate one of those really hard-to-find bugs.

Where to Go from Here

Finding out about a programming language is not a spectator sport. I'll try to make it as painless as possible, but you have to power up the ol' PC and get down to some serious programming. Limber up the fingers, break the spine on the book so that it lies flat next to the keyboard (and so that you can't take it back to the bookstore), and dive in.

Part I
Introduction to C++ Programming

The 5th Wave   By Rich Tennant

"We've failed to meet our Oct.31 launch date for Treat this year, but we're developing a new more robust version that should be available by the first or second quarter of next year."

In this part . . .

*B*oth the newest, hottest flight simulator and the simplest yet most powerful accounting programs use the same basic building blocks. In this part, you discover the basic features you need to write your killer application.

Chapter 1

Writing Your First C++ Program

• •

• •

*O*kay, so here we are: No one here but just you and me. Nothing left to do but get started. Might as well lay out a few fundamental concepts.

A computer is an amazingly fast but incredibly stupid machine. A computer can do anything you tell it (within reason), but it does *exactly* what it's told — nothing more and nothing less.

Perhaps unfortunately for us, computers don't understand any reasonable human language — they don't speak English either. Okay, I know what you're going to say: "I've seen computers that could understand English." What you really saw was a computer executing a *program* that could meaningfully understand English. (I'm still a little unclear on this computer-understanding-language concept, but then I don't know that my son understands my advice, either, so I'll let it slide.)

Computers understand a language variously known as *computer language* or *machine language*. It's possible but extremely difficult for humans to speak machine language. Therefore, computers and humans have agreed to sort of meet in the middle, using intermediate languages such as C++. Humans can speak C++ (sort of), and C++ is converted into machine language for the computer to understand.

Grasping C++ Concepts

In the early 1970s, a consortium of really clever people worked on a computer system called Multix. The goal of Multix was to give all houses inexpensive computer access to graphics, e-mail, stock data, pornography (just kidding), whatever. Of course, this was a completely crazy idea at the time, and the entire concept failed.

A small team of engineers working for Bell Labs decided to save some portion of Multix in a very small, lightweight operating system that they dubbed Unix (*Un*-ix, the single task version of *Mult*-ix, get it?).

Unfortunately for these engineers, they didn't have one large machine but a number of smaller machines, each from a different manufacturer. The standard development tricks of the day were all machine-dependent — they would have to rewrite the same program for each of the available machines. Instead, these engineers invented a small, powerful language named *C.*

C caught on like wildfire. Eventually, however, new programming techniques (most notably object-oriented programming) left the C programming language behind. Not to be outdone, the engineering community added equivalent new features to the C language. The result was called C++.

The C++ language consists of two basic elements:

✔ **Semantics:** This is a vocabulary of commands that humans can understand and that can be converted into machine language, fairly easily.

and

✔ **Syntax:** This is a language structure (or *grammar*) that allows humans to combine these C++ commands into a program that actually does something (well, *maybe* does something).

Think of the semantics as the building blocks of your C++ program and the syntax as the correct way to put them together.

What's a program?

A C++ program is a text file containing a sequence of C++ commands put together according to the laws of C++ grammar. This text file is known as the *source file* (probably because it's the source of all frustration). A C++ source file carries the extension .CPP just as a Microsoft Word file ends in .DOC or an MS-DOS (remember that?) batch file ends in .BAT. The concept extension .CPP is just a convention.

The point of programming in C++ is to write a sequence of commands that can be converted into a machine-language program that actually *does* what we want done. The resulting *machine-executable* files carry the extension .EXE. The act of creating an executable program from a C++ program is called *compiling* or *building* (the subtle difference between the two is described in Chapter 22).

That sounds easy enough — so what's the big deal? Keep going.

How do I program?

To write a program, you need two specialized computer programs. One (an editor) is what you use to write your code as you build your .CPP source file. The other (a compiler) converts your source file into a machine-executable .EXE file that carries out your real-world commands (open spreadsheet, make rude noise, deflect incoming asteroid, whatever).

Nowadays, tool developers generally combine compiler and editor into a single package — a development *environment*. After you finish entering the commands that make up your program, you need only click a button to create the executable file.

The most popular of all C++ environments is a Microsoft product, Visual C++.NET (pronounced "Visual-C-plus-plus-DOT-net"). All programs in this book compile and execute with Visual C++.NET; however, many of you may not already own Visual C++.NET — and at $250 bucks a pop, street price, this may be a problem.

Fortunately, there *are* public-domain C++ environments. We use one of them in this book — the Dev-CPP environment. A recent version of Dev-CPP environment is included on CD-ROM enclosed at the back of this book (or you can download the *absolutely most recent* version off the Web at www.bloodshed.net).

You can download quite a range of public-domain programs from the Internet. Some of these programs, however, are not free — you're encouraged — or required — to pay some (usually small) fee. You don't *have* to pay to use Dev-C++, but you can contribute to the cause if you like. See the Web site for details.

I have tested the programs in this book with Dev-C++ version 4.9.8.0; they should work with other versions as well. You can check out my Web site at www.stephendavis.com for a list of any problems that may arise with future versions of Dev-C++ or Windows.

Dev-C++ is not some bug-ridden, limited edition C++ compiler from some fly-by-night group of developers. Dev-C++ is a full-fledged C++ environment. Dev-C++ supports the entire C++ language and executes all the programs in this book (and any other C++ book) just fine, thank you.

Dev-C++ does generate Windows-compatible 32-bit programs, but it does not easily support creating programs that have the classic Windows look. If you want to do that, you'll have to break open the wallet and go for a commercial package like Visual Studio.NET. Having said that, I strongly recommend that you work through the examples in this book first to learn C++ *before* you tackle Windows development. They are two separate things and (for the sake of sanity) should remain so in your mind.

Follow the steps in the next section to install Dev-C++ and build your first C++ program. This program's task is to convert a temperature value entered by the user from degrees Celsius to degrees Fahrenheit.

The programs in this book are compatible with Visual C++.NET and the C++ section of Visual Studio.NET (which are essentially the same thing). Use the documentation in the Visual C++ .NET for instructions on installing C++. True, the error messages generated by Visual C++.NET are different (and often just as difficult to decipher), but the territory will seem mysteriously familiar. Even though you're using a different songbook, you shouldn't have much trouble following the tune.

Installing Dev-C++

The CD-ROM that accompanies this book includes the most recent version of the Dev-C++ environment at the time of this writing.

The Dev-C++ environment comes in an easy-to-install, compressed executable file. This executable file is contained in the `DevCPP` directory on the accompanying CD-ROM. Here's the rundown on installing the environment:

1. **Navigate to and double-click the file** `devcpp4980.exe`, **or (in Windows) click Start⇨Run.**

   - Double-clicking the file installs the environment automatically. (Note that 4.9.8.0, the version number, will be different on any newer version of Dev-C++ you downloaded off the Web.)

   - If you clicked Start⇨Run, type **x:\devcpp\devcpp4980** in the Run window that appears, where *x* is the letter designation for your CD-ROM drive (normally **D** but perhaps **E** — if one doesn't work, try the other).

     Dev-C++ begins with a warning (shown in Figure 1-1) that you'd better uninstall any older version of Dev-C++ you may have hanging around, and then reboot and start over. (Starting an installation with a threat is an inauspicious way to begin a relationship, but everything gets better from here.)

Figure 1-1:
You must
uninstall
earlier
versions of
Dev-C++
before you
begin the
installation
process.

2. **If you don't have to uninstall an old version of Dev-C++, skip to Step 4; if you do have to uninstall, abort the current installation process by closing the Run window.**

   Don't get upset if you've never even heard of Dev-C++ and you still get the warning message. It's just a reminder.

3. **Okay, if you're on this step, you're uninstalling: Open the Dev-CPP folder and double-click the** Uninstall.exe **file there.**

   The uninstall program does its thing, preparing the way for the new installation; the End User Legal Agreement (commonly known as the *EULA*) appears.

4. **Read the EULA and then click OK if you can live with its provisions.**

   Nope, the package really won't install itself if you don't accept. Assuming you *do* click OK, Dev-C++ opens the window shown in Figure 1-2 and offers you some installation options. The defaults are innocuous, with two exceptions:

   • You must leave the *Mingw compiler system. . .* option enabled.

   • The *Associate C and C++ Files to Dev-C++* option means that double-clicking a .CPP file automatically opens Dev-C++ rather than some other program (such as Visual C++ .NET, for example). It is possible, but difficult, to undo this association.

   Don't check this option if you also have Visual Studio.NET installed. Dev-C++ and Visual Studio.NET coexist peacefully on the same machine, but what Visual Studio has done, let no man cast assunder. You can still open your .CPP files with Dev-C++ by right-clicking on the file and selecting Open With. Personally, I prefer to use this option, even with Visual Studio.NET installed. It doesn't cause any problems, and Dev-C++ starts a *lot* faster than Visual Studio.

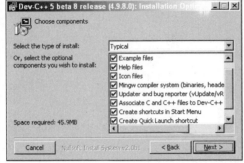

Figure 1-2:
The default
installation
options
should be
acceptable
to most
users.

5. **Click the Next button.**

   The installation program asks where you want it to install Dev-C++, using a message like that shown in Figure 1-3.

Figure 1-3:
The default
location for
the Dev-C++
environment
is provided.

6. **Accept the default directory,** c:\Dev-CPP.

   Don't install Dev-C++ in the directory \Program Files with all the other executables. That's because Dev-C++ doesn't do well with directories that contain spaces in their names. I haven't experimented much along these lines, but I believe you can use any other directory name without any special characters other than '_'. It's safer just to accept the default.

7. **Make sure you have enough room for the program, wherever you decide to put it.**

   The Dev-C++ environment uses only a paltry 45MB, but it's always good practice to check.

8. **Click Install.**

   At first, nothing seems to happen. Then Dev-C++ gets going, copying a whole passel of files to the Dev-CPP directory — putting absolutely nothing in the Windows home directory. Figure 1-4 displays the eventual result.

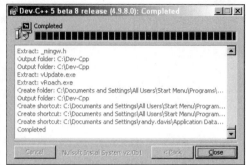

Figure 1-4:
The Dev-
C++
installation
process
unzips a
large
number of
mostly small
files.

While the installation is going on, Dev-C++ presents a window that asks whether you want to *install for all users* once it's done copying files onto your hard drive. That question boils down to this: If someone else logs on to your computer, do you want her or him to be able to execute Dev-C++? (The answer is "Yes" in my case.)

9. **Choose whether you want to install for all users, and then click the Close button to complete installation of the package.**

   Dev-C++ starts immediately, so you can set its options properly for your needs. (Yep, there's more work to do. But you knew that. Read on.)

Setting the options

As you probably know if you've spent more than a coffee break's worth of time installing software, setting options is a procedure unto itself. In this case, Dev-C++ has two options that must be set before you can use it. Set 'em as follows:

1. **Choose Tools⇨Compiler Options.**

   You can change these settings at any time, but now is as good as any.

2. **Choose the Settings tab.**

3. **Choose Code Generation from the menu on the left.**

   Make sure that the Enable Exception Handling is enabled, as shown in Figure 1-5. (If it isn't, click on the option box to display the two choices and select Yes.)

4. **Choose Linker and make sure the Generate Debugging Information option is enabled.**

   Figure 1-6 shows you what to look for.

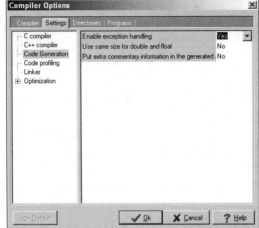

Figure 1-5:
The Enable
Exception
Handling
option must
be enabled.

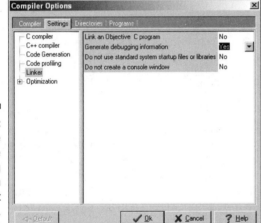

Figure 1-6:
The
Generate
Debugging
Information
option must
be enabled.

5. **Choose OK.**

   Installation is now complete! (Your options are saved automatically.)

Creating Your First C++ Program

In this section, you create your first C++ program. You first enter the C++ code into a file called CONVERT.CPP, and then convert the C++ code into an executable program.

Entering the C++ code

The first step to creating any C++ program is to enter C++ instructions using a text editor. The Dev-C++ user interface is built around a program editor specifically designed to create C++ programs.

1. **Click Start⇨Programs⇨Bloodshed Dev-C++⇨Dev-C++ to start up the Dev-C++ tool.**

   The Dev-C++ interface looks fundamentally like that of any other Windows program — perhaps a little clunkier, but a Windows application nonetheless.

   This is a lot of clicking. My personal preference is to create a shortcut on the desktop. To create a shortcut, double-click My Computer. Now double-click the Local Disk (C:). Finally, double-click Dev-CPP — whew! Right-click the file `devcpp.exe` and choose Create Shortcut from the drop down menu. Drag the `Shortcut to devcpp.exe` file onto your desktop (or some other easily accessible place). From now on, you can just double-click the shortcut to start Dev-C++.

2. **Choose File⇨New⇨Source File.**

   Dev-C++ opens a blank window wherein you get to enter your new code. Don't worry if you find yourself wishing you knew what to enter right now — that's why you bought this book.

3. **Enter the following program exactly as written.**

   Don't worry too much about indentation or spacing — it isn't critical whether a given line is indented two or three spaces, or whether there are one or two spaces between two words. C++ is case sensitive, however, so you need to make sure everything is lowercase.

   You can cheat and copy the `Conversion.cpp` file contained on the enclosed CD-ROM in directory `\CPP_Programs\Chap01`.

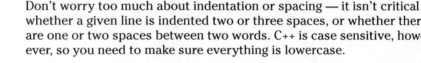

```
//
//   Program to convert temperature from Celsius degree
//   units into Fahrenheit degree units:
//   Fahrenheit = Celsius  * (212 - 32)/100 + 32
//
#include <cstdio>
#include <cstdlib>
#include <iostream>
using namespace std;

int main(int nNumberofArgs, char* pszArgs[])
{
```

```
// enter the temperature in Celsius
int celsius;
cout << "Enter the temperature in Celsius:";
cin >> celsius;

// calculate conversion factor for Celsius
// to Fahrenheit
int factor;
factor = 212 - 32;

// use conversion factor to convert Celsius
// into Fahrenheit values
int fahrenheit;
fahrenheit = factor * celsius/100 + 32;

// output the results (followed by a NewLine)
cout << "Fahrenheit value is:";
cout << fahrenheit << endl;

// wait until user is ready before terminating program
// to allow the user to see the program results
system("PAUSE");
return 0;
}
```

4. **Choose Save As under the File menu. Then type in the program name and press Enter.**

I know that it may not seem all that exciting, but you've just created your first C++ program!

For purposes of this book, I created a folder CPP_Programs. Within this, I created Chap01. Finally, I saved the program with the name Conversion. cpp. Note that Dev-C++ won't work properly with directory names that contain spaces. (It doesn't have a problem with names longer than eight characters in length — thank goodness!)

Building your program

After you've saved your Conversion.cpp C++ source file to disk, it's time to generate the executable machine instructions.

To build your Conversion.cpp program, you choose Execute⇨Compile from the menu or press F9 — or you can even click that cute little icon with four colored squares on the menu bar (use the Tool Tips to see which one I'm talking about). In response, Dev-C++ opens a compiling window. Nothing will happen at first (sshh . . . it's thinking). After a second or two, Dev-C++ seems to take off, compiling your program with gusto. If all goes well, a window like that shown in Figure 1-7 appears.

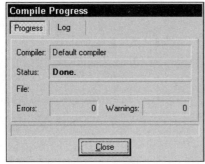

Figure 1-7:
The user is rewarded with a simple Done message if his program is error free.

Dev-C++ generates a message if it finds any type of error in your C++ program — and coding errors are about as common as snow in Alaska. You'll undoubtedly encounter numerous warnings and error messages, probably even when entering the simple `Conversion.cpp`. To demonstrate the error-reporting process, let's change Line 17 from `cin >> celsius;` to `cin >>> celsius;`.

This seems an innocent enough offense — forgivable to you and me perhaps, but not to C++. Dev-C++ opens a Compiler tab, as shown in Figure 1-8. The message `parse error before '>` is perhaps a little terse, but descriptive. To get rid of the message, remove the extra `>` and recompile.

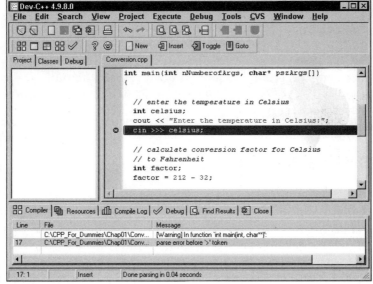

Figure 1-8:
Bad little programs generate error messages in the Compiler window.

Why is C++ so picky?

In the example given here, C++ could tell right away — and without a doubt — that I had screwed up. However, if C++ can figure out what I did wrong, why doesn't it just fix the problem and go on?

The answer is simple but profound. C++ *thinks* that I mistyped the >> symbol, but it may be mistaken. What could have been a mistyped command may actually be some other, completely unrelated error. Had the compiler simply corrected the problem, C++ would have masked the real problem.

Finding an error buried in a program that builds without complaining is difficult and time-consuming. It's far better to let the compiler find the error for you if at all possible. Generating a compiler error is a waste of the computer's time — forcing me to find a mistake that C++ could have caught is a waste of *my* time. Guess which one I vote for?

The term *parse* means to convert the C++ commands into something that the machine-code-generating part of the process can work with.

There was once a language that tried to fix simple mistakes like this for you. From my personal experience, I can tell you it was a waste of time — because (except for very simple cases) the compiler was almost always wrong. At least it warned me of the problem so I could fix it myself.

Executing Your Program

It's now time to execute your new creation . . . that is, to run your program. You will run the CONVERT.EXE program file and give it input to see how well it works.

To execute the Conversion program, click Execute➪Run or press Ctrl+F10. (I have no idea how they selected function keys. I would think that an action as common as executing a program would warrant its own function key — something without a Control or Shift key to hold down — but maybe that's just me.)

A window opens immediately, requesting a temperature in Celsius. Enter a known temperature, such as 100 degrees. After you press Enter, the program returns with the equivalent temperature of 212 degrees Fahrenheit as follows:

```
Enter the temperature in Celsius:100
Fahrenheit value is:212
Press any key to continue . . .
```

The message `Press any key` gives you the opportunity to read what you've entered before it goes away. Press Enter, and the window (along with its contents) disappears. Congratulations! You just entered, built, and executed your first C++ program.

Dev-C++ is not Windows

Notice that Dev-C++ is not truly intended for developing Windows programs. In theory, you can write a Windows application by using Dev-C++, but it isn't easy. (That's *so* much easier in Visual Studio.NET.)

Windows programs show the user a very visually oriented output, all nicely arranged in onscreen windows. Convesion.exe is a 32-bit program that executes *under* Windows, but it's not a "Windows" program in the visual sense.

If you don't know what *32-bit program* means, don't worry about it. As I said earlier, this book isn't about writing Windows programs. The C++ programs you write in this book have a *command line interface* executing within an MS-DOS box.

Budding Windows programmers shouldn't despair — you didn't waste your money. Learning C++ is a prerequisite to writing Windows programs. I think that they should be mastered separately: C++ first, Windows second.

Dev-C++ help

Dev-C++ provides a Help menu item. Choose `Help` followed by `Help on Dev C++` to open up a typical Windows help box. Help is provided on various aspects of the Dev-C++ development package but not much else. Noticeably lacking is help on the C++ language itself. Click a topic of interest to display help.

Reviewing the Annotated Program

Entering data in someone else's program is about as exciting as watching someone else drive a car. You really need to get behind the wheel itself. Programs are a bit like cars as well. All cars are basically the same with small differences and additions — OK, French cars are a lot different than other cars, but the point is still valid. Cars follow the same basic pattern — steering wheel in front of you, seat below you, roof above you and stuff like that.

Similarly, all C++ programs follow a common pattern. This pattern is already present in this very first program. We can review the Conversion program by looking for the elements that are common to all programs.

Examining the framework for all C++ programs

Every C++ program you write for this book uses the same basic framework, which looks a lot like this:

```
//
//   Template - provides a template to be used as the starting
//              point
//
// the following include files define the majority of
// functions that any given program will need
#include <cstdio>
#include <cstdlib>
#include <iostream>
using namespace std;

int main(int nNumberofArgs, char* pszArgs[])
{
    // your C++ code starts here

    // wait until user is ready before terminating program
    // to allow the user to see the program results
    system("PAUSE");
    return 0;
}
```

Without going into all the boring details, execution begins with the code contained in the open and closed braces immediately following the line beginning main( ).

I have copied this code into a file called `Template.cpp` located in the main `CPP_Programs` folder on the enclosed CD-ROM.

Clarifying source code with comments

The first few lines in `Conversion.cpp` appear to be freeform text. Either this code was meant for human eyes or C++ is a lot smarter than I give it credit for. These first six lines are known as comments. *Comments* are the programmer's explanation of what he or she is doing or thinking when writing a particular code segment. The compiler ignores comments. Programmers (*good* programmers, anyway) don't.

A C++ comment begins with a double slash (//) and ends with a newline. You can put any character you want in a comment. A comment may be as long as you want, but it's customary to keep comment lines to no more than 80 characters across. Back in the old days — "old" is relative here — screens were limited to 80 characters in width. Some printers still default to 80 characters across when printing text. These days, keeping a single line to under 80 characters is just a good practical idea (easier to read, less likely to cause eyestrain, the usual).

A newline was known as a *carriage return* back in the days of typewriters — when the act of entering characters into a machine was called *typing* and not *keyboarding*. A *newline* is the character that terminates a command line.

C++ allows a second form of comment in which everything appearing after a /* and before a */ is ignored; however, this form of comment isn't normally used in C++ anymore. (Later in this book, I describe the one case in which this type of comment is applied.)

It may seem odd to have a command in C++ (or any other programming language) that's specifically ignored by the computer. However, all computer languages have some version of the comment. It's critical that the programmer explain what was going through her mind when she wrote the code. A programmer's thoughts may not be obvious to the next colleague who picks up her program and tries to use it or modify it. In fact, the programmer herself may forget what her program meant if she looks at it months after writing the original code and has left no clue.

Basing programs on C++ statements

All C++ programs are based on what are known as C++ *statements*. This section reviews the statements that make up the program framework used by the `Conversion.cpp` program.

A *statement* is a single set of commands. All statements other than comments end with a semicolon. (There's a reason that comments don't end with a semicolon, but it's obscure. To my mind, comments *should* end in semicolons as well, for consistency's sake. Why nobody asked me about that remains a mystery.)

Program execution begins with the first C++ statement after the open brace and continues through the listing, one statement at a time.

As you look through the program, you can see that spaces, tabs, and newlines appear throughout the program. In fact, I place a newline after every statement in this program. These characters are collectively known as *white space* because you can't see them on the monitor.

You may add white space anywhere you like in your program to enhance readability — except in the middle of a word:

```
See wha

t I mean?
```

Although C++ may ignore white space, it doesn't ignore case. In fact, it's case sensitive to the point of obsession. The variable `fullspeed` and the variable `FullSpeed` have nothing to do with each other. While the command `int` may be understood completely, C++ has no idea what `INT` means.

Writing declarations

The line `int nCelsius;` is a declaration statement. A *declaration* is a statement that defines a variable. A *variable* is a "holding tank" for a value of some type. A variable contains a *value,* such as a number or a character.

The term variable stems from algebra formulae of the following type:

```
x = 10
y = 3 * x
```

In the second expression, `y` is set equal to 3 times x, but what is `x`? The variable `x` acts as a holding tank for a value. In this case, the value of `x` is 10, but we could have just as well set the value of `x` to 20 or 30 or –1. The second formula makes sense no matter what the value of `x`.

In algebra, you're allowed to begin with a statement, such as `x = 10`. In C++, the programmer must first define the variable `x` before she can use it.

In C++, a variable has a type and a name. The variable defined on Line 11 is called `celsius` and declared to hold an integer. (Why they couldn't have just said *integer* instead of *int,* I'll never know. It's just one of those things you learn to live with.)

The name of a variable has no particular significance to C++. A variable must begin with the letters A through Z or a through z. All subsequent characters must be a letter, a digit 0 through 9 or an underscore (_). Variable names can be as long as you want to make them.

It's convention that variable names begin with a lowercase letter. Each new word *within* a variable begins with a capital letter, as in `myVariable`.

Try to make variable names short but descriptive. Avoid names such as `x` because x has no particular meaning. A variable name such as `lengthOfLine Segment` is much more descriptive.

Generating output

The lines beginning with `cout` and `cin` are known as input/output statements, often contracted to I/O statements. (Like all engineers, programmers love contractions and acronyms.)

The first I/O statement says output the phrase *Enter the temperature in Celsius* to *cout* (pronounced "see-out"). `cout` is the name of the standard C++ output device. In this case, the standard C++ output device is your monitor.

The next line is exactly the opposite. It says, in effect, *Extract a value from the C++ input device and store it in the integer variable* `celsius`. The C++ input device is normally the keyboard. What we've got here is the C++ analog to the algebra formula $x = 10$ just mentioned. For the remainder of the program, the value of `celsius` is whatever the user enters there.

Calculating Expressions

All but the most basic programs perform calculations of one type or another. In C++, an *expression* is a statement that performs a calculation. Said another way, an expression is a statement that *has a value*. An *operator* is a command that generates a value.

For example, in the Conversion example program — specifically in the two lines marked as a `calculation expression` — the program declares a variable *factor* and then assigns it the value resulting from a calculation. This particular command calculates the difference of 212 and 32; the operator is the minus sign (-), and the expression is `212-32`.

Storing the results of expression

The spoken language can be very ambiguous. The term *equals* is one of those ambiguities. The word *equals* can mean that two things have the same value as in "5 cents equals a nickel." Equals can also imply assignment, as in math when you say that "y equals 3 times *x*."

To avoid ambiguity, C++ programmers call the *assignment operator,* which says (in effect), *Store the results of the expression to the right of the* equal *sign in the variable to the left.* Programmers say that "factor is *assigned the value* 212 minus 32."

Never say "factor is *equal to* 212 minus 32." You'll hear this from some lazy types, but you and I know better.

Examining the remainder of Conversion.cpp

The second expression in Conversion.cpp presents a slightly more complicated expression than the first. This expression uses the same mathematical symbols: * for multiplication, / for division and, + for addition. In this case, however, the calculation is performed on variables and not simply on constants.

The value contained in the variable called factor (calculated immediately prior, by the way) is multiplied by the value contained in celsius (which was input from the keyboard). The result is divided by 100 and summed with 32. The result of the total expression is assigned to the integer variable fahrenheit.

The final two commands output the string Fahrenheit value is: to the display, followed by the value of fahrenheit — and all so fast that the user scarcely knows it's going on.

Chapter 2

Declaring Variables Constantly

●●

●●

*T*he most fundamental of all concepts in C++ is the *variable* — a variable is like a small box. You can store things in the box for later use, particularly numbers. The concept of a variable is borrowed from mathematics. A statement such as

```
x = 1
```

stores the value 1 in the variable x. From that point forward, the mathematician can use the variable x in place of the constant 1 — until she changes the value of *x* to something else.

Variables work the same way in C++. You can make the assignment

```
x = 1;
```

From that point forward in the program, until the value of x is changed, any references to x are the same as referencing 1. That is, the *value of* x is 1.

Unfortunately, C++ has a few more concerns about variables than the mathematician does. This chapter deals with the care and feeding of variables in C++.

Declaring Variables

C++ saves numeric values in small storage boxes known as *variables.* Mathematicians throw variables around with abandon. A mathematician might (for example) write down something like the following:

```
(x + 2) =  y / 2
x + 4 = y
solve for x and y
```

Any reader who's had algebra realizes right off that the mathematician has introduced the variables x and y. But C++ isn't that smart (computers may be fast, but they're stupid).

You have to announce each variable to C++ before you can use it. You have to say something soothing like this:

```
int x;
x = 10;

int y;
y = 5;
```

These lines of code *declare* that a variable x exists, that it is of type int, and that a variable y of type int also exists. (The next section discusses variable types.) You can declare variables (almost) anywhere you want in your program — as long as you *declare the variable before you use it.*

Declaring Different Types of Variables

If you're on friendly terms with math (hey, aren't we all?), you probably think of a variable in mathematics as an amorphous box capable of holding whatever you might choose to store in it. You might easily write something like the following:

```
x = 1
x = 2.3
x = "this is a sentence"
x = Texas
```

Alas, C++ is not that flexible. (On the other hand, C++ can do things that people can't do, such as add a billion numbers or so in a second, so let's not get too uppity.) To C++, there are different types of variables just as there are different types of storage bins. Some storage bins are so small that they can only handle a single number. It takes a larger bin to handle a sentence. Of course, no bin is large enough to hold Texas (maybe Rhode Island or Delaware).

You have to tell C++ what size bin you need before you can use a C++ variable. In addition, different types of variables have different properties. So far, you have only seen the int type of variable in this chapter:

```
int x;
x = 1;
```

The variable type `int` is the C++ equivalent of an *integer* — a number that has no fractional part. (Integers are also known as *counting numbers* or *whole numbers*.)

Integers are great for most calculations. You can make it up through most (if not all) of elementary school with integers. It isn't until you reach age 11 or so that they start mucking up the waters with fractions. The same is true in C++: More than 90 percent of all variables in C++ are declared to be of type `int`.

Unfortunately, `int` variables don't always work properly in a program. If (for example) you worked through the temperature-conversion program in Chapter 1, the program has a potential problem — it can only handle integer temperatures — whole numbers that don't have a fractional part. This limitation of using only integers doesn't affect daily use because it isn't likely that someone (other than a meteorologist) would get all excited about entering a fractional temperature (such as 10.5 degrees). The lurking problem is not at all obvious: The conversion program lops off the fractional portion of temperatures that it calculates, and just keeps going without complaint. This can result in a lapse of accuracy that can be serious — for example, you wouldn't want to come up a half mile short of the runway on your next airplane trip due to a navigational round-off.

Reviewing the limitations of integers in C++

The `int` variable type is the C++ version of an integer. `int` variables suffer the same limitations as their counting-number integer equivalents in math do.

Integer round-off

Consider the problem of calculating the average of three numbers. Given three `int` variables — `nValue1`, `nValue2`, and `nValue3` — an equation for calculating the average is

```
int nAverage; int nValue1; int nValue2; int nValue3;
nAverage =(nValue1 + nValue2 + nValue3) / 3;
```

Because all three values are integers, the sum is assumed to be an integer. Given the values 1, 2, and 2, the sum is 5. Divide that by 3, and you get 1⅔, or 1.666. Given that all three variables `nValue1`, `nValue2`, and `nValue3` are integers, the sum is also assumed to be an integer. The result of the division is also an integer. The resulting value of `nAverage` is unreasonable but logical: 1.

Lopping off the fractional part of a number is called *truncation,* or rounding off. For many applications, truncation isn't a big deal. Some folks might consider its results reasonable (not mathematicians or bookies, of course), but integer truncation can create math mayhem in computer programs. Consider the following equivalent formulation:

```
int nAverage; int nValue1; int nValue2; int nValue3;
nAverage = nValue1/3 + nValue2/3 + nValue3/3;
```

Plugging in the same 1, 2, and 2 values, the resulting value of nAverage is (talk about logical-but-unreasonable) 0. To see how this can occur, consider that 13 truncates to 0, 23 truncates to 0, and 23 truncates to 0. The sum of 0, 0, and 0 is zero. (Sort of like that old song: "Nothing from nothing leaves nothing, ya gotta be something . . .") You can see that integer truncation can be completely unacceptable.

Limited range

A second problem with the int variable type is its limited range. A normal int variable can store a maximum value of 2,147,483,647 and a minimum value of –2,147,483,648 — roughly from positive 2 billion to negative 2 billion, for a total range of about 4 billion.

Two billion is a very large number: plenty big enough for most uses. But it's not large enough for some applications — for example, computer technology. In fact, your computer probably executes faster than 2 gigahertz, depending upon how old your computer is. (*Giga* is the prefix meaning billion.) A single strand of communications fiber — the kind that's been strung from one end of the country to the other — can handle way more than 2 billion bits per second.

C++ offers a little help by allowing you declare an integer to be unsigned, meaning that it cannot be negative. An unsigned int value type can represent a number from 0 to 4,294,967,295, should the need arise for some unimaginable reason.

You can declare a variable simply unsigned. The int is implied.

Solving the truncation problem

The limitations of int variables can be unacceptable in some applications. Fortunately, C++ understands decimal numbers. A decimal number can have a nonzero fractional part. (Mathematicians also call those *real numbers.*) Decimal numbers avoid many of the limitations of int type integers. Notice that a decimal number "can have" a nonzero fractional part. In C++, the number 1.0 is just as much a decimal number as 1.5. The equivalent integer is written simply as 1. Decimals numbers can also be negative, like –2.3.

When you declare variables in C++ that are decimal numbers, you identify them as `double` precision floating-point values. (Yes, there *is* such a critter as a "`single` precision floating-point variable," but stick with me here.) The term *floating-point* means the decimal point is allowed to float back and forth, identifying as many "decimal places" as necessary to express the value. Floating-point variables are declared in the same way as `int` variables:

```
double dValue1;
```

From this point forward, the variable `dValue1` is declared to be a `double`. Once declared, you cannot change the type of a variable. `dValue1` is now a `double` and will be a `double` for the remainder of its natural instructions. To see how floating-point numbers fix the truncation problem inherent with integers, convert all the `int` variables to `double`. Here's what you get:

```
double dValue;
dValue = 1.0/3.0 + 2.0/3.0 + 2.0/3.0;
```

is equivalent to

```
dValue = 0.333... + 0.666... + 0.666...;
```

which results in the value

```
dValue = 1.666...;
```

I have written the value `1.6666 . . .` as if the number of trailing 6s goes on forever. This is (not necessarily) the case. There's a limit to the number of digits of accuracy of a `double` variable — but it's a lot more than I can keep track of.

The programs `IntAverage` and `FloatAverage` are available on the enclosed CD in the `CPP_Programs\Chap02` directory to demonstrate this averaging example.

Looking at the limits of floating-point numbers

Although floating-point variables can solve many calculation problems such as truncation, they have some limitations themselves — in effect, the reverse of those associated with integer variables. `double` variables can't be used as counting numbers, they're more difficult for the computer to handle, and they also suffer from round-off error (though not nearly to the same degree as `int` variables).

Counting

You cannot use floating-point variables in applications where counting is important. This includes C++ constructs, which requires counting ability. C++ can't verify which whole number value is meant by a given floating-point number.

For example, it's clear that 1.0 is 1. But what about 0.9 or 1.1? Should these also be considered as 1? C++ simply avoids the problem by insisting on using `int` values when counting is involved.

Calculation speed

Historically, a computer processor can process integer arithmetic quicker than it can floating-point arithmetic. Thus, while a processor can add 1 million integer numbers in a given amount of time, the same processor may be able to perform only 200,000 floating-point calculations during the same period. (Not surprisingly, I couldn't even get around to *reading* the first value.)

Calculation speed is becoming less of a problem as microprocessors increase their capabilities. Most modern processors contain special calculation circuitry for performing floating-point calculations almost as fast as integer calculations.

Loss of accuracy

Floating-point variables cannot solve all computational problems. Floating-point variables have a limited precision of about 6 digits — an extra-economy size, double-strength version of float can handle some 15 significant digits with room left over for lunch.

To evaluate the problem, consider that 13 is expressed as 0.333 . . . in a continuing sequence. The concept of an infinite series makes sense in math, but not to a computer. The computer has a finite accuracy. Average 1, 2, and 2 (for example), and you get 1.666667.

C++ can correct for many forms of round-off error. For example, in output, C++ can determine that instead of 0.999999, that the user really meant 1. In other cases, even C++ cannot correct for round-off error.

Not-so-limited range

Although the `double` data type has a range much larger than that of an integer, it's still limited. The maximum value for an `int` is a skosh more than 2 billion. The maximum value of a `double` variable is roughly 10 to the 38th power. That's 1 followed by 38 zeroes; it eats 2 billion for breakfast. (It's even more than the national debt, at least at the time of this writing.)

Only the first 13 digits or so have any meaning; the remaining 25 digits suffer from floating-point round-off error.

Declaring Variable Types

So far this chapter has been trumpeting that variables must be declared and that they must be assigned a type. Fortunately (ta-dah!), C++ provides a number of different variable types. See Table 2-1 for a list of variables, their advantages, and limitations.

Table 2-1		C++ Variables
Variable	*Example*	*Purpose*
int	1	A simple counting number, either positive or negative.
unsigned int	1U	A counting number that's only non-negative.
long	10L	A potentially larger version of int. There is no difference between long and int with Dev-C++ and Microsoft Visual C++.NET.
unsigned long	10UL	A nonnegative long integer.
float	1.0F	A single precision real number. This smaller version takes less memory than a double but has less accuracy and a smaller range.
double	1.0	A standard floating-point variable.
char	'c'	A single char variable stores a single alphabetic or digital character. Not suitable for arithmetic.
string	"this is a string"	A string of characters forms a sentence or phrase.
bool	true	The only other value is false. No I mean, it's *really* false. Logically false. Not "false" as in fake or ersatz or . . . never mind.

It may seem odd that the standard floating length variable is called double while the "off size" is float. In days gone by, memory was an expensive asset — you could reap significant space savings by using a float variable. This is no longer the case. That, combined with the fact that modern processors perform double precision calculations at the same speed as float, makes the double the default. Bigger is better, after all.

The following statement declares a variable `lVariable` as type `long` and sets it equal to the value 1, while `dVariable` is a double set to the value `1.0`:

```
// declare a variable and set it to 1
long lVariable;
lVariable = 1;

// declare a variable of type double and set it to 1.0
double dVariable;
dVariable = 1.0;
```

You can declare a variable and initialize it in the same statement:

```
int nVariable = 1;  // declare a variable and
                    // initialize it to 1
```

Although such declarations are common, the only benefit to initializing a variable in the declaration is that it saves typing.

A `char` variable can hold a single character; a *string* (which isn't really a variable but works like one for most purposes) holds a string of characters. Thus, `'C'` is a `char` that contains the character C, whereas `"C"` is a string with one character in it. A rough analogy is that a 'C' corresponds to a nail in your hand, whereas "C" corresponds to a nail gun with one nail left in the magazine. (Chapter 9 describes strings in detail.)

If an application requires a string, you've gotta provide one, even if the string contains only a single character. Providing nothing but the character just won't do the job.

Types of constants

A *constant* is an explicit number or character (such as 1, 0.5, or 'c') that doesn't change. As with variables, every constant has a type. In an expression such as `n = 1;` (for example), the constant 1 is an `int`. To make 1 a `long` integer, write the statement as `n = 1L;`. The analogy is as follows: 1 represents a single ball in the bed of a pickup truck, whereas `1L` is a single ball in the bed of a dump truck. The ball is the same, but the capacity of its container is much larger.

Following the `int` to `long` comparison, 1.0 represents the value 1, but in a floating-point container. Notice, however, that the default for floating-point constants is `double`. Thus, 1.0 is a `double` number and not a `float`.

`true` is a constant of type `bool`. However, `"true"` (note the quotation marks) is a string of characters that spell out the word *true*. In addition, in keeping with C++'s attention to case, `true` is a constant, but `TRUE` has no meaning.

Special characters

You can store any printable character you want in a `char` or `string` variable. You can also store a set of non-printable characters that is used as character constants. See Table 2-2 for a description of these important non-printable characters.

Table 2-2	Special Characters
Character Constant	*Action*
`'\n'`	newline
`'\t'`	tab
`'\0'`	null
`'\\'`	backslash

You have already seen the newline character at the end of strings. This character breaks a string and puts the parts on separate lines. A newline character may appear anywhere within a string. For example,

```
"This is line 1\nThis is line 2"
```

appears on the output as

```
This is line 1
This is line 2
```

Similarly, the \t tab character moves output to the next tab position. (This position can vary, depending on the type of computer you're using to run the program.) Because the backslash character is used to signify special characters, a character pair for the backslash itself is required. The character pair \\ represents the backslash.

C++ collision with file names

Windows uses the backslash character to separate folder names in the path to a file. (This is a remnant of MS-DOS that Windows has not been able to shake.) Thus, `Root\FolderA\File` represents `File` within `FolderA`, which is a subdirectory of `Root`.

Unfortunately, MS-DOS's use of backslash conflicts with the use of backslash to indicate an escape character in C++. The character \\ is a backslash in C++. The MS-DOS path `Root\FolderA\File` is represented in C++ string as `Root\\FolderA\\File`.

Are These Calculations Really Logical?

C++ provides a logical variable called `bool`. The type `bool` comes from *Boolean*, the last name of the inventor of the logical calculus. There are two values for a boolean variable: `true` and `false`.

There are actually calculations that result in the value `bool`. For example, `"x is equal to y"` is either `true` or `false`.

Mixed Mode Expressions

C++ allows you to mix variable types in a single expression. That is, you are allowed to add an integer with a `double` precision floating-point value. In the following expression, for example, nValue1 is allowed to be an `int`:

```
// in the following expression the value of nValue1
// is converted into a double before performing the
// assignment
int nValue1 = 1;
nValue1 + 1.0;
```

An expression in which the two operands are not the same type is called a *mixed-mode expression*. Mixed-mode expressions generate a value whose type is equal to the more capable of the two operands. In this case, nValue1 is converted to a `double` before the calculation proceeds. Similarly, an expression of one type may be assigned to a variable of a different type, as in the following statement:

```
// in the following assignment, the whole
// number part of fVariable is stored into nVariable
double dVariable = 1.0;
int nVariable;
nVariable = dVariable;
```

You can lose precision or range if the variable on the left side of the assignment is smaller. In the previous example, C++ truncates the value of dVariable before storing it in nVariable.

Converting a larger value type into a smaller value type is called *demotion*, whereas converting values in the opposite direction is known as *promotion*. Programmers say that the value of `int` variable nVariable1 is promoted to a `double` as expressions such as the following:

```
int nVariable1 = 1;
double dVariable = nVariable1;
```

Naming conventions

You may have noticed that the name of each variable begins with a special character that seems to have nothing to do with the name. These special characters are shown in the following table. You can immediately recognize dVariable as a variable of type double by using this convention.

Character	Type
n	int
l	long
f	float
d	double
c	character
sz	string

These leading characters help the programmer keep track of the variable type. Thus, you can immediately identify the following as a mixed-mode assignment of a long variable to an int variable:

```
nVariable = lVariable;
```

These leading characters have no significance to C++. You don't need to adopt any naming scheme at all if you don't want to. Here's what you get:

```
double myVariable;
int someIntValue;
double nThisDoesntEvenMatch;
```

I used this first-letter-naming convention in this chapter to simplify the discussion; many programmers use this naming scheme all the time.

Mixed-mode expressions are not a good idea. Avoid forcing C++ to do your conversions for you.

Chapter 3

Performing Mathematical Operations

● ●

In This Chapter

▶ Defining mathematical operators in C++

▶ Using the C++ mathematical operators

▶ Identifying expressions

▶ Increasing clarity with special mathematical operators

● ●

A mathematician uses more than just the variables described in Chapter 2. A mathematician must do something with those variables: She can add them together, subtract them, multiply them, and perform an almost endless list of other operations.

C++ offers the same set of basic operations: C++ programs can multiply, add, divide, and so forth. Programs have to be able to perform these operations in order to get anything done. What good is an insurance program if it can't calculate how much you're supposed to (over) pay?

C++ operations look like the arithmetic operations you would perform on a piece of paper, except you have to declare any variables before you can use them (as detailed in Chapter 2):

```
int var1;
int var2 = 1;
var1 = 2 * var2;
```

Two variables, var1 and var2, are declared. var2 is initialized to 1. var1 is assigned the value resulting from the calculation two times the value of var2.

This chapter describes the complete set of C++ mathematical operators.

Performing Simple Binary Arithmetic

A *binary operator* is one that has two arguments. If you can say `var1 op var2`, `op` must be a binary operator. The most common binary operators are the simple operations you performed in grade school. The binary operators are flagged in Table 3-1.

Table 3-1	Mathematical Operators in Order of Precedence	
Precedence	*Operator*	*Meaning*
1	+ (unary)	Effectively does nothing
1	- (unary)	Returns the negative of its argument
2	++ (unary)	Increment
2	-- (unary)	Decrement
3	* (binary)	Multiplication
3	/ (binary)	Division
3	% (binary)	Modulo
4	+ (binary)	Addition
4	- (binary)	Subtraction
5	=, *=,%=,+=,-= (special)	Assignment types

Multiplication, division, modulus, addition, and subtraction are the operators used to perform arithmetic. In practice, they work just like the familiar arithmetic operations as well. For example, using the binary operator for division with a `float` variable looks like this:

```
float var = 133 / 12;
```

Each of the binary operators has the conventional meaning that you studied in grammar school — with one exception. You may not have encountered modulus in your studies.

The *modulus* operator (%) works much like division, except it produces the remainder *after* division instead of the quotient. For example, 4 goes into 15 three times with a remainder of 3. Expressed in C++ terms, 15 modulus 4 is 3.

```
int var = 15 % 4; // var is initialized to 3
```

Because programmers are always trying to impress nonprogrammers with the simplest things, C++ programmers define modulus as follows:

```
IntValue % IntDivisor
```

This expression is equal to

```
IntValue - (IntValue / IntDivisor) * IntDivisor
```

Try it out on this example:

```
15 % 4 is equal to 15 - (15/4) * 4
                   15 - 3 * 4
                   15 - 12
                   3
```

Modulus is not defined for floating-point variable because it depends on the round-off error inherent in integers. (I discuss round-off errors in Chapter 2.)

Decomposing Expressions

The most common type of statement in C++ is the expression. An *expression* is a C++ statement with a value. Every expression has a type (such as `int`, `double`, `char`, and so on). A statement involving any mathematical operator is an expression since all these operators return a value. For example, $1 + 2$ is an expression whose value is 3 and type is `int`. (Remember that constants without decimal points are `int`s.)

Expressions can be complex or extremely simple. In fact, the statement 1 is an expression because it has a value (1) and a type (`int`). There are five expressions in the following statement:

```
z = x * y + w;
```

The expressions are

```
x * y + w
x * y
x
y
w
```

An unusual aspect of C++ is that an expression is a complete statement. Thus, the following is a legal C++ statement:

```
1;
```

The type of the expression 1 is int.

Determining the Order of Operations

All operators perform some defined function. In addition, every operator has a *precedence* — a specified place in the order in which the expressions are evaluated. Consider, for example, how precedence affects solving the following problem:

```
int var = 2 * 3 + 1;
```

If the addition is performed before the multiplication, the value of the expression is 2 times 4 or 8. If the multiplication is performed first, the value is 6 + 1 or 7.

The precedence of the operators determines who goes first. Table 3-1 shows that multiplication has higher precedence than addition, so the result is 7. (The concept of precedence is also present in arithmetic. C++ adheres to the common arithmetic precedence.)

So what happens when we use two operators of the same precedence in the same expression? Well, it looks like this:

```
int var = 8 / 4 / 2;
```

But is this 8 divided by 2 or 4, or is it 2 divided by 2 or 1? When operators of the same precedence appear in the same expression, they are evaluated from left to right (the same rule applied in arithmetic). Thus, the answer is 8 divided by 4, which is 2 divided by 2 (which is 1).

The expression

```
x / 100 + 32
```

divides x by 100 before adding 32. But what if the programmer wanted to divide x by *100 plus 32?* The programmer can change the precedence by bundling expressions together in parentheses (shades of algebra!), as follows:

```
x/(100 + 32)
```

This expression has the same effect as dividing x by 132.

The original expression

```
x./ 100 + 32
```

is identical to the expression

```
(x/100) + 32
```

In a given expression, C++ normally performs multiplication and division *before* addition or subtraction. Multiplication and division have higher precedence than addition and subtraction.

In summary: Precedence refers to the order in which operators are evaluated. An operator with higher precedence is executed first. You can override the precedence of an operator by using parentheses.

Performing Unary Operations

Arithmetic binary operators — those operators that take two arguments — are familiar to a lot of us from school days. You've probably been doing binary operations since the first grade in school. But consider the *unary operators,* which take a single argument (for example, –a). Many unary operations are not so well known.

The unary mathematical operators are plus, plus-plus, minus, and minus-minus (respectively, +, –, ++, and ––). Thus

```
int var1 = 10;
int var2 = -var1;
```

The latter expression uses the minus unary operator (–) to calculate the value negative 10.

The minus operator changes the sign of its argument. Positive numbers become negative and vice versa. The plus operator does not change the sign of its argument. It wouldn't be weird to say the plus operator has no effect at all.

The ++ and the –– operators might be new to you. These operators (respectively) add one to their arguments or subtract one from their arguments, so they're known (also respectively) as the *increment and decrement operators.*

Because they're dependent upon numbers that can be counted, they're limited to non-floating-point variables. For example, the value of var after executing the following expression is 11.

```
int var = 10;    // initalize var
var++;           // now increment it
                 // value of var is now 11
```

The increment and decrement operators are peculiar in that both come in two flavors: a *prefix* version and a *postfix* version (known as pre-increment and post-increment, respectively). Consider, for example, the increment operator (the decrement works in exactly the same way).

Suppose that the variable n has the value 5. Both ++n and n++ increment n to the value 6. The difference between the two is that the value of ++n in an expression is 6 while the value of n++ is 5. The following example illustrates this difference:

```
// declare three integer variables
int n1, n2, n3;

// the value of both n1 and n2 is 6
n1 = 5;
n2 = ++n1;

// the value of n1 is 6 but the value of n3 is 5
n1 = 5;
n3 = n1++;
```

Thus n2 is given the value of n1 after n1 has been incremented (using the pre-increment operator), whereas n3 gets the value of n1 before it is incremented using the post-increment operator.

Why define a separate increment operator?

The authors of C++ noted that programmers add 1 more than any other constant. To provide some convenience, a special add 1 instruction was added to the language.

In addition, most present-day computer processors have an increment instruction that is faster than the addition instruction. Back when C++ was created, however — with microprocessors being what they were — saving a few instructions was a big deal.

Using Assignment Operators

An *assignment operator* is a binary operator that changes the value of its left argument. The equal sign (=), a simple assignment operator, is an absolute necessity in any programming language. This operator puts the value of the right-hand argument into the left argument. The other assignment operators are odd enough that they seem to be someone's whim.

The creators of C++ noticed that assignments often follow the form of

```
variable = variable # constant
```

where # is some binary operator. Thus, to increment an integer operator by 2, the programmer might write

```
nVariable = nVariable + 2;
```

This expression says, "add two to the value of nVariable and store the results back into nVariable." Doing so changes the value of nVariable to 2 more than it was.

It's common to see the same variable on both the right and left side of an assignment.

Because the same variable appears on both sides of the = sign, the same Fathers of the C++ Republic decided to create a version of the assignment operator in which a binary operator is attached. This says, in effect, "Thou shalt perform whatever operation on a variable and store the results right back into the same variable."

Every binary operator has one of these nifty *assignment versions*. Thus, the assignment just given could have been written this way:

```
nVariable = nVariable + 2;
nVariable += 2;
```

Here the first line says (being very explicit now) "Take the value of nVariable, add 2, and store the results back into nVariable." The line is a second form if the same expression, saying (a bit more abruptly), "Add 2 to the value of nVariable."

Other than assignment itself, these assignment operators are not used all that often. However, as odd as they might look, sometimes they can actually make the resulting program easier to read.

Chapter 4

Performing Logical Operations

• •

In This Chapter

▶ Using sometimes-illogical logical operators

▶ Defining logical variables

▶ Operating with bitwise logical operators logically, a bit at a time

• •

*T*he most common statement in C++ is the expression. Most expressions involve the arithmetic operators such as addition (+), subtraction (-) and multiplication (*). This chapter describes these types of expressions.

There is a whole other class of operators known as the *logical operators*. In comparison with the arithmetic operators, most people don't think nearly as much about operations.

It isn't that people don't deal with logical operations — after all, people compute AND and OR constantly. I won't eat cereal unless the bowl contains cereal AND the bowl has milk in it AND the cereal is coated with sugar (lots of sugar). I'll have a Scotch IF it's single-malt AND someone else paid for it. People use such logical operations all the time, it's just that they don't write them down as machine instructions (or think of them in that light).

Logical operators fall into two types. The AND and OR operators are what I will call *simple logical operators*. There is a second type of logical operator that people don't use in their daily business — the *bitwise* operator — that's unique to the computer world. We'll start with the simple and sneak up on the bitwise here.

Why Mess with Logical Operations?

C++ programs have to make decisions. A program that can't make decisions is of limited use. The temperature-conversion program laid out in Chapter 1 is about as complex you can get without *some* type of decision-making. Invariably a computer program gets to the point where it has to figure out situations such as "Do *this* if the *a* variable is less than some value, do that *other* thing if it's not." That's what makes a computer appear to be intelligent — that it can make decisions. (By the same token, that same property makes a computer look really stupid when the program makes the wrong decision.) Making decisions, right or wrong, requires the use of logical operators.

Using the Simple Logical Operators

The simple logical operators, shown in Table 4-1, evaluate to `true` or `false`.

Table 4-1	Simple Operators Representing Daily Logic
Operator	*Meaning*
==	Equality; `true` if the left-hand argument has the same value as the right
!=	Inequality; opposite of equality
>, <	Greater than, less than; `true` if the left-hand argument is greater than or less than the right-hand argument
>=, <=	Greater than or equal to, less than or equal to; `true` if either > or == is `true`, OR either < or == is `true`
&&	AND; `true` if both the left-and right-hand arguments are `true`
||	OR; `true` if either the left-or the right-hand argument is `true`
!	NOT; `true` if its argument is `false`

The first six entries in Table 4-1 are comparison operators. The equality operator is used to compare two numbers. For example, the following is `true` if the value of n is 0, and is `false` otherwise:

```
n == 0;
```

Looks can be deceiving. Don't confuse the equality operator (==) with the assignment operator (=). Not only is this a common mistake, but it's a mistake that the C++ compiler generally cannot catch — that makes it more than twice as bad.

```
n = 0;   // programmer meant to say n == 0
```

The greater-than (>) and less-than (<) operators are similarly common in everyday life. The following expression logical comparison is true:

```
int n1 = 1;
int n2 = 2;
n1 < n2;
```

It's easy to forget which operator is "greater than" and which is "less than." Just remember that the operator is `true` if the arrow points to the *smaller* of the two.

You may think that n1 is greater than or less than n2; however, this ignores the possibility that n1 and n2 are equal. The greater-than-or-equal-to operator (`<=`) and the less-than-or-equal-to operator (`>=`) include that bit of mathematical nuance. They are similar to the less-than and greater-than operators, with one major exception: They include equality; the other operators don't.

The `&&` (AND) and `||` (OR) can combine with the other logic operators, like this:

```
// true if n2 is greater than n1 but n2 smaller than n3
// (this is the most common way determining that n2 is in
// the range of n1 to n3, exclusive)
(n1 < n2) && (n2 < n3);
```

Storing logical values

The result of a logical operation can be assigned to a variable of type `bool`:

```
int n1 = 1;
int n2 = 2;
bool b;
b = (n1 == n2);
```

This expression highlights the difference between the assignment operator `=` and the comparison operator `==`. The expression says, "Compare the variables n1 and n2. Store the results of this comparison in the variable b."

The assignment operators are about as low down on the precedence totem pole as you can get. The equality operator is executed before the assignment. The parentheses are not required — so the following is an equally valid form of logical confusion:

```
b = n1 == n2; // compare n1 with n2; generate a true if n1
              // if n1 has the same value as n2, false if not
              // store the result, true or false, in b
```

Whoa. Better look at that again. Note the difference between the operators.

The following program demonstrates the use of a `bool` variable:

```
// BoolTest - compare variables input from the
//            keyboard and store the results off
//            into a logical variable
#include <cstdio>
#include <cstdlib>
#include <iostream>
using namespace std;

int main(int nNumberofArgs, char* pszArgs[])
{
    // set output format for bool variables
    // to true and false instead
    // of 1 and 0
    cout.setf(cout.boolalpha);

    // initialize two arguments
    int nArg1;
    cout << "Input value 1: ";
    cin >> nArg1;

    int nArg2;
    cout << "Input value 2: ";
    cin >> nArg2;

    bool b;
    b = nArg1 == nArg2;

    cout << "The statement, " << nArg1
         << " equals "        << nArg2
         << " is "            << b
         << endl;

    // wait until user is ready before terminating program
    // to allow the user to see the program results
    system("PAUSE");
    return 0;
}
```

The first line `cout.setf()` makes sure that our `bool` variable b is output as `"true"` or `"false"`. The next section explains why this is necessary.

The program inputs two values from the keyboard and displays the result of the equality comparison:

```
Input value 1: 5
Input value 2: 5
The statement, 5 equals 5 is true
Press any key to continue . . .
```

The special value `endl` inserts a newline. The difference between the value `endl` and the character `'\n'` as described in Chapter 2 is subtle and explained in Chapter 24.

Using logical int variables

C++ hasn't always had a `bool` type variable. Back in the old days (before that guy on TV kept walking around saying "Can you hear me now?"), C++ used `int` variables to store logical values. A value of 0 was considered `false` and all other values `true`. By the same token, a logical operator generated a 0 for `false` and a 1 for `true`. (Thus, 0 was false while `10 > 5` returned a 1.)

C++ retains a high degree of compatibility between `bool` and `int` in order to support the older programs that still have that quirk. You get completely different output from the `BitTest` program if you remove the line `cout.setf(cout.boolalpha)`:

```
Input value 1: 5
Input value 2: 5
The statement, 5 equals 5 is 1
Press any key to continue . . .
```

Variables of type `int` and `bool` can be mixed in expressions as well. For example, Dev-C++ allows the following bizarre statement without batting an eyelid:

```
int n;
n = nArg1 == nArg2;
```

Continue to use type `bool` to hold logical values despite this wart that modern C++ inherits from its forefathers. Other compilers may not be as forgiving.

Be careful performing logical operations on floating-point variables

Real numbers are those numbers that can have a fractional part. Because of this, real numbers cannot be counting numbers. That is, you can say the first (1st), second (2nd), third, fourth, and so on because the relationship of 1, 2, and 3 are known exactly. It does not make sense to speak of the 4.5th number in a sequence. (This brings to mind the number between the fourth and fifth, but it has no real meaning.)

Similarly the C++ type `float`, which is the C++ representation, is not a counting number. Even worse (unlike a real number), a floating-point number can't have an infinite number of digits beyond the decimal point if a computer is going to make any use of it. Because of this limitation, be careful when you use comparison operators on floating-point numbers. Consider the following example:

```
float f1 = 10.0;
float f2 = f1 / 3;
f1 == (f2 * 3.0);    // are these two equal?
```

The comparison in the preceding example is *not necessarily true*. A floating-point variable cannot hold an unlimited number of significant digits. Thus, f2 is not equal to the number we'd call "three-and-a-third," but rather to 3.3333..., stopping after some number of decimal places.

A float variable supports about 6 digits of accuracy while a double supports 13 digits. I say "about" because the computer is likely to generate a number like 3.3333347 due to vagaries in floating point calculations.

Now, in pure math, the number of threes after the decimal point is infinite — but no computer built can handle infinity. So, after multiplying 3.3333 by 3, you get 9.9999 instead of the 10 you'd get if you multiplied "three-and-a-third" — in effect, a *round-off error*. Such small differences may be unnoticeable to a person, but not to the computer. Equality means exactly that — *exact* equality.

Modern processors are very sophisticated in performing such calculations. The processor may, in fact, accommodate the round-off error, but from inside C++, you can't predict exactly what any given processor will do.

Problems can arise even in a straightforward calculation, such as the following:

```
float f1 = 10.0;
float f2 = 100 % 30;
f1 == f2;                 // are these two equal?
```

Theoretically, f1 and f2 *should* be equal (after you apply that percentlike operator that Chapter 3 identifies as modulus). There doesn't appear to be any problem with round off. So far. But you can't be sure — you have no idea how the computer that eventually runs your program is going to represent floating-point numbers internally. To flatly claim that there's no round-off error lurking here makes unwarranted assumptions about CPU internals.

The safer comparison is as follows:

```
float f1 = 10.0;
float f2 = f1 / 3;
float f3 = f2 * 3.0;
(f1 - f3) < 0.0001 && (f3 - f1) < 0.0001;
```

This comparison is `true` if `f1` and `f3` are within some small delta from each other, which should still be `true` even if you take some small round-off error into account.

Short circuits and C++

The `&&` and `||` perform what is called *short-circuit evaluation*. Consider the following:

```
condition1 && condition2
```

If `condition1` is *not* `true`, the result is *not* `true`, no matter what the value of `condition2`. (For example, `condition2` could be `true` *or* `false` without changing the result.) The same situation occurs in the following:

```
condition1 || condition2
```

If `condition1` is `true`, the result is `true`, no matter what the value of `condition2`.

To save time, C++ (wisely) cuts to the chase and evaluates `condition1` first. C++ does not evaluate `condition2` if `condition1` is `false` (in the case of `&&`) or `condition1` is `true` (in the case of `||`). This is known as short circuit evaluation.

Expressing Binary Numbers

C++ variables are stored internally as so-called binary numbers. Binary numbers are stored as a sequence of 1 and 0 values known as *bits*. Most of the time, you don't really need to deal with which particular bits you use to represent numbers. Sometimes, however, it's actually practical and convenient to tinker with numbers at the bit level — so C++ provides a set of operators for that purpose.

Fortunately, you won't have to deal too often with C++ variables at the bit level, so it's pretty safe to consider the remainder of this chapter a Deep Techie excursion.

The so-called *bitwise* logical operators operate on their arguments at the bit level. To understand how they work, let's first examine how computers store variables.

The decimal number system

The numbers we've been familiar with from the time we could first count on our fingers are known as *decimal numbers* because they're based on the number 10. (Coincidence? I don't think so . . .) In general, the programmer expresses C++ variables as decimal numbers. Thus you could specify the value of var as (say) 123 — but consider the implications.

A number such as 123 refers to $1 * 100 + 2 * 10 + 3 * 1$. Each of these base numbers — 100, 10, and 1 — are powers of 10.

```
123 = 1 * 100 + 2 * 10 + 3 * 1
```

Expressed in a slightly different (but equivalent) way, 123 looks like this:

```
123 = 1 * 10² + 2 * 10¹ + 3 * 10⁰
```

Remember that *any* number *to the zero power* is 1.

Other number systems

Well, okay, using 10 as the basis (or *base*) of our counting system probably stems from those 10 human fingers, the original counting tools. An alternative base for a counting system could just as easily have been 20 (maybe the inventor of base 10 had shoes on at the time).

If our numbering scheme had been invented by dogs, it might well be based on 8 (one digit of each paw is out of sight on the back part of the leg). Mathematically, such an *octal* system would have worked just as well:

```
123₁₀ = 1 * 8² + 7 * 8¹ + 3 * 8⁰ = 173₈
```

The small 10 and 8 here refer to the numbering system, 10 for decimal (base 10) and 8 for octal (base 8). A counting system may use any positive base.

The binary number system

Computers have essentially two fingers. (Maybe that's why computers are so stupid: without an opposing thumb, they can't grasp anything. And then again, maybe not.) Computers prefer counting using base 2. The number 123_{10} would be expressed this way:

```
123₁₀ = 0*128 + 1*64 + 1*32 + 1*16 + 1*8 + 0*4 +1*2 + 1*1
      = 01111011₂
```

Computer convention expresses binary numbers by using 4, 8, 16, 32 or even 64 binary digits even if the leading digits are zero. This is also because of the way computers are built internally.

Because the term *digit* refers to a multiple of ten, a *binary digit* is called a *bit* (an abbreviation of *binary digit*). Eight bits make up a *byte*. (Calling a binary digit a *byte-it* didn't seem like a good idea.) A short word is two bytes; a long word is four bytes.

With such a small base, you have to use a *large* number of bits to express numbers. Human beings don't want the hassle of using an expression such as 01111011_2 to express such a mundane value as 123_{10}. Programmers prefer to express numbers by using an even number of bits. The octal system — which is based on 3 bits — has been almost completely replaced by the *hexadecimal* system, which is based on 4-bit digits.

Hexadecimal uses the same digits for the numbers 0 through 9. For the digits between 9 and 16, hexadecimal uses the first six letters of the alphabet: A for 10, B for 11, etc. Thus, 123_{10} becomes $7B_{16}$, like this:

```
123 = 7 * 16¹ + B (i.e. 11) * 16⁰ = 7B₁₆
```

Programmers prefer to express hexadecimal numbers in 2, 4, or 8 hexadecimal digits even when the leading digit in each case is 0.

Finally, who wants to express a hexadecimal number such as $7B_{16}$ by using a subscript? Terminals don't even *support* subscripts. Even on a word processor such as the one I'm using now, it's a drag to change fonts to and from subscript mode just to type two lousy digits. Therefore, programmers (no fools they) use the convention of beginning a hexadecimal number with a 0x. (Why? Well, the reason for such a strange convention goes back to the early days of C, in a galaxy far, far, away . . . never mind.) Thus, 7B becomes 0x7B. Using this convention, the hexadecimal number 0x7B is equal to 123 decimal while 0x123 hexadecimal is equal to 291 decimal.

You can use all the mathematical operators on hexadecimal numbers, in the same way you'd apply them to decimal numbers. (Well, okay, most of us can't perform a multiplication such as 0xC * 0xE in our heads, but that has more to do with the multiplication tables we learned in school than it has to do with any limitation in the number system.)

Roman numeral expressions

On a historical note, I should mention that some numbering systems actually *hinder* computations. The Roman numeral system is a (so to speak) classic example that greatly hindered the development of math.

Adding two Roman numerals isn't too difficult:

XIX + XXVI = XLV

Think this one out:

a) IX + VI: The I after the V cancels out the I before the X so the result is V carry the X.

b) X + XX: Plus the carry X is XXXX, which is expressed as XL.

Subtraction is only slightly more difficult.

Ah, but *multiplying* two Roman numerals all but requires a bachelor's degree in mathematics. (You end up with rules like *X promotes the digits on the right by 1 letter so that X –* IV becomes XL.*) Division practically required a Ph.D., and higher operations such as integration would have been completely impossible.

Love those Arabic numerals . . .

Performing Bitwise Logical Operations

All C++ numbers can be expressed in binary form. Binary numbers use only the digits 1 and 0 to represent a value. The following Table 4-2 defines the set of operations that work on numbers *one bit at a time,* hence the term *bitwise* operators.

Table 4-2	Bitwise Operators
Operator	*Function*
~	NOT: Toggle each bit from 1 to 0 and from 0 to 1
&	AND each bit of the left-hand argument with that on the right
|	OR each bit of the left-hand argument with that on the right
^	XOR (exclusive OR) each bit of the left-hand argument with that on the right

Bitwise operations can potentially store a lot of information in a small amount of memory. There are a lot of traits in the world that have only two (or, at most, four) possibilities — that are either this way or that way. You are either married or you're not (you might be divorced but you are still not currently married). You are either male or female (at least that's what my driver's license says). In C++, you can store each of these traits in a single bit — in this way, you can pack 32 separate properties into a single 32-bit `int`.

In addition, bit operations can be extremely fast. There is no performance penalty paid for that 32-to-1 saving.

Even though memory is cheap these days, it's not unlimited. Sometimes, when you're storing large amounts of data, this ability to pack a whole lot of properties into a single word is a big advantage.

The single bit operators

The bitwise operators — AND (&), OR (|) and NOT (~) — perform logic operations on single bits. If you consider 0 to be `false` and 1 to be `true` (it doesn't *have* to be this way, but it's a common convention), you can say things like the following for the NOT operator:

```
NOT 1 (true)  is 0 (false)
NOT 0 (false) is 1 (true)
```

The AND operator is defined as following:

```
1 (true) AND 1 (true)  is 1 (true)
1 (true) AND 0 (false) is 0 (false)
```

It's a similar situation for the OR operator:

```
1 (true)  OR 0 (false) is 1 (true)
0 (false) OR 0 (false) is 0 (false)
```

The definition of the AND operator appears in Table 4-3.

Table 4-3	Truth Table for the AND Operator	
AND	*1*	*0*
1	1	0
0	0	0

You read this table as the column corresponding to the value of one of the arguments while the row corresponds to the other. Thus, 1 & 0 is 0. (Column 1 and row 0.) The only combination that returns anything other than 0 is 1 & 1. (This is known as a truth table.)

Similarly, the truth table for the OR operator is shown in Table 4-4.

Table 4-4	Truth Table for the OR Operator	
XOR	*1*	*0*
1	1	1
0	1	0

One other logical operation that is not so commonly used in day-to-day living is the OR ELSE operator commonly contracted to XOR. XOR is true if either argument is `true` but not if both are `true`. The truth table for XOR is shown in Table 4-5.

Table 4-5	Truth Table for the XOR Operator	
XOR	*1*	*0*
1	0	1
0	1	0

Armed with these single bit operators, we can take on the C++ bitwise logical operations.

Using the bitwise operators

The bitwise operators operate on each bit separately.

The bitwise operators are used much like any other binary arithmetic operator. The NOT operator is the easiest to understand. To NOT a number is to NOT each bit that makes up that number (and to a programmer, that sentence makes perfect sense — honest). Consider this example:

```
~0110₂ (0x6)
 1001₂ (0x9)
```

Thus we say that ~0x6 equals 0x9.

The following calculation demonstrates the & operator:

```
        0110₂
    &
        0011₂
        0010₂
```

Beginning with the most significant bit, 0 AND 0 is 0. In the next bit, 1 AND 0 is 0. In bit 3, 1 AND 1 is 1. In the least significant bit, 0 AND 1 is 0.

The same calculation can be performed in hexadecimal by first converting the number in binary, performing the operation and then converting the result back.

```
    0x6             0110₂
    &               &
    0x3             0011₂
    0x2             0010₂
```

In shorthand, we say that 0x6 & 0x3 equals 0x2.

(Try this test: What is the value of 0x6 | 0x3? Get this in 7 seconds, and you can give yourself 7 pats on the back.)

A simple test

The following program illustrates the bitwise operators in action. The program initializes two variables and outputs the result of ANDing, ORing, and XORing them.

```cpp
// BitTest - initialize two variables and output the
//           results of applying the ~,& , | and ^
//           operations
#include <cstdio>
#include <cstdlib>
#include <iostream>
using namespace std;

int main(int nNumberofArgs, char* pszArgs[])
{
    // set output format to hexadecimal
    cout.setf(cout.hex);

    // initialize two arguments
    int nArg1;
    nArg1 = 0x1234;

    int nArg2;
    nArg2 = 0x00ff;

    // now perform each operation in turn
    // first the unary NOT operator
```

```
cout << "Arg1         = 0x" << nArg1 << "\n";
cout << "Arg2         = 0x" << nArg2 << "\n";
cout << "~nArg1       = 0x" << ~nArg1 << "\n";
cout << "~nArg2       = 0x" << ~nArg2 << "\n";

// now the binary operators
cout << "nArg1 & nArg2 = 0x"
     << (nArg1 & nArg2)
     << "\n";
cout << "nArg1 | nArg2 = 0x"
     << (nArg1 | nArg2)
     << "\n";
cout << "nArg1 ^ nArg2 = 0x"
     << (nArg1 ^ nArg2)
     << "\n";

// wait until user is ready before terminating program
// to allow the user to see the program results
system("PAUSE");
return 0;
}
```

The first expression in our program, cout.setf(ios::hex), sets the output format from the default decimal to hexadecimal (you'll have to trust me for now that it works).

The remainder of the program is straightforward. The program assigns nArg1 the test value 0x1234 and nArg2 the value 0x00ff. The program then outputs all combinations of bitwise calculations. The process looks like this:

```
Arg1          = 0x1234
Arg2          = 0xff
~nArg1        = 0xffffedcb
~nArg2        = 0xffffff00
nArg1 & nArg2 = 0x34
nArg1 | nArg2 = 0x12ff
nArg1 ^ nArg2 = 0x12cb
Press any key to continue . . .
```

Do something logical with logical calculations

Running through simple and bitwise logical calculations in your head at parties is fun (well, okay, for *some* of us), but a program has to make actual, practical *use* of these values to make them worth the trouble. Coming right up: Chapter 5 demonstrates how logical calculations are used to control program flow.

Chapter 5

Controlling Program Flow

● ●

In This Chapter

▶ Controlling the flow through the program

▶ Executing a group of statements repetitively

▶ Avoiding infinite loops

● ●

*T*he simple programs that appear in Chapters 1 through 4 process a fixed number of inputs, output the result of that calculation, and quit. However, these programs lack any form of flow control. They cannot make tests of any sort. Computer programs are all about making decisions. If the user presses a key, the computer responds to the command.

For example, if the user presses Ctrl+C, the computer copies the currently selected area to the Clipboard. If the user moves the mouse, the pointer moves on the screen. If the user clicks the right mouse button with the Windows key depressed, the computer crashes. The list goes on and on. Programs that don't make decisions are necessarily pretty boring.

Flow-control commands allow the program to decide what action to take, based on the results of the C++ logical operations performed (see Chapter 4). There are basically three types of flow-control statements: the branch, the loop, and the switch.

Controlling Program Flow with the Branch Commands

The simplest form of flow control is the *branch statement*. This instruction allows the program to decide which of two paths to take through C++ instructions, based on the results of a logical expression (see Chapter 4 for a description of logical expressions).

In C++, the branch statement is implemented using the if statement:

```
if (m > n)
{
    // Path 1
    // ...instructions to be executed if
    // m is greater than n
}
else
{
    // Path 2
    // ...instructions to be executed if not
}
```

First, the logical expression m > n is evaluated. If the result of the expression is true, control passes down the path marked Path 1 in the previous snippet. If the expression is false, control passes to Path 2. The else clause is optional. If it is not present, C++ acts as if it is present but empty.

Actually, the braces are optional (sort of) if there's only one statement to execute as part of the if. If you lose the braces, however, it's embarrassingly easy to make a mistake that the C++ compiler can't catch. The braces serve as a guide marker; it's much safer to include 'em. (If your friends try to entice you into *not* using braces, "Just say No.")

The following program demonstrates the if statement (note all the lovely braces):

```
// BranchDemo - input two numbers. Go down one path of the
//              program if the first argument is greater than
//              the first or the other path if not
#include <cstdio>
#include <cstdlib>
#include <iostream>
using namespace std;

int main(int nNumberofArgs, char* pszArgs[])
{
    // input the first argument...
    int arg1;
    cout << "Enter arg1: ";
    cin  >> arg1;

    // ...and the second
    int arg2;
    cout << "Enter arg2: ";
    cin  >> arg2;

    // now decide what to do:
    if (arg1 > arg2)
```

```
    {
        cout << "Argument 1 is greater than argument 2"
            << endl;
    }
    else
    {
        cout << "Argument 1 is not greater than argument 2"
            << endl;
    }

    // wait until user is ready before terminating program
    // to allow the user to see the program results
    system("PAUSE");
    return 0;
}
```

Here the program reads two integers from the keyboard and compares them. If the expression "arg1 is greater than arg2" is true, control flows to the output statement cout << "Argument 1 is greater than argument 2". If arg1 is not greater than arg2, control flows to the else clause where the statement cout << "Argument 1 is not greater than argument 2\n" is executed. Here's what that operation looks like:

```
Enter arg1: 5
Enter arg2: 6
Argument 1 is not greater than argument 2
Press any key to continue . . .
```

Executing Loops in a Program

Branch statements allow you to control the flow of a program's execution from one path of a program or another. This is a big improvement, but still not enough to write full-strength programs.

Consider the problem of updating the computer display. On the typical PC display, 1 million pixels are drawn to update the entire display. A program that can't execute the same code repetitively would need to include the same set of instructions over and over 1,000 times.

What we really need is a way for the computer to execute the same sequence of instructions thousands and millions of times. Executing the same command multiple times requires some type of looping statements.

Looping while a condition is true

The simplest form of looping statement is the `while` loop. Here's what the `while` loop looks like:

```
while(condition)
{
    // ... repeatedly executed as long as condition is true
}
```

The *condition* is tested. This condition could be `if var > 10` or `if var1 == var2` or anything else you might think of. If it is true, the statements within the braces are executed. Upon encountering the closed brace, C++ returns control to the beginning, and the process starts over. The effect is that the C++ code *within the braces is executed repeatedly* as long as the condition is `true`. (Kind of reminds me of how I get to walk around the yard with my dog until she . . . well, until we're done.)

If the condition were `true` the first time, what would make it be `false` in the future? Consider the following example program:

```
// WhileDemo - input a loop count. Loop while
//             outputting astring arg number of times.
#include <cstdio>
#include <cstdlib>
#include <iostream>
using namespace std;

int main(int nNumberofArgs, char* pszArgs[])
{
    // input the loop count
    int loopCount;
    cout << "Enter loopCount: ";
    cin  >> loopCount;

    // now loop that many times
    while (loopCount > 0)
    {
        loopCount = loopCount - 1;
        cout << "Only " << loopCount << " loops to go\n";
    }

    // wait until user is ready before terminating program
    // to allow the user to see the program results
    system("PAUSE");
    return 0;
}
```

WhileDemo begins by retrieving a loop count from the user, which it stores in the variable `loopCount`. The program then executes a `while` loop. The `while` first tests `loopCount`. If `loopCount` is greater than zero, the program enters the body of the loop (the *body* is the code between the braces) where it decrements `loopCount` by 1 and outputs the result to the display. The program then returns to the top of the loop to test whether `loopCount` is still positive.

When executed, the program `WhileDemo` outputs the results shown in this next snippet. Here I entered a loop count of 5. The result is that the program loops 5 times, each time outputting a countdown.

```
Enter loopCount: 5
Only 4 loops to go
Only 3 loops to go
Only 2 loops to go
Only 1 loops to go
Only 0 loops to go
Press any key to continue . . .
```

If the user enters a negative loop count, the program skips the loop entirely. That's because the specified condition is never `true`, so control never enters the loop. In addition, if the user enters a very large number, the program loops for a long time before completing.

A separate, less frequently used version of the `while` loop known as the `do . . . while` appears identical except the condition isn't tested until the bottom of the loop:

```
do
{
    // ...the inside of the loop
} while (condition);
```

Because the condition isn't tested until the end, the body of the `do . . . while` is always executed at least once.

The condition is only checked at the beginning of the `while` loop or at the end of the `do . . . while` loop. Even if the condition ceases to be `true` at some time during the execution of the loop, control does not exit the loop until the condition is retested.

Using the autoincrement/ autodecrement feature

Programmers very often use the autoincrement ++ or the autodecrement -- operators with loops that count something. Notice, from the following snippet extracted from the `WhileDemo` example, that the program decrements the loop count by using assignment and subtraction statements, like this:

```
// now loop that many times
while (loopCount > 0)
{
    loopCount = loopCount - 1;
    cout << "Only " << loopCount << " loops to go\n";
}
```

A more compact version uses the *autodecrement* feature, which does what you may well imagine:

```
while (loopCount > 0)
{
    loopCount--;
    cout << "Only " << loopCount << " loops to go\n";
}
```

The logic in this version is the same as in the original. The only difference is the way that loopCount is decremented.

Because the autodecrement both decrements its argument *and* returns its value, the decrement operation can actually be combined with the while loop. In particular, the following version is the smallest loop yet.

```
while (loopCount-- > 0)
{
    cout << "Only " << loopCount << " loops to go\n";
}
```

Believe it or not, the loopcount— > 0 is the version that most C++ programmers would use. It's not that C++ programmers like being cute (although they do). In fact, the more compact version (which embeds the autoincrement or autodecrement feature in the logical comparison) is easier to read, especially as you gain experience.

Both loopCount— and —loopCount expressions decrement loopCount. The former expression, however, returns the value of loopCount *before* being decremented; the latter expression does so *after* being decremented.

How often should the autodecrement version of WhileDemo execute when the user enters a loop count of 1? If you use the pre-decrement version, the value of —loopCount is 0, and the body of the loop is never entered. With the post-decrement version, the value of loopCount— is 1, and control enters the loop.

Beware thinking that the version of the program with the autodecrement command executes faster (since it contains fewer statements). It probably executes exactly the same. Modern compilers are pretty good at getting the number of machine-language instructions down to a minimum, no matter which of the decrement instructions shown here you actually use.

Using the for loop

The most common form of loop is the `for` loop. The `for` loop is preferred over the more basic `while` loop because it's generally easier to read (there's really no other advantage).

The `for` loop has the following format:

```
for (initialization; conditional; increment)
{
    // ...body of the loop
}
```

Execution of the `for` loop begins with the *initialization clause,* which got its name because it's normally where counting variables are initialized. The initialization clause is only executed once when the `for` loop is first encountered.

Execution continues with the *conditional clause.* This clause works a lot like the `while` loop: as long as the conditional clause is `true`, the `for` loop continues to execute.

After the code in the body of the loop finishes executing, control passes to the `increment` clause before returning to check the conditional clause — thereby repeating the process. The `increment` clause normally houses the autoincrement or autodecrement statements used to update the counting variables.

The following `while` loop is equivalent to the `for` loop:

```
{
    initialization;
    while(conditional)
    {
        {
            // ...body of the loop
        }
        increment;
    }
}
```

All three clauses are optional. If the initialization or increment clauses are missing, C++ ignores them. If the conditional clause is missing, C++ performs the `for` loop forever (or until something else passes control outside the loop).

The `for` loop is best understood by example. The following `ForDemo` program is nothing more than the `WhileDemo` converted to use the `for` loop construct:

```
// ForDemo1 - input a loop count. Loop while
//               outputting astring arg number of times.
#include <cstdio>
#include <cstdlib>
#include <iostream>
using namespace std;

int main(int nNumberofArgs, char* pszArgs[])
{
    // input the loop count
    int loopCount;
    cout << "Enter loopCount: ";
    cin  >> loopCount;

    // count up to the loop count limit
    for (; loopCount > 0;)
    {
        loopCount = loopCount - 1;
        cout << "Only " << loopCount << " loops to go\n";
    }

    // wait until user is ready before terminating program
    // to allow the user to see the program results
    system("PAUSE");
    return 0;
}
```

The program reads a value from the keyboard into the variable loopCount. The for starts out comparing loopCount to zero. Control passes into the for loop if loopCount is greater than zero. Once inside the for loop, the program decrements loopCount and displays the result. That done, the program returns to the for loop control. Control skips to the next line after the for loop as soon as loopCount has been decremented to zero.

 All three sections of a for loop may be empty. An empty initialization or increment section does nothing. An empty comparison section is treated like a comparison that returns true.

This for loop has two small problems. First, it's destructive — not in the sense of what my puppy does to a slipper, but in the sense that it changes the value of loopCount, "destroying" the original value. Second, this for loop counts "backward" from large values down to smaller values. These two problems are addressed if you add a dedicated counting variable to the for loop. Here's what it looks like:

```
// ForDemo2 - input a loop count. Loop while
//               outputting astring arg number of times.
#include <cstdio>
#include <cstdlib>
```

```cpp
#include <iostream>
using namespace std;

int main(int nNumberofArgs, char* pszArgs[])
{
    // input the loop count
    int loopCount;
    cout << "Enter loopCount: ";
    cin  >> loopCount;

    // count up to the loop count limit
    for (int i = 1; i <= loopCount; i++)
    {
        cout << "We've finished " << i << " loops\n";
    }

    // wait until user is ready before terminating program
    // to allow the user to see the program results
    system("PAUSE");
    return 0;
}
```

This modified version of WhileDemo loops the same as it did before. Instead of modifying the value of loopCount, however, this ForDemo2 version uses a counter variable.

Control begins by declaring a variable and initializing it to the value contained in loopCount. It then checks the variable i to make sure that it is positive. If so, the program executes the output statement, decrements i and starts over.

When declared within the initialization portion of the for loop, the index variable is only known within the for loop itself. Nerdy C++ programmers say that the scope of the variable is the for loop. In the example just given, the variable i is not accessible from the return statement because that statement is not within the loop. Note, however, that not all compilers are strict about sticking to this rule. The Dev-C++ compiler (for example) generates a warning if you use i outside the for loop — but it uses the variable anyway.

Avoiding the dreaded infinite loop

An *infinite loop* is an execution path that continues forever. An infinite loop occurs any time the condition that would otherwise terminate the loop can't occur — usually the result of a coding error.

Consider the following minor variation of the earlier loop:

```
while (loopCount > 0)
    {
        cout << "Only " << loopCount << " loops to go\n";
    }
```

The programmer forgot to decrement the variable loopCount as in the loop example below. The result is a loop counter that never changes. The test condition is either always false or always true. The program executes in a never-ending (infinite) loop.

I realize that nothing's infinite. Eventually the power will fail, the computer will break, Microsoft will go bankrupt, and dogs will sleep with cats. . . . Either the loop will stop executing, or you won't care anymore.

You can create an infinite loop in many more ways than shown here, most of which are much more difficult to spot than this one.

Applying special loop controls

C++ defines two special flow-control commands known as break and continue. Sometimes the condition for terminating the loop occurs at neither the beginning nor the end of the loop, but in the middle. Consider a program that accumulates numbers of values entered by the user. The loop terminates when the user enters a negative number.

The challenge with this problem is that the program can't exit the loop until the user has entered a value, but must exit before the value is added to the sum.

For these cases, C++ defines the break command. When encountered, the break causes control to exit the current loop immediately. Control passes from the break statement to the statement immediately following the closed brace at the end of the loop.

The format of the break commands is as follows:

```
while(condition) // break works equally well in for loop
{
    if (some other condition)
    {
        break;   // exit the loop
    }
}                // control passes here when the
                 // program encounters the break
```

Armed with this new break command, my solution to the accumulator problem appears as the program BreakDemo.

```cpp
// BreakDemo - input a series of numbers.
//             Continue to accumulate the sum
//             of these numbers until the user
//             enters a negative number.
#include <cstdio>
#include <cstdlib>
#include <iostream>
using namespace std;

int main(int nNumberofArgs, char* pszArgs[])
{
    // input the loop count
    int accumulator = 0;
    cout << "This program sums values entered"
         << "by the user\n";
    cout << "Terminate the loop by entering "
         << "a negative number\n";

    // loop "forever"
    for(;;)
    {
        // fetch another number
        int value = 0;
        cout << "Enter next number: ";
        cin  >> value;

        // if it's negative...
        if (value < 0)
        {
            // ...then exit
            break;
        }

        // ...otherwise add the number to the
        // accumulator
        accumulator = accumulator + value;
    }

    // now that we've exited the loop
    // output the accumulated result
    cout << "\nThe total is "
         << accumulator
         << "\n";

    // wait until user is ready before terminating program
    // to allow the user to see the program results
    system("PAUSE");
    return 0;
}
```

After explaining the rules to the user (entering a negative number to terminate, and so on), the program enters what looks like an infinite for loop.

Once within the loop, `BreakDemo` retrieves a number from the keyboard. Only after the program has read a number can it test to see whether the number it just read matches the exit criteria. If the input number is negative, control passes to the `break`, causing the program to exit the loop. If the input number is *not* negative, control skips over the `break` command to the expression that sums the new value into the accumulator. After the program exits the loop, it outputs the accumulated value and then exits.

When performing an operation on a variable repeatedly in a loop, make sure that the variable is initialized properly before entering the loop. In this case, the program zeros `accumulator` before entering the loop where `value` is added to it.

The result of an example run appears as follows:

```
This program sums values entered by the user
Terminate the loop by entering a negative number
Enter next number: 1
Enter next number: 2
Enter next number: 3
Enter next number: -1

The total is 6
Press any key to continue . . .
```

The `continue` command is used less frequently. When the program encounters the `continue` command, it immediately moves back to the top of the loop. The rest of the statements in the loop are ignored for the current iteration.

The following example snippet ignores negative numbers that the user might input. Only a zero terminates this version (the complete program appears on the CD-ROM as `ContinueDemo`):

```cpp
while(true)// this while() has the same effect as for(;;)
{
    // input a value
    cout << "Input a value:";
    cin  >> value;

    // if the value is negative...
    if (value < 0)
    {
        // ...output an error message...
        cout << "Negative numbers are not allowed\n";

        // ...and go back to the top of the loop
        continue;
    }

    // ...continue to process input like normal
}
```

Nesting Control Commands

Return to our PC-screen-repaint problem. Surely it must need a loop structure of some type to write each pixel from left to right on a single line. (Do Middle Eastern terminals scan from right to left? I have no idea.) What about repeatedly repainting each scan line from top to bottom? (Do PC screens in Australia scan from bottom to top? Beats me.) For this particular task, you need to include the left-to-right scan loop within the top-to-bottom scan loop.

A loop command within another loop is known as a *nested loop*. As an example, you can modify the BreakDemo program into a program that accumulates any number of sequences. In this NestedDemo program, the inner loop sums numbers entered from the keyboard until the user enters a negative number. The outer loop continues accumulating sequences until the sum is 0. Here's what it looks like:

```
// NestedDemo - input a series of numbers.
//              Continue to accumulate the sum
//              of these numbers until the user
//              enters a 0. Repeat the process
//              until the sum is 0.
#include <cstdio>
#include <cstdlib>
#include <iostream>
using namespace std;

int main(int nNumberofArgs, char* pszArgs[])
{
    // the outer loop
    cout << "This program sums multiple series\n"
         << "of numbers. Terminate each sequence\n"
         << "by entering a negative number.\n"
         << "Terminate the series by entering two\n"
         << "negative numbers in a row\n";

    // continue to accumulate sequences
    int accumulator;
    do
    {
        // start entering the next sequence
        // of numbers
        accumulator = 0;
        cout << "Start the next sequence\n";

        // loop forever
        for(;;)
        {
            // fetch another number
            int value = 0;
```

```
        cout << "Enter next number: ";
        cin  >> value;

        // if it's negative...
        if (value < 0)
        {
            // ...then exit
            break;
        }

        // ...otherwise add the number to the
        // accumulator
        accumulator = accumulator + value;
    }

    // output the accumulated result...
    cout << "The total for this sequence is "
         << accumulator
         << endl << endl;

    // ...and start over with a new sequence
    // if the accumulated sequence was not zero
} while (accumulator != 0);

// we're about to quit
cout << "Thank you" << endl;

// wait until user is ready before terminating program
// to allow the user to see the program results
system("PAUSE");
return 0;
}
```

Switching to a Different Subject?

One last control statement is useful in a limited number of cases. The switch statement resembles a compound if statement by including a number of different possibilities rather than a single test:

```
switch(expression)
{
    case c1:
        // go here if the expression == c1
        break;
    case c2:
        // go here if expression == c2
        break;
    default:
        // go here if there is no match
}
```

The value of expression must be an integer (int, long, or char). The case values c1, c2, and c3 must be constants. When the switch statement is encountered, the expression is evaluated and compared to the various case constants. Control branches to the case that matches. If none of the cases match, control passes to the default clause.

Consider the following example code snippet:

```
int choice;
cout << "Enter a 1, 2 or 3:";
cin  >> choice;

switch(choice)
{
    case 1:
      // do "1" processing
      break;

    case 2:
      // do "2" processing
      break;

    case 3:
      // do "3" processing
      break;

    default:
      cout << "You didn't enter a 1, 2 or 3\n";
}
```

Once again, the switch statement has an equivalent, in this case multiple if statements; however, when there are more than two or three cases, the switch structure is easier to understand.

The break statements are necessary to exit the switch command. Without the break statements, control falls through from one case to the next. (Look out below!)

Part II

Becoming a Functional C++ Programmer

The 5th Wave   By Rich Tennant

THE GREAT THING ABOUT OBJECT-ORIENTED PROGRAMMING IS, IT'S MADE SOFTWARE DEVELOPMENT AS EASY AS PUTTING ONE FOOT IN FRONT OF THE OTHER.

In this part . . .

*I*t's one thing to perform operations such as addition and multiplication — even when we're logical (AND and OR or other operations). It's another thing to write real programs. This section introduces the features necessary to make the leap into programmerdom.

You'll find the program BUDGET1 on the enclosed CD-ROM. This largish program demonstrates the concepts of functional programming. You may want to visit this program and its documentation once you've mastered functional programming concepts.

Chapter 6

Creating Functions

*T*he programs developed in prior chapters have been small enough that they can be easily read as a single unit. Larger, real-world programs can be many thousands (or millions!) of lines long. Developers need to break up these monster programs into smaller chunks that are easier to conceive, develop, and maintain.

C++ allows programmers to divide their code into exactly such chunks (known as *functions*). As long as a function has a simple description and a well-defined interface to the outside world, it can be written and debugged without worrying about the code that surrounds it.

This divide-and-conquer approach reduces the difficulty of creating a working program of significant size. This is a simple form of encapsulation — see Chapter 15 for more details on encapsulation.

Writing and Using a Function

Functions are best understood by example. This section starts with the example program `FunctionDemo`, which simplifies the `NestedDemo` program I discussed in Chapter 5 by defining a function to contain part of the logic. Then this section explains how the function is defined and how it is invoked, using `FunctionDemo` as a pattern for understanding both the problem and the solution.

The NestedDemo program in Chapter 5 contains an inner loop (which accumulates a sequence of numbers) surrounded by an outer loop (which repeats the process until the user quits). Separating the two loops would simplify the program by allowing the reader to concentrate on each loop independently.

The following FunctionDemo program shows how NestedDemo can be simplified by creating the function sumSequence().

Function names are normally written with a set of parentheses immediately following the term, like this:

```
// FunctionDemo - demonstrate the use of functions
//                by breaking the inner loop of the
//                NestedDemo program off into its own
//                function
#include <cstdio>
#include <cstdlib>
#include <iostream>
using namespace std;

// sumSequence - add a sequence of numbers entered from
//               the keyboard until the user enters a
//               negative number.
//               return - the summation of numbers entered
int sumSequence(void)
{
    // loop forever
    int accumulator = 0;
    for(;;)
    {
        // fetch another number
        int value = 0;
        cout << "Enter next number: ";
        cin  >> value;

        // if it's negative...
        if (value < 0)
        {
            // ...then exit from the loop
            break;
        }

        // ...otherwise add the number to the
        // accumulator
        accumulator= accumulator + value;
    }

    // return the accumulated value
    return accumulator;
}

int main(int nNumberofArgs, char* pszArgs[])
{
```

```
        cout << "This program sums multiple series\n"
             << "of numbers. Terminate each sequence\n"
             << "by entering a negative number.\n"
             << "Terminate the series by entering two\n"
             << "negative numbers in a row\n"
             << endl;

        // accumulate sequences of numbers...
        int accumulatedValue;
        for(;;)
        {
            // sum a sequence of numbers entered from
            // the keyboard
            cout << "Enter next sequence" << endl;
            accumulatedValue = sumSequence();

            // terminate the loop if sumSequence() returns
            // a zero
            if (accumulatedValue == 0)
            {
                break;
            }

            // now output the accumulated result
            cout << "The total is "
                 << accumulatedValue
                 << "\n"
                 << endl;
        }

        cout << "Thank you" << endl;

        // wait until user is ready before terminating program
        // to allow the user to see the program results
        system("PAUSE");
        return 0;
}
```

Defining the sumSequence () function

The statement int sumSequence(void) begins the definition of the sumSequence() function. The block of code contained in the braces is the *function body*. The function sumSequence() accumulates a sequence of values entered from the keyboard. This code section is identical to that found in the inner loop of NestedDemo.

Calling the function sumSequence ( )

Let's concentrate on the main program contained in the braces following `main()`. This section of code looks similar to the outer loop in `NestedDemo`.

The main difference is the expression `accumulatedValue = sumSequence();` that appears where the inner loop would have been. The `sumSequence()` statement invokes the function of that name. A value returned by the function is stored in the variable `accumulatedValue`. Then this value is displayed. The main program continues to loop until `sumSequence()` returns a sum of zero, which indicates that the user has finished calculating sums.

Divide and conquer

The `FunctionDemo` program has split the outer loop in `main()` from the inner loop into a function `sumSequence()`. This division wasn't arbitrary: `sumSequence()` performs a separate role — worth considering by itself — apart from the control features within `FunctionDemo`.

A good function is easy to describe. You shouldn't have to use more than a single sentence, with a minimum of such words as *and*, *or*, *unless*, or *but*. For example, here's a simple, straightforward definition:

"The function `sumSequence` accumulates a sequence of integer values entered by the user."

This definition is concise and clear. It's a world away from the `ContinueDemo` program description:

"sums a sequence of positive values AND generates an error if the user enters a negative number AND displays the sum AND starts over again until the user enters two zero-length sums."

The output of a sample run of this program appears much like that generated by the `NestedDemo` program, as follows:

```
This program sums multiple series
of numbers. Terminate each sequence
by entering a negative number.
Terminate the series by entering two
negative numbers in a row

Enter next sequence
Enter next number: 1
Enter next number: 2
```

```
Enter next number: 3
Enter next number: -1
The total is 6

Enter next sequence
Enter next number: 1
Enter next number: 2
Enter next number: -1
The total is 3

Enter next sequence
Enter next number: -1
Thank you
Press any key to continue . . .
```

Understanding the Details of Functions

Functions are so fundamental to creating C++ programs that getting a handle on the details of defining, creating, and testing them is critical. Armed with the example `FunctionDemo` program, consider the following definition of *function:*

A function is a logically separated block of C++ code. The function construct has the following form:

```
<return type> name(<arguments to the function>)
{
    // ...
    return <expression>;
}
```

The *arguments* to a function are values that can be passed to the function to be used as input information. The *return value* is a value that the function returns. For example, in the call to the function `square(10)`, the value 10 is an argument to the function `square()`. The returned value is 100.

Both the arguments and the return value are optional. If either is absent, the keyword `void` is used instead. That is, if a function has a `void` argument list, the function does not take any arguments when called (this was the case with the `FunctionDemo` program). If the return type is `void`, the function does not return a value to the caller.

In the example `FunctionDemo` program, the name of the function is `sumSequence()`, the return type is `int`, and no arguments exist.

The default argument type to a function is void, meaning that it takes no arguments. A function int fn(void) may be declared as int fn().

The function construct made it possible for me to write two distinct parts of the FunctionDemo program separately. I concentrated on creating the sum of a sequence of numbers when writing the sumSequence() function. I didn't think about other code that may call the function.

Similarly, when writing main(), I concentrated on handling the summation returned by sumSequence() while thinking only of what the function did — not how it worked.

Understanding simple functions

The simple function sumSequence() returns an integer value that it calculates. Functions may return any of the regular types of variables. For example, a function might return a double or a char (int, double, and char are a few of the variable types discussed in Chapter 2).

If a function returns no value, the return type of the function is labeled void.

A function may be labeled by its return type — for example, a function that returns an int is often known as an integer function. A function that returns no value is known as a void function.

For example, the following void function performs an operation, but returns no value:

```
void echoSquare()
{
    int value;
    cout << "Enter a value:";
    cin >> value;
    cout << "\n The square is:" << (value * value) << "\n";
    return;
}
```

Control begins at the open brace and continues through to the return statement. The return statement in a void function is not followed by a value.

The return statement in a void function is optional. If it isn't present, execution returns to the calling function when control encounters the close brace.

Understanding functions with arguments

Simple functions are of limited use because the communication from such functions is one-way — through the return value. Two-way communication is through function arguments.

Functions with arguments

A *function argument* is a variable whose value is passed to the calling function during the call operation. The following SquareDemo example program defines and uses a function square() that returns the square of a double precision float passed to it:

```
// SquareDemo - demonstrate the use of a function
//              which processes arguments

#include <cstdio>
#include <cstdlib>
#include <iostream>
using namespace std;

// square - returns the square of its argument
//          doubleVar - the value to be squared
//          returns - square of doubleVar
double square(double doubleVar)
{
    return doubleVar * doubleVar;
}

// sumSequence - accumulate the square of the number
//               entered at the keyboard into a sequence
//               until the user enters a negative number
double sumSequence(void)
{
    // loop forever
    double accumulator= 0.0;
    for(;;)
    {
        // fetch another number
        double dValue = 0;
        cout << "Enter next number: ";
        cin  >> dValue;

        // if it's negative...

        if (dValue < 0)
        {
            // ...then exit from the loop
```

```
                    break;
            }

            // ...otherwise calculate the square
            double value = square(dValue);

            // now add the square to the
            // accumulator
            accumulator= accumulator + value;
        }

        // return the accumulated value
        return accumulator;
}

int main(int nNumberofArgs, char* pszArgs[])
{
    cout << "This program sums multiple series\n"
         << "of numbers squared. Terminate each sequence\n"
         << "by entering a negative number.\n"
         << "Terminate the series by entering two\n"
         << "negative numbers in a row\n"
         << endl;

    // Continue to accumulate numbers...
    double accumulatedValue;
    for(;;)
    {
        // sum a sequence of numbers entered from
        // the keyboard
        cout << "Enter next sequence" << endl;
        accumulatedValue = sumSequence();

        // terminate if the sequence is zero or negative
        if (accumulatedValue <= 0.0)
        {
            break;
        }

        // now output the accumulated result
        cout << "\nThe total of the values squared is "
             << accumulatedValue
             << endl;
    }

    cout << "Thank you" << endl;

    // wait until user is ready before terminating program
    // to allow the user to see the program results
    system("PAUSE");
    return 0;
}
```

This is the same `FunctionDemo()` program, except that `SquareDemo()` accumulates the square of the values entered. The function `square()` returns the value of its one argument multiplied by itself. The change to the `sumSequence()` function is simple — rather than accumulate the value entered, the function now accumulates the result returned from `square()`.

Functions with multiple arguments

Functions may have multiple arguments that are separated by commas. Thus, the following function returns the product of its two arguments:

```
int product(int arg1, int arg2)
{
    return arg1 * arg2;
}
```

main ( ) exposed

The "keyword" `main()` from our standard program template is nothing more than a function — albeit a function with strange arguments — but a function nonetheless.

When a program is built, C++ adds some boilerplate code that executes before your program ever starts (you can't see this code without digging into the bowels of the C++ library functions). This code sets up the environment in which your program operates. For example, this boilerplate code opens the default input and output channels `cin` and `cout`.

After the environment has been established, the C++ boilerplate code calls the function `main()`, thereby beginning execution of your code. When your program finishes, it exits from `main()`. This enables the C++ boilerplate to clean up a few things before turning control over to the operating system that kills the program.

Overloading Function Names

C++ allows the programmer to assign the same name to two or more functions. This multiple use of names is known as *overloading* functions.

In general, two functions in a single program cannot share the same name. If they did, C++ would have no way to distinguish them. Note, however, that the name of the function includes the number and type of its arguments — but does *not* include its return argument. Thus the following are not the same functions:

```
void someFunction(void)
{
    // ....perform some function
}
void someFunction(int n)
{
    // ...perform some different function
}
void someFunction(double d)
{
    // ...perform some very different function
}
void someFunction(int n1, int n2)
{
    // ....do something different yet
}
```

C++ still knows that the functions someFunction(void), someFunction(int), someFunction(double), and someFunction(int, int) are not the same. Like so many things that deal with computers, this has an analogy in the human world.

void as an argument type is optional. sumFunction(void) and sumFunction() are the same function. A function has a shorthand name, such as someFunction(), in same way that I have the shorthand name Stephen (actually, my nickname is Randy, but work with me on this one). If there aren't any other Stephens around, people can talk about Stephen behind his back. If, however, there *are* other Stephens, no matter how handsome they might be, people have to use their full names — in my case, Stephen Davis. As long as we use the entire name, no one gets confused — however many Stephens might be milling around. Similarly, the full name for one of the someFunctions() is someFunction(int). As long as this *full* name is unique, no confusion occurs.

The analogies between the computer world (wherever that is) and the human world are hardly surprising because humans build computers. (I wonder . . . if dogs had built computers, would the standard unit of memory be a gnaw instead of a byte? Would requests group in packs instead of queues?)

Here's a typical application that uses overloaded functions with unique full names:

```
int intVariable1, intVariable2; // equivalent to
                                // int Variable1;
                                // int Variable2;
double doubleVariable;

// functions are distinguished by the type of
// the argument passed
```

```
someFunction();              // calls someFunction(void)
someFunction(intVariable1);  // calls someFunction(int)
someFunction(doubleVariable); // calls someFunction(double)
someFunction(intVariable1, intVariable2); // calls
                             // someFunction(int, int)

// this works for constants as well
someFunction(1);             // calls someFunction(int)
someFunction(1.0);           // calls someFunction(double)
someFunction(1, 2);          // calls someFunction(int, int)
```

In each case, the type of the arguments matches the full name of the three functions.

The return type is not part of the extended name (which is also known as the *function signature*) of the function. The following two functions have the same name — so they can't be part of the same program:

```
int someFunction(int n);     // full name of the function
                             // is someFunction(int)
double someFunction(int n);  // same name
```

You're allowed to mix variable types as long as the source variable type is *more restrictive than the target type.* Thus an int can be promoted to a double. The following is acceptable:

```
int someFunction(int n);
double d = someFunction(10); // promote returned value
```

The int returned by someFunction() is promoted into a double. Thus the following would be confusing:

```
int someFunction(int n);
double someFunction(int n);
double d = someFunction(10);// promote returned int?
                            // or use returned double as is
```

Here C++ does not know whether to use the value returned from the double version of someFunction() or promote the value returned from int version.

Defining Function Prototypes

The programmer may provide the remainder of a C++ source file, or module, the extended name (the name and functions) during the definition of the function.

The target functions `sumSequence()` and `square()` — appearing earlier in this chapter — are both defined in the code that appears before the actual call. This doesn't have to be the case: A function may be defined anywhere in the module. (A *module* is another name for a C++ source file.)

However, something has to tell the calling function the full name of the function to be called. Consider the following code snippet:

```
int main(int nNumberofArgs, char* pszArgs[])
{
    someFunc(1, 2);
}
int someFunc(double arg1, int arg2)
{
    // ...do something
}
```

`main()` doesn't know the full name of the function `someFunc()` at the time of the call. It may surmise from the arguments that the name is `someFunc(int, int)` and that its return type is `void` — but as you can see, this is incorrect.

I know, I know — C++ could be less lazy and look ahead to determine the full name of `someFunc()`s on its own, but it doesn't. It's like my crummy car; it gets me there, and I've learned to live with it.

What is needed is some way to inform `main()` of the full name of `someFunc()` before it is used. This is handled by what we call a *function prototype*.

A prototype declaration appears the same as a function with no body. In use, a prototype declaration looks like this:

```
int someFunc(double, int);
int main(int nNumberofArgs, char* pszArgs[])
{
    someFunc(1, 2);
}
int someFunc(double arg1, int arg2)
{
    // ...do something
}
```

The prototype declaration tells the world (at least that part of the world after the declaration) that the extended name for `someFunc()` is `someFunction(double, int)`. The call in `main()` now knows to cast the 1 to a double before making the call. In addition, `main()` knows that the value returned by `someFunc()` is an `int`.

Variable Storage Types

Function variables are stored in three different places. Variables declared within a function are said to be local. In the following example, the variable `localVariable` is local to the function `fn()`:

```
int globalVariable;
void fn()
{
    int localVariable;
    static int staticVariable;
}
```

The variable `localVariable` doesn't exist until execution passes through its declaration within the function `fn()`. `localVariable` ceases to exist when the function returns. Upon return, whatever value that is stored in `localVariable` is lost. In addition, only `fn()` has access to `localVariable` — other functions cannot reach into the function to access it.

By comparison, the variable `globalVariable` is created when the program begins execution — and exists as long as the program is running. All functions have access to `globalVariable` all the time.

The static variable `staticVariable` is a sort of mix between a local and a global variable. The variable `staticVariable` is created when execution first reaches the declaration — at roughly when the function `fn()` is called. The variable is not destroyed when program execution returns from the function. If `fn()` assigns a value to `staticVariable` once, it'll still be there the next time `fn()` is called. The declaration is ignored every subsequent time execution passes through.

In case anyone asks, there is a fourth type, `auto`, but today it has the same meaning as `local`, so you rarely (if ever) see that declaration type anymore. So whoever asked you about it is probably just being a show off (or showing his age).

Including Include Files

It's common to place function prototypes in a separate file (called an *include file*) that the programmer can then include in her C++ source files. Doing so sets the stage for a C++ *preprocessor* program (which runs before the actual compiler takes over) to insert the contents of a file such as `filename`, at the point of a statement such as `#include "filename"`.

A definition for a typical math include file looks like this:

```
// math include file:
// provide prototypes for functions that might be useful
// in more than one program

// abs - return the absolute value of the argument
double abs(double d);

// square - return the square of the argument
double square(double d);
```

A program uses the math include file like this:

```
// MyProgram -
#include "math"

using namespace std;
// my code continues here
```

The #include directive says, in effect, *Replace this directive with the contents of the* math *file.*

The #include directive doesn't have the format of a C++ statement because it's interpreted by a separate interpreter that executes before the C++ compiler starts doing its thing. In particular, the # must be in column one and an end-of-line terminates the include statement. The actual file name must be enclosed in either quotes or brackets. Brackets are used for C++ library functions. Use the quotes for any includes that you create.

The C++ environment provides include files such as cstdio and iostream. In fact, it's iostream that contains the prototype for the setf() function used in Chapter 4 to set output to hex mode.

For years, programmers followed the custom of using the extension .h to designate include files. In more recent years, the C++ ISO standard removed the .h extension from standard include files. (For example, the include file cstdio was previously known as stdio.h.) Many programmers still stubbornly cling to the ".h gold standard" for their own programs. (What's in a name? Evidence that even high-tech folks have traditions.)

Chapter 7

Storing Sequences in Arrays

· ·

In This Chapter

▶ Considering the need for something like an array

▶ Introducing the array data type

▶ Using an array

▶ Using the most common type of array — the character string

· ·

*A*n *array* is a sequence of variables that shares the same name and that is referenced using an index. Arrays are useful little critters that allow you to store a large number of values of the same type and that are related in some way — for example, the batting averages of all the players on the same team might be a good candidate for storage within an array. Arrays can be multidimensional, too, allowing you, for example, to store an array of batting averages within an array of months, which allows you to work with the batting averages of the team as they occur by month. If you think about it long enough, you get a headache.

In this chapter, you find out how to initialize and use arrays for fun and profit. You also find out about an especially useful form of array, a *string,* which in C++ is really just an array of type `char`.

Considering the Need for Arrays

Consider the following problem. You need a program that can read a sequence of numbers from the keyboard. You guessed it — the program stops reading in numbers as soon as you enter a negative number. Unlike similar programs in Chapters 5 and 6, this program is to output all the numbers entered before displaying the average.

You could try to store numbers in a set of independent variables, as in

```
cin >> value1;
if (value1 >= 0)
{
    cin >> value2;
    if (value2 >= 0)
    {
        . . .
```

You can see that this approach can't handle sequences involving more than just a few numbers. Besides, it's ugly. What we need is some type of structure that has a name like a variable but that can store more than one value. May I present to you, Ms. A. Ray.

An array solves the problem of sequences nicely. For example, the following snippet declares an array `valueArray` that has storage for up to 128 `int` values. It then populates the array with numbers entered from the keyboard.

```
int value;

// declare an array capable of holding up to 128 ints
int valueArray[128];

// define an index used to access subsequent members of
// of the array; don't exceed the 128 int limit
for (int i = 0; i < 128; i++)
{
    cin >> value;

    // exit the loop when the user enters a negative
    // number
    if (value < 0)
    {
        break;
    }
    valueArray[i] = value;
}
```

The second line of this snippet declares an array `valueArray`. Array declarations begin with the type of the array members: in this case, `int`. This is followed by the name of the array. The last element of an array declaration is an open and closed bracket containing the maximum number of elements that the array can hold. In this code snippet, `valueArray` can store up to 128 integers.

This snippet reads a number from the keyboard and stores it into each subsequent member of the array `valueArray`. You access an individual element of an array by providing the name of the array followed by brackets containing the index. The first integer in the array is `valueArray[0]`, the second is `valueArray[1]`, and so on.

In use, `valueArray[i]` represents the *i*th element in the array. The index variable i must be a counting variable — that is, i must be a `char`, an `int`, or a `long`. If `valueArray` is an array of `int`s, `valueArray[i]` is an `int`.

Using an array

The following program inputs a sequence of integer values from the keyboard until the user enters a negative number. The program then displays the numbers input and reports their sum.

```cpp
// ArrayDemo - demonstrate the use of arrays
//             by reading a sequence of integers
//             and then displaying them in order
#include <cstdio>
#include <cstdlib>
#include <iostream>
using namespace std;

// prototype declarations
int sumArray(int integerArray[], int sizeOfloatArray);
void displayArray(int integerArray[], int sizeOfloatArray);

int main(int nNumberofArgs, char* pszArgs[])
{
    // input the loop count
    int nAccumulator = 0;
    cout << "This program sums values entered "
         << "by the user\n";
    cout << "Terminate the loop by entering "
         << "a negative number\n";
    cout << endl;

    // store numbers into an array
    int inputValues[128];

    int numberOfValues;
    for(numberOfValues = 0;
        numberOfValues < 128;
        numberOfValues++)
    {
        // fetch another number
        int integerValue;
        cout << "Enter next number: ";
        cin >> integerValue;

        // if it's negative...
        if (integerValue < 0)
```

```
        {
            // ...then exit
            break;
        }

        // ... otherwise store the number
        // into the  storage array
        inputValues[numberOfValues] = integerValue;
    }

    // now output the values and the sum of the values
    displayArray(inputValues, numberOfValues);
    cout << "The sum is "
         << sumArray(inputValues, numberOfValues)
         << endl;

    // wait until user is ready before terminating program
    // to allow the user to see the program results
    system("PAUSE");
    return 0;
}

// displayArray - display the members of an
//                array of length sizeOfloatArray
void displayArray(int integerArray[], int sizeOfArray)
{
    cout << "The value of the array is:" << endl;
    for (int i = 0; i < sizeOfArray; i++)
    {
        cout.width(3);
        cout << i << ": " << integerArray[i] << endl;
    }
    cout << endl;
}

// sumArray - return the sum of the members of an
//            integer array
int sumArray(int integerArray[], int sizeOfArray)
{
    int accumulator = 0;
    for (int i = 0; i < sizeOfArray; i++)
    {
        accumulator += integerArray[i];
    }
    return accumulator;
}
```

The program ArrayDemo begins with a prototype declaration of the functions
sumArray() and displayArray() that it will need later. The main body of
the program contains an input loop (boring). This time, however, the input
values are stored off in the array inputValues.

If the input value is negative, control exits the loop by executing the `break`. If not, `integerValue` is copied into the array. The `int` variable `numberOfValues` is used as an index into the array. `numberOfValues` was initialized to 0 up at the beginning of the `for` loop. The index is incremented on each iteration of the loop. The test in the `for` loop keeps the program from storing more than the 128 integers allocated by the program. (The program goes immediately to the output portion after 128 entries whether or not the user enters a negative number.)

The array `inputValues` is declared as 128 integers long. If you're thinking that this is enough, don't count on it. Writing more data than an array causes your program to perform erratically and often to crash. No matter how large you make the array, always put a check to make sure that you do not exceed the limits of the array.

The main function ends by calling `displayArray()` to print the contents of the array and the sum.

The Dev-C++ environment can help keep you and your functions straight. Figure 7-1 shows the contents of the Classes tab. The name and prototype of each function appear there. Double-clicking a function name takes you straight to the function in the .CPP source file.

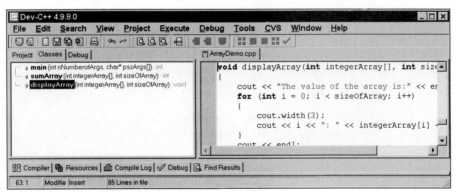

Figure 7-1:
The Classes tab displays information about the functions that make up the program.

The `displayArray()` function contains the typical `for` loop used to traverse an array. Each entry in the array is added to the variable `accumulator`. The `sizeOfArray` passed to the function indicates the number of values contained in `integerArray`.

Notice, yet again, that the index is initialized to 0 and not to 1. In addition, notice how the `for` loop terminates before `i` is equal to `sizeOfArray`. None of the elements after the `sizeOfArray` element contains valid data. The output appears as follows:

```
This program sums values entered by the user
Terminate the loop by entering a negative number

Enter next number: 1
Enter next number: 2
Enter next number: 3
Enter next number: -1
The value of the array is:
   0: 1
   1: 2
   2: 3

The sum is 6
Press any key to continue . . .
```

Just to keep nonprogrammers guessing, the term *iterate* means to traverse through a set of objects such as an array. Programmers say that the sumArray() function iterates through the array. In a similar fashion, I "get irate" when my dog iterates from one piece of furniture to another.

Initializing an array

A local variable does not start life with a valid value, not even the value 0. Said another way, a local variable contains garbage until you actually store something in it. Locally declared arrays are the same — each element contains garbage until you actually assign something to it. You should initialize local variables when you declare them. This rule is even truer for arrays. It is far too easy to access uninitialized array elements thinking that they are valid values.

Fortunately, a small array may be initialized at the time it is declared. The following code snippet demonstrates how this is done:

```
float floatArray[5] = {0.0, 1.0, 2.0, 3.0, 4.0};
```

This initializes floatArray[0] to 0, floatArray[1] to 1, floatArray[2] to 2, and so on.

The number of initialization constants can determine the size of the array. For example, you could have determined that floatArray has five elements just by counting the values within the braces. C++ can count as well (here's at least one thing C++ can do for itself).

The following declaration is identical to the preceding one.

```
float floatArray[] = {0.0, 1.0, 2.0, 3.0, 4.0};
```

You may initialize all the elements in an array to a common value by listing only that value. For example, the following initializes all 25 locations in floatArray to 1.0.

```
float floatArray[25] = {1.0};
```

Accessing too far into an array

Mathematicians start counting arrays with 1. Most program languages start with an offset of 1 as well. C++ arrays begin counting at 0. The first member of a C++ array is valueArray[0]. That makes the last element of a 128-integer array integerArray[127] and not integerArray[128].

Unfortunately for the programmer, C++ does not check to see whether the index you are using is within the range of the array. C++ is perfectly happy giving you access to integerArray[200]. Our yard is only 128 integers long — that's 72 integers into someone else's yard. No telling who lives there and what he's storing at that location. Reading from integerArray[200] will return some unknown and unpredictable value. Writing to that location generates unpredictable results. It may do nothing — the house may be abandoned and the yard unused. On the other hand, it might overwrite some data, thereby confusing the neighbor and making the program act in a seemingly random fashion. Or it might crash the program.

The most common wrong way to access an array is to read or write location integerArray[128]. This is one integer beyond the end of the array. Although it's only one element beyond the end of the array, reading or writing this location is just as dangerous as using any other incorrect address.

Using arrays

On the surface, the ArrayDemo program doesn't do anything more than our earlier, non-array-based programs did. True, this version can replay its input by displaying the set of input numbers before calculating their sum, but this feature hardly seems earth shattering.

Yet, the ability to redisplay the input values hints at a significant advantage to using arrays. Arrays allow the program to process a series of numbers multiple times. The main program was able to pass the array of input values to displayArray() for display and then repass the same numbers to sumArray() for addition.

Defining and using arrays of arrays

Arrays are adept at storing sequences of numbers. Some applications require sequences of sequences. A classic example of this matrix configuration is the spreadsheet. Laid out like a chessboard, each element in the spreadsheet has both an x and a y offset.

C++ implements the matrix as follows:

```
int intMatrix[10][5];
```

This matrix is 10 elements in 1 dimension, and 5 in another, for a total of 50 elements. In other words, intMatrix is a 10-element array, each element of which is a 5-int array. As you might expect, one corner of the matrix is in intMatrix[0][0], while the other corner is intMatrix[9][4].

Whether you consider intMatrix to be 10 elements long in the x dimension and in the y dimension is a matter of taste. A matrix can be initialized in the same way that an array is

```
int intMatrix[2][3] = {{1, 2, 3}, {4, 5, 6}};
```

This line initializes the 3-element array intMatrix[0] to 1, 2, and 3 and the 3-element array intMatrix[1] to 4, 5, and 6, respectively.

Using Arrays of Characters

The elements of an array are of any type. Arrays of floats, doubles, and longs are all possible; however, arrays of characters have particular significance.

Creating an array of characters

Human words and sentences can be expressed as an array of characters. An array of characters containing my first name would appear as

```
char sMyName[] = {'S', 't', 'e', 'p', 'h', 'e', 'n'};
```

The following small program displays my name:

```
// CharDisplay - output a character array to
//               standard output, the MS-DOS window
```

```
#include <stdio.h>
#include <iostream.h>

// prototype declarations
void displayCharArray(char stringArray[],
                      int sizeOfloatArray);

int main(int nArg, char* pszArgs[])
{
    char charMyName[] = {'S', 't', 'e', 'p', 'h', 'e', 'n'};
    displayCharArray(charMyName, 7);
    cout << "\n";
    return 0;
}


// displayCharArray - display an array of characters
//                    by outputing one character at
//                    a time
void displayCharArray(char stringArray[],
                      int sizeOfloatArray)
{
    for(int i = 0; i< sizeOfloatArray; i++)
    {
        cout << stringArray[i];
    }
}
```

The program declares a fixed array of characters `charMyName` containing —
you guessed it — my name (what better name?). This array is passed to the
function `displayCharArray()` along with its length. The `displayCharArray()`
function is identical to the `displayArray()` function in the earlier example
program except that this version displays `char`s rather than `int`s.

This program works fine; however, it is inconvenient to pass the length of the
array around with the array itself. If we could come up with a rule for deter-
mining the end of the array, we wouldn't need to pass its length — you would
know that the array was complete when you encountered the special rule that
told you so.

Creating a string of characters

In many cases, all values for each element are possible. However, C++
reserves the special "character" 0 as the non-character. We can use '\0' to
mark the end of a character array. (The numeric value of '\0' is zero; however, the type of '\0' is `char`.)

The character \y is the character whose numeric value is y. The character \0 is the character with a value of 0, otherwise known as the null character. Using that rule, the previous small program becomes

```cpp
// DisplayString - output a character array to
//                 standard output, the MS-DOS window
#include <cstdio>
#include <cstdlib>
#include <iostream>
#include <string>
using namespace std;

// prototype declarations
void displayString(char stringArray[]);

int main(int nNumberofArgs, char* pszArgs[])
{
    char charMyName[] =
            {'S', 't', 'e', 'p', 'h', 'e', 'n', 0};
    displayString(charMyName);

    // wait until user is ready before terminating program
    // to allow the user to see the program results
    system("PAUSE");
    return 0;
}

// displayString - display a character string
//                 one character at a time
void displayString(char stringArray[])
{
    for(int i = 0; stringArray[i] != '\0'; i++)
    {
        cout << stringArray[i];
    }
}
```

The declaration of charMyName declares the character array with the extra null character \0 on the end. The displayString program iterates through the character array until a null character is encountered.

The function displayString() is simpler to use than its displayCharArray() predecessor because it is no longer necessary to pass along the length of the character array. This secret handshake of terminating a character array with a null is so convenient that it is used throughout C++ language. C++ even gives such an array a special name.

A *string of characters* is a null terminated character array. Confusingly enough, this is often shortened to simply *string,* even though C++ defines the separate type string.

The choice of '\0' as the terminating character was not random. Remember that zero is the only numeric value that converts to `false`; all other values translate to `true`. This means that the `for` loop could (and usually is) written as:

```
for(int i = 0; stringArray[i]; i++)
```

This whole business of null terminated character strings is so ingrained into the C++ language psyche that C++ uses a string of characters surrounded by double quotes to be an array of characters automatically terminated with a '\0' character. The following are identical declarations:

```
char szMyName[] = "Stephen";
char szAlsoMyName[] =
            {'S', 't', 'e', 'p', 'h', 'e', 'n', '\0'};
```

The naming convention used here is exactly that, a convention. C++ does not care. The prefix `sz` stands for *zero-terminated string*.

The string `Stephen` is eight characters long and not seven — the null character after the `n` is assumed. The string `""` is one character long consisting of just the null character.

Manipulating Strings with Character

The C++ programmer is often required to manipulate strings. C++ provides a number of standard string-manipulation functions to make the job easier. A few of these functions are listed in Table 7-1.

Table 7-1	String-Handling Functions
Name	*Operation*
`int strlen(string)`	Returns the number of characters in a string.
`void strcpy(target, source, n)`	Copies the source string into a target array.
`void strcat(target, source, n)`	Concatenates the source string onto the end of the target string.
`void strncpy(target, source, n)`	Copies a string up to *n* characters from the source string into a target array.

(continued)

Table 7-1 *(continued)*

Name	Operation
`void strncat(target, source, n)`	Concatenates the source string onto the end of the target string or 'n' characters, whichever comes first.
`int strnstr(string, pattern, n)`	Finds the first occurrence of one pattern string in another.
`int strncmp(source1, source2, n)`	Compares the first *n* characters in two strings. Returns a zero if the two strings match exactly.
`int strnicmp(source1, source2)`	Compares up to *n* characters in two strings without regard to case.

You need to add the statement #include <strings.h> to the beginning of any program that uses a str... function.

The current ANSI C++ standard suggests that you avoid the str...() functions. ANSI C++ says that these functions are *deprecated,* meaning that ANSI will leave them alone for now, but don't be surprised if they go away some day. That's why strings.h uses the older standard of ending all include files with a ".h". The ANSI standard suggests that you use the string type as defined in the next section. However, you will see a large number of programs that continue to use these functions.

The following Concatenate program inputs two strings from the keyboard and concatenates them into a single string.

```
// Concatenate - concatenate two strings
//                with a " - " in the middle
#include <cstdio>
#include <cstdlib>
#include <iostream>
using namespace std;

// the following include file is deprecated;
// however, it is required for the str functions
#include <strings.h>

int main(int nNumberofArgs, char* pszArgs[])
{
    // read first string...
    char szString1[256];
    cout << "Enter string #1:";
    cin >> szString1;
```

```
    // safer alternative
    // cin.getline(szString1, 128);

    // ...now the second string...
    char szString2[128];
    cout << "Enter string #2:";
    cin >> szString2;
    // safer alternative
    // cin.getline(szString1, 128);

    // accumulate both strings into a single buffer
    char szString[260];

    // copy the first string into the buffer...
    strncpy(szString, szString1, 128);

    // ...concatenate a " - " onto the first...
    strncat(szString, " - ", 4);

    // ...now add the second string...
    strncat(szString, szString2, 128);

    // ...and display the result
    cout << "\n" << szString << endl;

    // wait until user is ready before terminating program
    // to allow the user to see the program results
    system("PAUSE");
    return 0;
}
```

The Concatenate program reads two character strings and appends them together with a " - " in the middle.

The arguments to the str...() functions appear backward to any reasonable individual (you might consider this an acid test for "reasonable"). For example, the function strncat(target, source, count) tacks the second string source onto the end of the first argument target.

An example output from the program appears as follows:

```
Enter string #1:Chester
Enter string #2:Dog

Chester - Dog
Press any key to continue . . .
```

The program begins by reading a string from the keyboard. cin >> szString1 stops when any type of whitespace is encountered. Characters up to the first whitespace are read, the whitespace character is tossed, and the remaining characters are left in the input hopper for the next `cin>>` statement. Thus, if I were to enter "the Dog", `szString2` would be filled with "the", and the word "Dog" would be left in the input buffer.

The `cin >>` extractor knows nothing about the length of the string. `cin` is perfectly willing to read thousands of characters and stuff them into `szString1`, even though it is declared 256 characters long. This causes a dangerous overflow condition that hackers can (and will) exploit to put a virus in your program.

C++ provides work-arounds for many of the string overflow problems. For example, the function `getline()` inputs a line of text; however, this function accepts the length of the string as one of its arguments:

```
cin.getline(string, lengthOfTheString);
```

(Ignore the strange looking `cin.` format for now.)

The `strncpy()` and `strncat()` functions accept the length of the target buffer as one of their arguments. The call `strncpy(szString, szString1, 128)` says "copy the characters in `szString1` into `szString` until you copy a null character or until you've copied 128 characters, whichever comes first." The call specifically does not mean copy 128 characters every time.

There are both "counting" and "noncounting" versions of most of the `str...()` functions. The noncounting versions don't require the maximum number of characters to process as an argument. You can use these when you don't know the buffer size, but be aware that they are perfectly happy to write beyond the end of the target string.

String-ing Along Variables

ANSI C++ includes a type `string` designed to make it easier to manipulate strings of text.

I use the term *string* to refer to an array of characters terminated by a null and *string type* to refer to the type `string`. The `string` type includes operations for copying, concatenating, capitalizing, knotting, and simple magic tricks. `string` avoids the overrun problems inherent with null terminated strings. The functions that manipulate string objects are defined in the include file `<string>`.

The `string` type based StringConcatenate program appears as follows:

```
// StringConcatenate - concatenate two string type
//                 variables with a " - " in the middle
#include <cstdio>
#include <cstdlib>
#include <iostream>
#include <string>
using namespace std;

int main(int nNumberofArgs, char* pszArgs[])
{
    // read first string...
    string string1;
    cout << "Enter string #1:";
    cin >> string1;

    // ...now the second string...
    string string2;
    cout << "Enter string #2:";
    cin >> string2;

    // accumulate both strings into a single buffer
    string buffer;
    string divider = " - ";
    buffer = string1 + divider + string2;

    // ...and display the result
    cout << "\n" << buffer << endl;

    // wait until user is ready before terminating program
    // to allow the user to see the program results
    system("PAUSE");
    return 0;
}
```

This concatenate function defines two variables, string1 and string2 (clever, no?). A string type variable is not defined of any specified length — it can grow and shrink to fit the number of characters it contains (up to available memory, of course, or the cows come home, whichever is first). Not only do you not have to guess how big to make a target character array, but some nefarious user can't crash your program by inputting too many characters. The StringConcatenate program manipulates the string type variables as it would any other.

Notice that some operations have to be understood in a slightly different way from their arithmetic equivalent. For example, to add two string type variables together means to concatenate them. In addition, notice how C++ can convert a null terminated character string into a string type variable without being told to.

The `string` type is not intrinsic to C++ like `int` or `float`, meaning that its operations are not built into the syntax of the language. Operations on `string` type variables are defined in the `string` include file. The `string` class is discussed further in Chapter 27. I mention `string` here to demonstrate that it is often easier to use than manipulating null terminated character arrays yourself.

Chapter 8

Taking a First Look at C++ Pointers

So far, the C++ language has been fairly conventional compared with other programming languages. Sure, some computer languages lack (il-)logical operators (see Chapter 4 for more) and C++ has its own unique symbols, but there's nothing new in the way of concepts. C++ really separates itself from the crowd in definition and use of pointer variables. A *pointer* is a variable that "points at" other variables. I realize that's a circular argument, but let me put it this way: A pointer variable contains the address of a variable in memory.

This chapter introduces the pointer variable type. It begins with some concept definitions, flows through pointer syntax, and then introduces some of the reasons for the pointer mania that grips the C++ programming world.

Variable Size

My weight goes up and down all the time, but here I'm really referring to the size of a variable, not my own variable size. Memory is measured in bytes or bits. The following program gives you the size of the different variable types:

```cpp
// VariableSize - output the size of each type of
//                variable
#include <cstdio>
#include <cstdlib>
#include <iostream>
using namespace std;

int main(int nNumberofArgs, char* pszArgs[])
```

```
{
    bool    b;
    char    c;
    int     n;
    long    l;
    float   f;
    double  d;

    cout << "sizeof a bool   = "  << sizeof b << endl;
    cout << "sizeof a char   = " << sizeof c << endl;
    cout << "sizeof an int   = " << sizeof n << endl;
    cout << "sizeof a long   = " << sizeof l << endl;
    cout << "sizeof a float = " << sizeof f << endl;
    cout << "sizeof a double= " << sizeof d << endl;

    // wait until user is ready before terminating program
    // to allow the user to see the program results
    system("PAUSE");
    return 0;
}
```

sizeof is actually a C++ construct that returns the size of its argument in bytes. The variable size program generates the following output:

```
sizeof a bool   = 1
sizeof a char   = 1
sizeof an int   = 4
sizeof a long   = 4
sizeof a float = 4
sizeof a double= 8
Press any key to continue . . .
```

Don't be concerned if the compiler that you're using generates different results. For example, you may find that an int is smaller than a long. C++ doesn't say exactly how big a variable type must be; it just says that a long is the same size as or larger than an int and that a double is the same size as or larger than a float. The sizes output by the VariableSize program are typical for a 32-bit processor such as the Pentium class processors.

What's in an Address?

Like the saying goes: "Everyone has to be somewhere." Every C++ variable is stored somewhere in the computer's memory. Memory is broken into individual bytes with each byte carrying its own address numbered 0, 1, 2, and so on.

A variable intReader might be at address 0x100, whereas floatReader might be over at location 0x180. (By convention, memory addresses are expressed in hexadecimal.) Of course, intReader and floatReader might be somewhere else in memory entirely — only the computer knows for sure and only at the time that the program is executed.

This is somewhat analogous to a hotel. When you make your reservation, you may be assigned room 0x100. (I know that suite numbers are normally *not* expressed in hexadecimal, but bear with me.) Your buddy may be assigned 80 doors down in room 0x180. Each variable is assigned an address when it is created (more on that later in this chapter when we talk about scope).

Address Operators

The two pointer-related operators are shown in Table 8-1. The & operator says "tell me your hotel address," and * says "his address is."

Table 8-1	Pointer Operators
Operator	*Meaning*
& (unary)	The address of
* (unary)	(In an expression) the thing pointed at by
* (unary)	(In a declaration) pointer to

The following Layout program demonstrates how the & operator displays the layout of memory variables in memory:

```
// Layout - this program tries to give the
//          reader an idea of the layout of
//          local memory in her compiler
#include <cstdio>
#include <cstdlib>
#include <iostream>
using namespace std;

int main(int nNumberofArgs, char* pszArgs[])
{
    int    end;
    int    n;
    long   l;
    float  f;
    double d;

    // set output to hex mode
    cout.setf(ios::hex);
    cout.unsetf(ios::dec);
```

```
    // output the address of each variable
    // in order to get an idea of how variables are
    // laid out in memory
    cout << "--- = 0x" << &end << "\n";
    cout << "&n  = 0x" << &n  << "\n";
    cout << "&l  = 0x" << &l  << "\n";
    cout << "&f  = 0x" << &f  << "\n";
    cout << "&d  = 0x" << &d  << "\n";

    // wait until user is ready before terminating program
    // to allow the user to see the program results
    system("PAUSE");
    return 0;
}
```

The program declares a set of variables. It then applies the & operator to each one to find out where it lies in memory. The results of one execution of this program with Dev-C++ appear as follows:

```
--- = 0x0x22ff6c
&n  = 0x0x22ff68
&l  = 0x0x22ff64
&f  = 0x0x22ff60
&d  = 0x0x22ff58
Press any key to continue . . .
```

Your results may vary. The absolute address of program variables depends on a lot of factors. In general, it may even vary from one execution of the program to the next.

Notice how the variable n is exactly 4 bytes from the first variable declared (m2). The variable l appears 4 bytes down from that. The double variable d is a full 8 bytes from its neighboring variable f. Each variable has been allocated just the space needed for its type.

There is no requirement that the C++ compiler pack variables in memory with no spaces between them. Dev-C++ could have laid out the variables in memory in any other reasonable fashion.

Using Pointer Variables

A *pointer variable* is a variable that contains an address, usually the address of another variable. Returning to my hotel analogy for a moment, I might tell my son that I will be in room 0x100 on my trip. My son is a pointer variable of sorts. Anyone can ask him at any time, "Where's your father staying?" and he'll spill his guts without hesitation.

The following pseudo-C++ demonstrates how the two address operators shown in Table 8-1 are used:

```
mySon = &DadsRoom;  // tell mySon the address of Dad's Room
room = *mySon;       // "Dad's room number is"
```

The following C++ code snippet shows these operators used correctly:

```
void fn()
{
   int  intVar;
   int* pintVar;

   pintVar  = &intVar;  // pintVar now points to intVar
   *pintVar = 10;       // stores 10 into int location
                        // pointed at by pintVar
}
```

The function fn() begins with the declaration of intVar. The next statement declares the variable pintVar to be a variable of type pointer to an int. (By the way, pintVar is pronounced pee-int-Var, not pint-Var.)

Pointer variables are declared like normal variables except for the addition of the unary * character. This * character can appear anywhere between the base type name — in this case int — and the variable name; however, it is becoming increasingly common to add the * to the end of the type.

The * character is called the *asterisk character* (that's logical enough), but because asterisk is hard to say, many programmers have come to call it the *splat* character. Thus, they would say splat pintVar.

Many programmers adopt a naming convention in which the first character of the variable name indicates the type of the variable, such as n for int, d for double, and so on. A further aspect of this naming convention is to place a p at the beginning of a pointer variable name.

In an expression, the unary operator & means the address of. Thus, we would read the first assignment as store the address of intVar in pintVar.

To make this more concrete, assume that the memory for function fn() starts at location 0x100. In addition, assume that intVar is at address 0x102 and that pintVar is at 0x106. The layout here is simpler than the actual results from the Layout program; however, the concepts are identical.

The first assignment stores the value of & intVar (0x102) in the pointer variable pintVar. The second assignment in the small program snippet says "store 10 in the location pointed at by pintVar." The value 10 is stored in the address contained in pintVar, which is 0x102 (the address of intVar).

Comparing pointers and houses

A pointer is much like a house address. Your house has a unique address. Each byte in memory has an address that is unique. A house address is made up of both numbers and letters. For example, my address is 123 Main Street.

You can store a couch in the house at 123 Main Street — you can store a number in the byte located at 0x123456. Alternatively, you can take a piece of paper and write an address — I don't know, say, 123 Main Street. You can now store a couch at the house with the address written on the piece of paper. In fact, this is the way delivery people work — their job is to deliver a couch to the address written down on the shipping orders whether it's 123 Main Street or not. (I'm not maligning delivery people — they have brains — it's just that this is more or less the way things work.)

In C++, the following code snippet finds the address of myHouse and stores a couch at that houseAddress (loosely speaking):

```
House myHouse;
House* houseAddress;
houseAddress = &myHouse;
*houseAddress = couch;
```

In humanspeak, you would say myHouse is a House. houseAddress is the address of a House. Assign the address of myHouse to the House pointer, houseAddress. Now store a couch at the house located at the address stored in houseAddress.

Having said all that, take a look at the int and int* version of the earlier example code snippet:

```
int myInt;
int* intAddress;
intAddress = &myInt;
*intAddress = 10;
```

That is, myInt is an int. intAddress is a pointer to an int. Assign the address of myInt to the pointer intAddress. Finally, assign 10 to the int that intAddress points to.

Using different types of pointers

Every expression has a type as well as a value. The type of the expression intVar is pointer to an integer, written as int*. Comparing this with the declaration of pintVar, you see that the types match exactly:

```
int* pintVar = &intVar; // both sides of the assignment are
                        // of type int*
```

Similarly, because `pintVar` is of type `int*`, the type of `*pintVar` is `int`:

```
*pintVar = 10;        // both sides of the assignment are
                      // of type int
```

The type of the thing pointed to by `pintVar` is `int`. This is equivalent to saying that, if `houseAddress` is the address of a house, the thing pointed at by `houseAddress` must be a house. Amazing, but true.

Pointers to other types of variables are expressed the same way:

```
double doubleVar;
double* pdoubleVar = &doubleVar;
*pdoubleVar = 10.0;
```

A pointer on a Pentium class machine takes 4 bytes no matter what it points to. That is, an address on a Pentium is 4 bytes long, period.

Matching pointer types is extremely important. Consider what might happen if the following were allowed:

```
int    n1;
int*   pintVar;
pintVar  = &n1;
*pintVar = 100.0;
```

The second assignment attempts to store the 8-byte double value 100.0 into the 4-byte space allocated for `n1`. Actually, this isn't as bad as it looks — C++ is smart enough to demote the constant 100.0 to an `int` before making the assignment.

It is possible to cast one type of variable into another:

```
int iVar;
double dVar = 10.0;
iVar = (int)dVar;
```

Similarly, it is possible to cast one pointer type into another.

```
int* piVar;
double dVar = 10.0;
double* pdVar;
piVar = (int*)pdVar;
```

Consider, however, what catastrophes can arise if this type of casting about of pointers were to get loose. Save a variable into an area of the wrong size, and nearby variables can be wiped out. This is demonstrated graphically in the following LayoutError program.

```
// LayoutError - demonstrate the results of
//                a messing up a pointer usage
#include <cstdio>
#include <cstdlib>
#include <iostream>
using namespace std;

int main(int nNumberofArgs, char* pszArgs[])
{
    int     upper = 0;
    int     n     = 0;
    int     lower = 0;

    // output the values of the three variables before...
    cout << "the initial values are" << endl;
    cout << "upper = " << upper << endl;
    cout << "n     = " << n     << endl;
    cout << "lower = " << lower << endl;

    // now store a double into the space
    // allocated for an int
    cout << "\nStoring 13.0 into the location &n" << endl;
    double* pD = (double*)&n;
    *pD = 13.0;

    // display the results
    cout << "\nThe final results are:" << endl;
    cout << "upper = " << upper << endl;
    cout << "n     = " << n     << endl;
    cout << "lower = " << lower << endl;

    // wait until user is ready before terminating program
    // to allow the user to see the program results
    system("PAUSE");
    return 0;
}
```

The first three lines in main() declare three integers in the normal fashion. The assumption made here is that these three variables are laid out next to each other.

The next three executable lines output the value of the three variables. Not surprisingly, all three variables display as 0. The assignment *pD = 13.0; stores the double value 13.0 in the integer variable n. The three output statements display the values of all three variables after the assignment.

After assigning the double value 13.0 in the integer variable n, n is not modified at all; however, the nearby variable upper is filled with a garbage value. This is not good, as the output from the program shows:

```
the initial values are
upper = 0
```

```
n     = 0
lower = 0

Storing 13.0 into the location &n

The final results are:
upper = 1076494336
n     = 0
lower = 0
Press any key to continue . . .
```

The house equivalent goes something like this:

```
House* houseAddress = &"123 Main Street";
Hotel* hotelAddress;
hotelAddress = (Hotel*)houseAddress;
*hotelAddress = TheRitz;
```

houseAddress is initialized to point to my house. The variable hotelAddress is a pointer to a hotel. Now, the house address is cast into the address of a hotel and saved off into the variable hotelAddress. Finally, TheRitz is plopped down on top of my house. Because TheRitz is slightly bigger than my house (okay, a lot bigger than my house), it isn't surprising that TheRitz wipes out my neighbors' houses as well.

The type of pointer saves the programmer from stuffing an object into a space that is too big or too small. The assignment *pintVar = 100.0; actually causes no problem — because C++ knows that pintVar points to an int, C++ knows to demote the 100.0 to an int before making the assignment.

Passing Pointers to Functions

One of the uses of pointer variables is in passing arguments to functions. To understand why this is important, you need to understand how arguments are passed to a function.

Passing by value

You may have noticed that it is not normally possible to change the value of a variable passed to a function from within the function. Consider the following example code segment:

```
void fn(int intArg)
{
    intArg = 10;
    // value of intArg at this point is 10
}

void parent(void)
{
    int n1 = 0;
    fn(n1);
    // value of n1 at this point is 0
}
```

Here the parent() function initializes the integer variable n1 to zero. The value of n1 is then passed to fn(). Upon entering the function, intArg is equal to 10, the value passed. fn() changes the value of intArg before returning to parent(). Perhaps surprisingly, upon returning to parent(), the value of n1 is still 0.

The reason is that C++ doesn't pass a variable to a function. Instead, C++ passes the value contained in the variable at the time of the call. That is, the expression is evaluated, even if it is just a variable name, and the result is passed.

It is easy for a speaker to get lazy and say something like, "Pass the variable x to the function fn()." This really means to pass the value of the expression x.

Passing pointer values

Like any other intrinsic type, a pointer may be passed as an argument to a function:

```
void fn(int* pintArg)
{
  *pintArg = 10;
}

void parent(void)
{
    int n = 0;

    fn(&n);      // this passes the address of i
                 // now the value of n is 10
}
```

In this case, the address of n is passed to the function fn() rather than the value of n. The significance of this difference is apparent when you consider the assignment within fn().

Suppose n is located at address 0x102. Rather than the value 10, the call fn(&n) passes the value 0x102. Within fn(), the assignment *pintArg = 10 stores the value 10 into the int variable located at location 0x102, thereby overwriting the value 0. Upon returning to parent(), the value of n is 10 because n is just another name for 0x102.

Passing by reference

C++ provides a shorthand for passing arguments by address — a shorthand that enables you to avoid having to hassle with pointers. In the following example, the variable n is passed by reference.

```
void fn(int& intArg)
{
    intArg = 10;
}

void parent(void)
{
    int n = 0;
    fn(n);
                        // here the value of n is 10
}
```

In this case, a reference to n rather than its value is passed to fn(). The fn() function stores the value 10 into int location referenced by intArg.

Notice that reference is not an actual type. Thus, the function's full name is fn(int) and not fn(int&).

Making Use of a Block of Memory Called the Heap

The *heap* is an amorphous block of memory that your program can access as necessary. This section describes why it exists and how to use it.

Visual C++.NET allows the programmer to write code in what is known as *managed mode* in addition to the conventional, "unmanaged mode." In managed mode, the compiler handles the allocation and deallocation of memory. Managed programs rely upon the .NET framework. Only Visual C++.NET currently supports managed mode. This book only covers unmanaged mode programming.

Just as it is possible to pass a pointer to a function, it is possible for a function to return a pointer. A function that returns the address of a double is declared as follows:

```
double* fn(void);
```

However, you must be very careful when returning a pointer. In order to understand the dangers, you must know something about variable scope. (No, I don't mean a variable zoom rifle scope.)

Limiting scope

C++ variables have a property in addition to their value and type known as scope. Besides being a mouthwash, *scope* is the range over which a variable is defined.

Consider the following code snippet:

```
// the following variable is accessible to
// all functions and defined as long as the
// program is running(global scope)
int intGlobal;

// the following variable intChild is accessible
// only to the function and is defined only
// as long as C++ is executing child() or a
// function which child() calls (function scope)
void child(void)
{
    int intChild;
}

// the following variable intParent has function
// scope
void parent(void)
{
    int intParent = 0;
    child();

    int intLater = 0;
    intParent = intLater;
}

int main(int nArgs, char* pArgs[])
{
    parent();
}
```

Execution begins with main(). The function main() immediately invokes parent(). The first thing that the processor sees in parent() is the declaration of intParent. At that point, intParent goes into scope — that is, intParent is defined and available for the remainder of the function parent().

The second statement in parent() is the call to child(). Once again, the function child() declares a local variable, this time intChild. The variable intChild is within the scope of child(). Technically, intParent is not within the scope of child() because child() doesn't have access to intParent; however, the variable intParent continues to exist.

When child() exits, the variable intChild goes out of scope. Not only is intChild no longer accessible, but it no longer even exists. (The memory occupied by intChild is returned to the general pool to be used for other things.)

As parent() continues executing, the variable intLater goes into scope at the declaration. At the point that parent() returns to main(), both intParent and intLater go out of scope. The programmer may declare a variable outside of any function. This type of variable, known as a *global variable,* remains in scope for the duration of the program.

Because intGlobal is declared globally in this example, it is available to all three functions and remains available for the life of the program.

Examining the scope problem

The following code segment compiles without error but doesn't work (don't you just hate that):

```
double* child(void)
{
    double dLocalVariable;
    return &dLocalVariable;
}

void parent(void)
{
    double* pdLocal;
    pdLocal  = child();
    *pdLocal = 1.0;
}
```

The problem with this function is that dLocalVariable is defined only within the scope of the function child(). Thus, by the time the memory address of dLocalVariable is returned from child(), it refers to a variable that no longer exists. The memory that dLocalVariable formerly occupied is probably being used for something else.

This error is very common because it can creep up in a number of different ways. Unfortunately, this error does not cause the program to instantly stop. In fact, the program may work fine most of the time — that is, the program continues to work as long as the memory formerly occupied by dLocalVariable is not reused immediately. Such intermittent problems are the most difficult ones to solve.

Providing a solution using the heap

The scope problem originated because C++ took back the locally defined memory before the programmer was ready. What is needed is a block of memory controlled by the programmer. She can allocate the memory and put it back when she wants to — not because C++ thinks it's a good idea. Such a block of memory is called the *heap*.

Heap memory is allocated using the new command followed by the type of object to allocate. For example, the following allocates a double variable off the heap.

```
double* child(void)
{
    double* pdLocalVariable = new double;
    return pdLocalVariable;
}
```

Although the variable pdLocalVariable goes out of scope when the function child() returns, the memory to which pdLocalVariable refers does not. A memory location returned by new does not go out of scope until it is explicitly returned to the heap using a delete command:

```
void parent(void)
{
    // child() returns the address of a block
    // of heap memory
    double* pdMyDouble = child();

    // store a value there
    *pdMyDouble = 1.1;

    // ...
```

```
    // now return the memory to the heap
    delete pdMyDouble;
    pdMyDouble = 0;

    // ...
}
```

Here the pointer returned by `child()` is used to store a double value. After the function is finished with the memory location, it is returned to the heap. The function *parent()* sets the pointer to zero after the heap memory has been returned — this is not a requirement, but a very good idea. If the programmer mistakenly attempts to store something in `* pdMyDouble` after the `delete`, the program will crash immediately.

A program that crashes immediately upon encountering an error is much easier to fix than one that is intermittent in its behavior.

The whole problem of allocating and returning heap memory goes away in Visual C++.NET–managed mode. *Managed* refers to the fact that C++ handles the allocation and deallocation of memory references. This book deals only with unmanaged mode Visual C++.NET programs.

Chapter 9

Taking a Second Look at C++ Pointers

C++ allows the programmer to operate on pointer variables much as she would on simple types of variables. (The concept of pointer variables is introduced in Chapter 8.) How and why this is done along with its implications are the subjects of this chapter.

Defining Operations on Pointer Variables

Some of the same operators I cover in Chapter 3 can be applied to pointer types. This section examines the implications of applying these operators to both to pointers and to the array types (I discuss arrays in Chapter 7). Table 9-1 lists the three fundamental operations that are defined on pointers.

Table 9-1	The Three Operations Defined on Pointer Types	
Operation	*Result*	*Meaning*
pointer + offset	pointer	Calculate the address of the object integer entries from pointer
pointer - offset	pointer	The opposite of addition
pointer2 - pointer1	offset	Calculate the number of entries between pointer2 and pointer1

In this case, offset is of type long. (Although not listed in Table 9-1, C++ also supports operators related to addition and subtraction, such as ++ and +=.)

The real estate memory model (which I use so effectively in Chapter 8, if I do say so myself) is useful to explain how pointer arithmetic works. Consider a city block in which all houses are numbered sequentially. The house next to 123 Main Street has the address 124 Main Street (or 122 if you go backward, like Hebrew and Arabic).

Now it's pretty clear that the house four houses down from 123 Main Street must be 127 Main Street; thus, you can say 123 Main + 4 = 127 Main. Similarly, if I were to ask how many houses are there from 123 Main to 127 Main, the answer would be four — 127 Main - 123 Main = 4. (Just as an aside, a house is zero houses from itself: 123 Main - 123 Main = 0.)

Extending this concept one step further, it makes no sense to add 123 Main Street to 127 Main Street. In similar fashion, you can't add two addresses, nor can you multiply an address, divide an address, square an address, or take the square root — you get the idea.

Re-examining arrays in light of pointer variables

Now return to the wonderful array for just a moment. Once again, my neighborhood comes to mind. An array is just like my city block. Each element of the array corresponds to a house on that block. Here, however, the array elements are measured by the number of houses from the beginning of the block (the street corner). Say that the house right on the corner is 123 Main Street, which means that the house one house from the corner is 124 Main Street, and so on. Using array terminology, you would say cityBlock[0] is 123 Main Street, cityBlock[1] is 124 Main Street, and so on.

Take that same model back to the world of computer memory. Consider the case of an array of 32 1-byte characters called charArray. If the first byte of this array is stored at address 0x110, the array will extend over the range 0x110 through 0x12f. charArray[0] is located at address 0x110, charArray[1] is at 0x111, charArray[2] at 0x112, and so on.

Take this model one step further to the world of pointer variables. After executing the expression

```
ptr = &charArray[0];
```

the pointer ptr contains the address 0x110. The addition of an integer offset to a pointer is defined such that the relationships shown in Table 9-2 are true. Table 9-2 also demonstrates why adding an offset n to ptr calculates the address of the *n*th element in charArray.

Table 9-2	Adding Offsets	
Offset	*Result*	*Is the Address of*
+ 0	0x110	`charArray[0]`
+ 1	0x111	`charArray[1]`
+ 2	0x112	`charArray[2]`
...	...	...
+ n	0x110 + n	`charArray[n]`

The addition of an offset to a pointer is similar to applying an index to an array.

Thus, if

```
char* ptr = &charArray[0];
```

then

```
*(ptr + n) ← corresponds with → charArray[n]
```

 Because * has higher precedence than addition, * ptr + n adds n to the character that ptr points to. The parentheses are needed to force the addition to occur before the indirection. The expression *(ptr + n) retrieves the character pointed at by the pointer ptr plus the offset n.

In fact, the correspondence between the two forms of expression is so strong that C++ considers array[n] nothing more than a simplified version of *(ptr + n), where ptr points to the first element in array.

```
array[n] -- C++ interprets as → *(&array[0] + n)
```

In order to complete the association, C++ takes a second shortcut. If given

```
char charArray[20];
```

charArray is defined as &charArray[0];.

That is, the name of an array without a subscript present is the address of the array itself. Thus, you can further simplify the association to

```
array[n] --> C++ interprets as --> *(array + n)
```

Applying operators to the address of an array

The correspondence between indexing an array and pointer arithmetic is useful.

For example, a displayArray() function used to display the contents of an array of integers can be written as follows:

```
// displayArray - display the members of an
//                array of length nSize
void displayArray(int intArray[], int nSize)
{
    cout << "The value of the array is:\n";

    for(int n; n < nSize; n++)
    {
        cout << n << ": " << intArray[n] << "\n";
    }
    cout << "\n";
}
```

This version uses the array operations with which you are familiar. A pointer version of the same appears as follows:

```
// displayArray - display the members of an
//                array of length nSize
void displayArray(int intArray[], int nSize)
{
    cout << "The value of the array is:\n";

    int* pArray = intArray;
    for(int n = 0; n < nSize; n++, pArray++)
    {
        cout << n << ": " << *pArray << "\n";
    }
    cout << "\n";
}
```

The new displayArray() begins by creating a pointer to an integer pArray that points at the first element of intArray.

The p in the variable name indicates that the variable is a pointer, but this is just a convention, not a part of the C++ language.

The function then loops through each element of the array. On each loop, displayArray() outputs the current integer (that is, the integer pointed at by pArray) before incrementing the pointer to the next entry in intArray. displayArray() can be tested using the following version of main():

```
int main(int nNumberofArgs, char* pszArgs[])
{
    int array[] = {4, 3, 2, 1};
    displayArray(array, 4);

    // wait until user is ready before terminating program
    // to allow the user to see the program results
    system("PAUSE");
    return 0;
}
```

The output from this program is

```
The value of the array is:
0: 4
1: 3
2: 2
3: 1

Press any key to continue . . .
```

You may think this pointer conversion is silly; however, the pointer version of `displayArray()` is actually more common among C++ programmers in the know than the array version. For some reason, C++ programmers don't seem to like arrays.

The use of pointers to access arrays is nowhere more common than in the accessing of character arrays.

Expanding pointer operations to a string

A null terminated string is simply a character array whose last character is a null. C++ uses the null character at the end to serve as a terminator. This null terminated array serves as a quasi-variable type of its own. (See Chapter 7 for an explanation of string arrays.) Often C++ programmers use character pointers to manipulate such strings. The following code examples compare this technique to the earlier technique of indexing in the array.

Character pointers enjoy the same relationship with a character array that any other pointer and array share. However, the fact that strings end in a terminating null makes them especially amenable to pointer-based manipulation, as shown in the following `DisplayString()` program:

```
// DisplayString - display an array of characters both
//                 using a pointer and an array index
#include <cstdio>
#include <cstdlib>
#include <iostream>
```

```
using namespace std;

int main(int nNumberofArgs, char* pszArgs[])
{
    // declare a string
    char* szString = "Randy";
    cout << "The array is '" << szString << "'" << endl;

    // display szString as an array
    cout << "Display the string as an array: ";
    for(int i = 0; i < 5; i++)
    {
        cout << szString[i];
    }
    cout << endl;

    // now using typical pointer arithmetic
    cout << "Display string using a pointer: ";
    char* pszString = szString;
    while(*pszString)
    {
        cout << *pszString;
        pszString++;
    }
    cout << endl;

    // wait until user is ready before terminating program
    // to allow the user to see the program results
    system("PAUSE");
    return 0;
}
```

The program first makes its way through the array szString by indexing into the array of characters. The for loop chosen stops when the index reaches 5, the length of the string.

The second loop displays the same string using a pointer. The program sets the variable pszString equal to the address of the first character in the array. It then enters a loop that will continue until the char pointed at by pszString is equal to false — in other words, until the character is a null.

The integer value 0 is interpreted as false — all other values are true.

The program outputs the character pointed at by pszString and then increments the pointer so that it points to the next character in the string before being returned to the top of the loop.

The dereference and increment can be (and usually are) combined into a single expression as follows:

```
cout << *pszString++;
```

The output of the program appears as follows:

```
The array is 'Randy'
Display the string as an array: Randy
Display string using a pointer: Randy
Press any key to continue . . .
```

Justifying pointer-based string manipulation

The sometimes-cryptic nature of pointer-based manipulation of character strings might lead the reader to wonder, "Why?" That is, what advantage does the char* pointer version have over the easier-to-read index version?

The answer is partially (pre-)historic and partially human nature. When C, the progenitor to C++, was invented, compilers were pretty simplistic. These compilers could not perform the complicated optimizations that modern compilers can. As complicated as it might appear to the human reader, a statement such as *pszString++ could be converted into an amazingly small number of machine level instructions even by a stupid compiler.

Older computer processors were not very fast by today's standards. In the old days of C, saving a few computer instructions was a big deal. This gave C a big advantage over other languages of the day, notably Fortran, which did not offer pointer arithmetic.

In addition to the efficiency factor, programmers like to generate clever program statements. After C++ programmers learn how to write compact and cryptic but efficient statements, there is no getting them back to accessing arrays with indices.

Do not generate complex C++ expressions in order to create a more efficient program. There is no obvious relationship between the number of C++ statements and the number of machine instructions generated.

Applying operators to pointer types other than char

It is not too hard to convince yourself that szTarget + n points to szTarget [n] when szTarget is an array of chars. After all, a char occupies a single byte. If szTarget is stored at 0x100, the sixth element is located at 0x105.

It is not so obvious that pointer addition works in exactly the same way for an `int` array because an `int` takes 4 bytes for each `char`'s 1 byte (at least it does on a 32-bit Intel processor). If the first element in `intArray` were located at 0x100, the sixth element would be located at 0x114 (0x100 + (5 * 4) = 0x114) and not 0x104.

Fortunately for us, `array + n` points at `array[n]` no matter how large a single element of `array` might be. C++ takes care of the element size for us — it's clever that way.

Once again, the dusty old house analogy works here as well. (I mean dusty analogy, not dusty house.) The third house down from 123 Main is 126 Main, no matter how large the building might be, even if it's a hotel.

Contrasting a pointer with an array

There are some differences between indexing into an array and using a pointer. For one, the array allocates space for the data, whereas the pointer does not, as shown here:

```
void arrayVsPointer()
{
    // allocate storage for 128 characters
    char charArray[128];

    // allocate space for a pointer but not for
    // the thing pointed at
    char* pArray;
}
```

Here `charArray` allocates room for 128 characters. `pArray` allocates only 4 bytes — the amount of storage required by a pointer.

The following function does not work:

```
void arrayVsPointer()
{
    // this works fine
    char charArray[128];
    charArray[10] = '0';
    *(charArray + 10) = '0';

    // this does not work
    char* pArray;
    pArray[10] = '0';
    *(pArray + 10) = '0';
}
```

The expressions charArray[10] and *(charArray + 10) are equivalent and legal. The two expressions involving pArray are syntactically equivalent but don't make sense. Although they are both legal to C++, the uninitialized pointer pArray contains a random value. pArray has not been initialized to point to an array such as charArray so both pArray[10] and the equivalent *(pArray + 10) reference garbage.

The mistake of referencing memory with an uninitialized pointer variable is generally caught by the CPU when the program executes, resulting in the dreaded *segment violation* error that from time to time issues from your favorite applications under your favorite, or not-so-favorite, operating system. This problem is not generally a problem of the processor or the operating system but of the application.

A second difference between a pointer and the address of an array is the fact that charArray is a constant, whereas pArray is not. Thus, the following for loop used to initialize the array charArray does not work:

```
void arrayVsPointer()
{
char charArray[10];
for (int i = 0; i < 10; i++)
{
    *charArray = '\0';      // this makes sense...
    charArray++;            // ...this does not
}
}
```

The expression charArray++ makes no more sense than 10++. The following version is correct:

```
void arrayVsPointer()
{
char charArray[10];
char* pArray = charArray;
for (int i = 0; i < 10; i++)
{
    *pArray = '\0';      // this works great
    pArray++;
}
}
```

Declaring and Using Arrays of Pointers

If pointers can point to arrays, it seems only fitting that the reverse should be true. Arrays of pointers are a type of array of particular interest.

Just as arrays may contain other data types, an array may contain pointers. The following declares an array of pointers to ints:

```
int* pInts[10];
```

Given the preceding declaration, pnInt[0] is a pointer to an int value. Thus, the following is true:

```
void fn()
{
    int n1;
    int* pInts[3];
    pInts[0] = &n1;
    *pInts[0] = 1;
}
```

or

```
void fn()
{
    int n1, n2, n3;
    int* pInts[3] = {&n1,&n2,&n3};
    for (int i = 0; i < 3; i++)
    {
        *pInts[i] = 0;
    }
}
```

or even

```
void fn()
{
    int* pInts[3] = {(new int),
                     (new int),
                     (new int)};
    for (int i = 0; i < 3; i++)
    {
        *pInts[i] = 0;
    }
}
```

The latter declares three int objects off the heap.

This type of declaration isn't used very often except in the case of an array of pointers to character strings. The following two examples show why arrays of character strings are useful.

Utilizing arrays of character strings

Suppose I need a function that returns the name of the month corresponding to an integer argument passed to it. For example, if the program is passed a 1, it returns a pointer to the string "January"; if 2, it reports "February", and so on. The month 0 is assumed to be invalid as are any numbers greater than 12.

I could write the function as follows:

```
// int2month() - return the name of the month
char* int2month(int nMonth)
{
    char* pszReturnValue;

    switch(nMonth)
    {
        case 1: pszReturnValue = "January";
                break;
        case 2: pszReturnValue = "February";
                break;
        case 3: pszReturnValue = "March";
                break;
        // ...and so forth...
        default: pszReturnValue = "invalid";
    }
    return pszReturnValue;
}
```

The switch() control command is like a sequence of if statements.

A more elegant solution uses the integer value for the month as an index into an array of pointers to the names of the months. In use, this appears as follows:

```
// int2month() - return the name of the month
char* int2month(int nMonth)
{
    // first check for a value out of range
    if (nMonth < 1 || nMonth > 12)
    {
        return "invalid";
    }

    // nMonth is valid - return the name of the month
    char* pszMonths[] = {"invalid",
                         "January",
                         "February",
                         "March",
                         "April",
                         "May",
                         "June",
                         "July",
                         "August",
                         "September",
                         "October",
                         "November",
                         "December"};
    return pszMonths[nMonth];
}
```

Here `int2month()` first checks to make sure that `nMonth` is a number between 1 and 12, inclusive (the `default` clause of the `switch` statement handled that in the previous example). If `nMonth` is valid, the function uses it as an offset into an array containing the names of the months.

This technique of referring to character strings by index is especially useful when writing your program to work in different languages. For example, a program may declare a `ptrMonths` of pointers to Julian months in different languages. The program would initialize `ptrMonth` to the proper names, be they in English, French or German (for example) at execution time. In that way, `ptrMonth[1]` points to the correct name of the first Julian month, irrespective of the language.

Accessing the arguments to main ( )

The first argument to `main()` is an array of pointers to null terminated character strings. These strings contain the arguments to the program. The arguments to a program are the strings that appear with the program name when you launch it. These arguments are also known as *parameters*. For example, suppose that I entered the following command at the MS-DOS prompt:

```
MyProgram file.txt /w
```

MS-DOS executes the program contained in the file `MyProgram.exe`, passing it the arguments `file.txt`, and `/w`.

If you have never seen an MS-DOS prompt, please bear with me. There is an exact Windows analog that will appear here in just a second.

The variable `pszArgs` passed to `main()` is an array of pointers to the arguments to the program, whereas `nArg` is the number of arguments.

Consider the following simple program:

```cpp
// PrintArgs - write the arguments to the program
//             to the standard output
#include <cstdio>
#include <cstdlib>
#include <iostream>
using namespace std;

int main(int nNumberofArgs, char* pszArgs[])
{
    // print a warning banner
    cout << "The arguments to " << pszArgs[0] << "are:\n";

    // now write out the remaining arguments
    for (int i = 1; i < nNumberofArgs; i++)
```

```
    {
        cout << i << ":" << pszArgs[i] << "\n";
    }

    // that's it
    cout << "That's it\n";

    // wait until user is ready before terminating program
    // to allow the user to see the program results
    system("PAUSE");
    return 0;
}
```

As always, the function `main()` accepts two arguments. The first argument is an `int` that I have been calling (quite descriptively, as it turns out) `nNumberofArgs`. This variable is the number of arguments passed to the program. The second argument is an array of pointers of type `char[]*`, which I have been calling `pszArgs`. Each one of these `char*` elements points to an argument passed to the program.

Accessing program arguments DOS style

If I were to execute the `PrintArgs` program as

```
PrintArgs arg1 arg2 arg3 /w
```

from the command line of an MS-DOS window, `nArgs` would be 5 (one for each argument). The first argument is the name of the program. Thus, `pszArgs[0]` points to `PrintArgs`. The remaining elements in `pszArgs` point to the program arguments. The element `pszArgs[1]` points to `arg1`, and `pszArgs[2]` to `arg2`, for example. Because MS-DOS does not place any significance on `/w`, this string is also passed as an argument to be processed by the program.

Accessing program arguments Dev-C++ style

You can add arguments to your program when you execute it from Dev-C++ as well. Select Parameters under the Debug menu. Type whatever you like and then run the program by choosing Execute⇨Run or pressing Ctrl+F10 as usual. The program output appears as it would from the DOS prompt.

Accessing program arguments Windows-style

Windows passes arguments as a means of communicating with your program as well. Try the following experiment. Build your program as you would normally. Find the executable file using Windows Explorer. For example, the `PrintArgs` program should appear as `X:\CPP_Programs\Chap09\PrintArgs.exe`. Now grab a file and drop it onto the filename (it doesn't matter what file you choose because the program won't hurt it anyway). Bam! The PrintArgs program starts right up, and the name of the file that you dropped on the program appears.

Now try again, but drop several files at once. Select multiple file names by clicking several files while pressing the Ctrl key or by using the Shift key to select a group. The name of each file appears as output.

I dropped a few of the files that appear in my \Program Files\WinZip folder onto PrintsArgs as an example:

```
The arguments to C:\PrintArgs.exe
1:C:\Program Files\WinZip\WZINST.HLP
2:C:\Program Files\WinZip\WZCAB.DLL
3:C:\Program Files\WinZip\WZCAB3.DLL
4:C:\Program Files\WinZip\WZ32.DLL
5:C:\Program Files\WinZip\WZQKPICK.EXE
6:C:\Program Files\WinZip\WZQKSTRT.RTF
That's it
Press any key to continue . . .
```

Notice that the name of each file appears as a single argument, even though the file name may include spaces. Also note that Windows passes the full pathname of the file.

Using the drag-and-drop feature is an easy way to pass arguments to your program at startup.

Chapter 10

Debugging C++

*Y*ou may have noticed that your programs often don't work the first time. In fact, I have seldom, if ever, written a nontrivial C++ program that didn't have some type of error the first time I tried to execute it.

That leaves you with two alternatives: You can give up on programming now while you still have a chance, or you can find and fix your errors. This chapter assumes you'll use the latter approach. In this chapter, you find out how to track down and eradicate software bugs.

Identifying Types of Errors

Two types of errors exist — those that the C++ compiler can catch on its own and those that the compiler can't catch. Errors that C++ can catch are known as *compile-time errors*. Compile-time errors are relatively easy to fix because the compiler generally points you to the problem. Sometimes the description of the problem isn't quite correct. Sometimes the description isn't even close (it's easy to confuse a compiler), but after you learn the quirks of your own C++ environment, understanding its complaints isn't too difficult.

Errors that C++ can't catch show up as you try to execute the program. These are known as *run-time errors*. Run-time errors are harder to find than compile-time errors because you have no hint of what's gone wrong except for whatever errant output the program might generate. "Errant" being the key word here.

You can use two different techniques for finding bugs. You can add output statements at key points. You can get an idea of what's gone wrong with your program as these different output statements are executed. A second approach is to use a separate program called a *debugger*. A debugger enables you to control your program as it executes.

I cover both of these debugging techniques in this chapter.

Choosing the WRITE Technique for the Problem

Adding output statements to the C++ source code to find out what's going on within the program is known as using the WRITE statement approach. It gained this name back in the days of early programs when programs were written mostly in COBOL and FORTRAN. Fortran's output is through the WRITE command.

The following "buggy" program shows how the WRITE approach works.

The following program is supposed to read a series of numbers from the keyboard and return their average. Unfortunately, the program contains two errors, one that makes the program crash and one that causes the program to generate incorrect results.

The following steps route out the problem. First, enter the program as written (or copy the program ErrorProgram1.cpp from the CD-ROM).

```
// ErrorProgram - this program averages a series
//                of numbers, except that it contains
//                at least one fatal bug
#include <cstdio>
#include <cstdlib>
#include <iostream>
using namespace std;

int main(int nNumberofArgs, char* pszArgs[])
{
    cout << "This program is designed to crash!"
         << endl;
    int nSum;
    int nNums;

    // accumulate input numbers until the
    // user enters a negative number, then
    // return the average
    nNums = 0;
    while(true)
    {
        // enter another number to add
```

```
        int nValue;
        cout << "Enter another number:";
        cin  >> nValue;
        cout << endl;

        // if the input number is negative...
        if (nValue < 0)
        {
            // ...then output the average
            cout << "Average is: "
                 << nSum/nNums
                 << endl;
            break;

        }

        // not negative, add the value to
        // the accumulator
        nSum += nValue;
    }

    // wait until user is ready before terminating program
    // to allow the user to see the program results
    system("PAUSE");
    return 0;
}
```

Build and execute the program as normal. I enter my trusty 1, 2, and 3 followed by –1, but get quite a shock when the nasty message shown in Figure 10-1 appears instead of the expected average.

Figure 10-1 appeared using Dev-C++ 4.9.8.0. User results may differ with different C++ compilers, but the general idea that you did something really bad should stay the same.

Figure 10-1:
The initial version of Error Program terminates suddenly instead of generating the expected output.

```
C:\CPP_Programs\Chap10\ErrorProgram1.exe                          _ □ ×
This program is designed to crash!
Enter another number:1
Enter another number:2
Enter another number:3
Enter another number:-1
```

```
ErrorProgram1.exe - Application Error                              ×

     ⊗    The exception Integer division by zero.
          (0xc0000094) occurred in the application at location 0x0040134e.

          Click on OK to terminate the program
          Click on CANCEL to debug the program

               ┌──────────┐      ┌──────────┐
               │    OK    │      │  Cancel  │
               └──────────┘      └──────────┘
```

Catching bug #1

Though unexpected, the error message shown in Figure 10-1 contains some useful information. However, don't let the Cancel button get your hopes up. Despite the message, clicking on Cancel doesn't bring you any closer to finding the problem than does the OK button. Windows simply says that it can't really help you find the problem.

Fortunately, the first line of the error message is descriptive of the problem. "Application error" means that someone tapped Windows on the back with an important message that Windows wasn't expecting and didn't know what to do with. The message is "Integer division by zero." Apparently, someone divided a number by zero (pretty astute, huh?). The message also spits out the memory address where the division occurred, but this is of little use because you have no idea where in the program that address may be.

The divide by zero error message isn't always so straightforward. For example, suppose that the program lost its way and began executing instructions that aren't part of the program? (That happens a lot more often than you might think.) The CPU may just happen to execute a divide instruction with a denominator of zero, thereby generating a divide by zero error message and masking the source of the problem. (An errant program is like a train that's jumped the track — the program doesn't stop executing until it hits something really big.)

A review of the program reveals only one obvious division:

```
cout << "Average is: "
     << nSum/nNums
     << endl;
```

Just because division appears only once, it doesn't meant that this is the only place where division occurs. The compiler may have generated a division on its own as a result of some other C++ instruction that you wrote. In addition, the Standard C++ Library is just full of divisions.

I feel reasonably certain that at the time of the division, nNums must have been equal to zero. nNums is supposed to be a count of the number of values entered. You can add a cout statement to track the value of nNums within the while loop as follows:

```
while(true)
{
    // output
    cout << "nNums = " << nNums << endl;

    // ...the rest of program unchanged...
```

This addition generates the following output:

```
This program is designed to crash!
nNums = 0
Enter another number:1

nNums = 0
Enter another number:2

nNums = 0
Enter another number:3

nNums = 0
Enter another number:
```

You can see where nNums is initialized to 0, but where is it incremented? It isn't, and this is the bug. Clearly nNums should have been incremented during each loop of the input section. I edit the while loop into a for loop as follows:

```
for (int nNums = 0; ;nNums++)
```

Catching bug #2

Having fixed a bug, execute the program using the same 1, 2, 3, and –1 input that crashed the program earlier. This time, the program doesn't crash, but it doesn't work either. The output shown here includes a ridiculous value for average:

```
This program generates incorrect results
Enter another number:1

Enter another number:2

Enter another number:3

Enter another number:-1

Average is: 1456814
Press any key to continue...
```

Apparently, either nSum or nNums (or both) isn't being calculated properly. To get any farther, you need to know the value of these variables. In fact, it would help to know the value of nValue as well because nValue is used to calculate nSum.

Now you modify the for loop as follows to learn the values of the nSum, nNums, and nValue (this version of the program appears on the CD-ROM as ErrorProgram2.cpp):

```cpp
// ErrorProgram - this program averages a series
//                of numbers, except that it contains
//                at least one fatal bug
#include <cstdio>
#include <cstdlib>
#include <iostream>
using namespace std;

int main(int nNumberofArgs, char* pszArgs[])
{
    cout << "This program generates incorrect results"
         << endl;

    // accumulate input numbers until the
    // user enters a negative number, then
    // return the average
    int nSum;

    for (int nNums = 0; ;nNums++)
    {
        // enter another number to add
        int nValue;
        cout << "Enter another number:";
        cin  >> nValue;
        cout << endl;

        // if the input number is negative...
        if (nValue < 0)
        {
            // ...then output the average
            cout << "\nAverage is: "
                 << nSum/nNums
                 << "\n";
            break;

        }
        // output critical information
        cout << "nSum = " << nSum   << "\n";
        cout << "nNums= " << nNums   << "\n";
        cout << "nValue= "<< nValue << "\n";
        cout << endl;

        // not negative, add the value to
        // the accumulator
        nSum += nValue;
    }

    // wait until user is ready before terminating program
    // to allow the user to see the program results
    system("PAUSE");
    return 0;
}
```

Notice the addition of the output statements to display nSum, nNums, and nValue on each iteration through the loop.

The result of executing the program with the now standard 1, 2, 3, and –1 input is shown next. Even on the first loop, the value of nSum is unreasonable. In fact, at this point during the first loop, the program has yet to add a new value to nSum. You would think that the value of nSum should be 0.

```
This program generates incorrect results
Enter another number:1

nSum = 4370436
nNums= 0
nValue= 1

Enter another number:2

nSum = 4370437
nNums= 1
nValue= 2

Enter another number:3

nSum = 4370439
nNums= 2
nValue= 3

Enter another number:-1


Average is: 1456814
Press any key to continue . . .
```

On careful examination of the program, nSum is declared, but it isn't initialized to anything. The solution is to change the declaration of nSum to the following:

```
int nSum = 0;
```

Note: Until a variable has been initialized, the value of that variable is indeterminate.

When you have convinced yourself that you have found the problem, "clean up" the program as follows (this version is ErrorProgram3.cpp on the enclosed CD-ROM):

```
// ErrorProgram - this program averages a series
//                of numbers
#include <cstdio>
#include <cstdlib>
#include <iostream>
```

```
using namespace std;

int main(int nNumberofArgs, char* pszArgs[])
{
    // accumulate input numbers until the
    // user enters a negative number, then
    // return the average
    int nSum = 0;

    for (int nNums = 0; ;nNums++)
    {
        // enter another number to add
        int nValue;
        cout << "Enter another number:";
        cin  >> nValue;
        cout << endl;

        // if the input number is negative...
        if (nValue < 0)
        {
            // ...then output the average
            cout << "\nAverage is: "
                 << nSum/nNums
                 << "\n";
            break;

        }
        // not negative, add the value to
        // the accumulator
        nSum += nValue;
    }

    // wait until user is ready before terminating program
    // to allow the user to see the program results
    system("PAUSE");
    return 0;
}
```

Now rebuild the program and retest with the 1, 2, 3, and –1 sequence. This time you see the expected average value of 2. After testing the program with a number of other inputs, you convince yourself that the program is now executing properly.

Calling for the Debugger

For small programs, the WRITE technique works reasonably well. Adding output statements is simple enough, and the programs rebuild quickly so the cycle time is short enough. Problems with this approach don't really become obvious until the programs become large and complex.

In large programs, the programmer often generally doesn't know where to begin adding output statements. The constant cycle of adding write statements, executing the program, adding write statements, and on and on becomes tedious. Further, in order to change an output statement, the programmer must rebuild the entire program. For a large program, this rebuild time can be significant. (I have worked on programs that took most of the night to rebuild.)

Finally, finding pointer problems with the WRITE approach is almost impossible. A pointer written to the display in hex means nothing, and as soon as you attempt to dereference the pointer, the program blows.

A second, more sophisticated technique is based on a separate utility known as a debugger. This approach avoids the disadvantages of the WRITE statement approach. However, this approach involves learning to use a debugger.

Defining the debugger

A debugger is actually a tool built into Dev-C++, Microsoft Visual Studio.NET, and most other development environments (though they differ, most debuggers work on the same principles).

The programmer controls the debugger through commands by means of the same interface as the editor. You can access these commands in menu items or by using hot keys.

The debugger allows the programmer to control the execution of her program. She can execute one step at a time in the program, she can stop the program at any point, and she can examine the value of variables. To appreciate the power of the debugger, you need to see it in action.

Finding commonalities among us

Unlike the C++ language, which is standardized across manufacturers, each debugger has its own command set. Fortunately, most debuggers offer the same basic commands. The commands you need are available in both the ubiquitous Microsoft Visual C++.NET and the Dev-C++ environments. In addition, in both environments, you can access debugger commands via menu items or function keys. Table 10-1 lists the command hot keys you use in both environments.

Table 10-1	Debugger Commands for Microsoft Visual C++.NET and Dev-C++	
Command	*Visual C++*	*Dev-C++*
Start executing in debugger	F5	F8
Step in	F11	Shift-F7
Step over (Next Step)	F10	F7
Continue	F5	Ctl-F7
View variable	Menu only	<Add Watch>
Set breakpoint*	Crl+B or click	Ctl+F5
Add watch	Menu only	F4
Program reset	Shift+F5	Ctl+Alt+F2

Clicking in the trough to the left of the C++ source code listing is an alternate way to set a breakpoint in both environments.

Running a test program

The best way to learn how to fix a program using the debugger is to go through the steps to fix a buggy program. The following program has several problems that need to be discovered and fixed. This version is found on the CD-ROM as Concatenate1.cpp.

```
// Concatenate - concatenate two strings
//                with a " - " in the middle
//                (this version crashes)
#include <cstdio>
#include <cstdlib>
#include <iostream>
#include <string.h>

using namespace std;
void stringEmUp(char* szTarget,
                char* szSource1,
                char* szSource2,
                int nLength);

int main(int nNumberofArgs, char* pszArgs[])
{
    cout << "This program concatenates two strings\n"
         << "(This version may crash.)" << endl;
    char szStrBuffer[256];
```

```
        // create two strings of equal length...
        char szString1[16];
        strncpy(szString1, "This is a string", 16);
        char szString2[16];
        strncpy(szString2, "THIS IS A STRING", 16);

        // ...now string them together
        stringEmUp(szStrBuffer,
                szString1,
                szString2,
                16);

        // output the result
        cout << "<" << szStrBuffer << ">" << endl;

        // wait until user is ready before terminating program
        // to allow the user to see the program results
        system("PAUSE");
        return 0;
}

void stringEmUp(char* szTarget,
                char* szSource1,
                char* szSource2,
                int nLength)
{
    strcpy(szTarget, szSource1);
    strcat(szTarget, " - ");
    strcat(szTarget, szSource2);
}
```

The program compiles uneventfully. Execute the program. Rather than generate the proper output, the program may return with almost anything. The first time I tried it, the program opened a console window and then immediately went away, without giving me any idea of what might be wrong. You'll need to dive into the program using the debugger if you're to have any hope of tracking down the problem.

Single-stepping through a program

The best first step when tracking down a program problem is to execute the program in debugger mode. Sometimes, the debugger can give you more information about the problem. The first time I executed the program under Dev-C++ using the debugger (by pressing F8), I received the error message "An Access Violation (Segmentation Fault) raised in your program."

This is a little help, but you'll need more information in order to track down the problem.

A Segmentation Fault usually indicates an errant pointer of some type.

You'll have to reset the program back to the beginning before trying again. Click OK to acknowledge the error and then the Program Reset from the Debug menu or the Stop Execution command from the Debug toolbar to make sure that everything within the debugger is reset back to the beginning. It's always a good idea to reset the debugger before starting again — doing so is necessary if the program is not at the starting point, and resetting the debugger won't hurt anything if the program is already at the beginning.

To see exactly where the problem occurs, execute just a part of the program. The debugger lets you do this through what is known as a *breakpoint*. The debugger stops the program if execution ever passes through a breakpoint. The debugger then gives control back to the programmer.

Now set a breakpoint at the first executable statement by clicking in the trough just to the left of the reference to cout immediately after main() or pressing F5 as shown in Table 10-1. A small red circle with a check appears. The display now appears like the one shown in Figure 10-2.

Now execute the program under the debugger again, either by selecting the Debug item under the Debug menu, by clicking the blue check mark on the debug toolbar, or by pressing F8. Program execution starts like normal but immediately stops on the first line. The line containing the breakpoint turns from red to blue, indicating that execution has halted at that point.

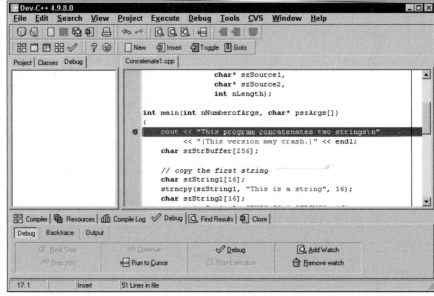

Figure 10-2:
A breakpoint shows up as a small red circle with a check.

You can now select Next Step either from the Debug menu, from the debug toolbar, or by pressing F7 to execute one line at a time in the program. The blue marking moves to the next executable statement, skipping over both declarations. (A declaration is not a command and is not executed. A declaration simply allocates space for a variable.) Executing a single C++ statement is also known as *single stepping*. You can switch to the Console window to see that the single output statement has executed, as shown in Figure 10-3.

Figure 10-3:
You can
click the
Console
window at
any time to
see any
program
output.

```
C:\CPP_Programs\Chap10\Concatenate1.exe                    _ □ ×
This program concatenates two strings
(This version may crash.)
```

Execute the Next Step two more times to move the point of execution to the call to `StringEmUp()`. So far, so good. When you select Next Step one more time, however, the program crashes ignominiously just as before. You now know that the problem is encountered somewhere within the `StringEmUp()` function.

When the program crashes within a function, either the function contains a bug, or the arguments passed to the function are incorrect.

The Next Step command treats a function call like a single command. This is known as *stepping over* the function. However, a function consists of a number of C++ statements of its own. You need to execute each of the statements within the function in order to better see what's going on. I need a different type of single step command, one that steps into the function. This functionality is provided by the Step Into debugger command.

Restart the program by selecting the Program Reset menu item from the Debug menu, by clicking on Stop Execution from the debug toolbar, or by pressing Alt+F2. This time, you want to save a little time executing right up to function call before stopping. Click the existing red circle to toggle the existing breakpoint off. The dot disappears. Next click in the trough across from the call to the function to set a new breakpoint, as shown in Figure 10-4.

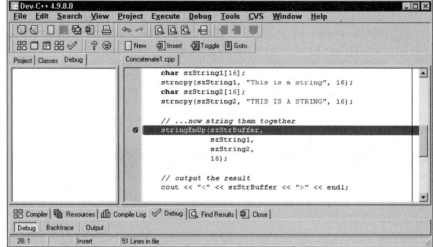

Figure 10-4:
A breakpoint on the function call allows the programmer to execute up to the call.

You can have as many breakpoints active in a program at one time as you like. There is no (reasonable) limit.

Now start the program over again. This time, execution stops on the function call. Step into the function. The display appears like the one shown in Figure 10-5.

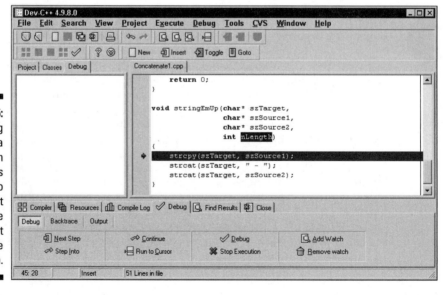

Figure 10-5:
Stepping into a function moves control to the first executable statement within the function.

You know that the program is about to crash. You could understand better what's going on in the program if you could see the value of the arguments to the function. This is the function of Add Watch. A watch displays the value of a variable each time execution is halted. The easiest way to set a watch is to select the variable on the display and press F4. Figure 10-6 shows a watch set on all four arguments to the function.

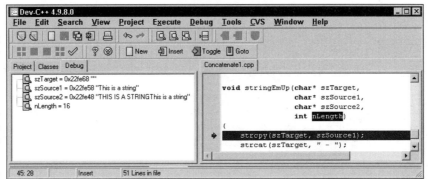

Figure 10-6:
Setting a
watch
allows the
programmer
to monitor
the value of
a variable.

The numbers next to each name in the watch window are that variable's address, which aren't of much use in this case. szTarget appears to be an empty string — this makes sense because you've yet to copy anything there. The value of szSource1 looks okay, but the value of szSource2 includes both the "this is a string" and the "THIS IS A STRING" messages. Something seems to be amiss.

The answer actually lies in the final argument. The length of the two strings is not 16 characters but 17! The main program has failed to allocate room for the terminating null. The program terminates as soon as you execute the first statement within stringEmUp(), the call to strcpy().

The length of a string always includes the terminating null.

Now you update the program. This time, let C++ calculate the size of the string because it just naturally includes sufficient space. The resulting program Concatenate2 works properly:

```
// Concatenate - concatenate two strings
//                with a " - " in the middle
//                (this version crashes)
#include <cstdio>
#include <cstdlib>
#include <iostream>
#include <string.h>

using namespace std;
void stringEmUp(char* szTarget,
```

```
                          char* szSource1,
                          char* szSource2);

int main(int nNumberofArgs, char* pszArgs[])
{
    cout << "This program concatenates two strings\n"
         << "(This version shouldn't crash.)" << endl;
    char szStrBuffer[256];

    // define two strings...
    char szString1[] = "This is a string";
    char szString2[] = "THIS IS A STRING";

    // ...now string them together
    stringEmUp(szStrBuffer,
               szString1,
               szString2);

    // output the result
    cout << "<" << szStrBuffer << ">" << endl;

    // wait until user is ready before terminating program
    // to allow the user to see the program results
    system("PAUSE");
    return 0;
}

void stringEmUp(char* szTarget,
                char* szSource1,
                char* szSource2)
{
    strcpy(szTarget, szSource1);
    strcat(szTarget, " - ");
    strcat(szTarget, szSource2);
}
```

This version of the program generates the expected result:

```
This program concatenates two strings
(This version shouldn't crash.)
<This is a string - THIS IS A STRING>
Press any key to continue . . .
```

Congratulations! You're now a debugging expert.

Part III
Introduction to Classes

In this part . . .

The feature that differentiates C++ from other languages is C++'s support for object-oriented programming. *Object-oriented* is about the most hyped term in the computer world (okay, maybe *.com* has it beat). Computer languages, editors, and databases all claim to be object-oriented, sometimes with justification, but most of the time without.

Check out the BUDGET2 program on the enclosed CD-ROM to see an example program that can help you orient objects of object-oriented concepts.

What is it about being object-oriented that makes it so desired around the world? Read on to find out.

Chapter 11

Examining Object-Oriented Programming

*W*hat, exactly, is object-oriented programming? Object-oriented programming, or OOP as those in the know prefer to call it, relies on two principles you learned before you ever got out of Pampers: abstraction and classification. To explain, let me tell you a little story.

Abstracting Microwave Ovens

Sometimes when my son and I are watching football (which only happens when my wife can't find the switcher), I whip up a terribly unhealthy batch of nachos. I dump some chips on a plate, throw on some beans, cheese, and lots of jalapeños, and nuke the whole mess in the microwave oven for five minutes.

To use my microwave, I open the door, throw the stuff in, and punch a few buttons. After a few minutes, the nachos are done. (I try not to stand in front of the microwave while it's working lest my eyes start glowing in the dark.)

Now think for a minute about all the things I don't do to use my microwave:

✔ I don't rewire or change anything inside the microwave to get it to work. The microwave has an interface — the front panel with all the buttons and the little time display — that lets me do everything I need.

✔ I don't have to reprogram the software used to drive the little processor inside my microwave, even if I cooked a different dish the last time I used the microwave.

✔ I don't look inside my microwave's case.

✔ Even if I were a microwave designer and knew all about the inner workings of a microwave, including its software, I would still use it to heat my nachos without thinking about all that stuff.

These are not profound observations. You can deal with only so much stress in your life. To reduce the number of things that you deal with, you work at a certain level of detail. In object-oriented (OO) computerese, the level of detail at which you are working is called the *level of abstraction*. To introduce another OO term while I have the chance, I *abstract away* the details of the microwave's innards.

When I'm working on nachos, I view my microwave oven as a box. (As I'm trying to knock out a snack, I can't worry about the innards of the microwave oven and still follow the Cowboys on the tube.) As long as I operate the microwave only through its interface (the keypad), there should be nothing I can do to

✔ Cause the microwave to enter an inconsistent state and crash.

✔ Turn my nachos into a blackened, flaming mass.

✔ Burst into flames!

Preparing functional nachos

Suppose that I were to ask my son to write an algorithm for how Dad makes nachos. After he understood what I wanted, he would probably write "open a can of beans, grate some cheese, cut the jalapeños," and so on. When it came to the part about microwaving the concoction, he would write something like "cook in the microwave for five minutes."

That description is straightforward and complete. But it's not the way a functional programmer would code a program to make nachos. Functional programmers live in a world devoid of objects such as microwave ovens and other appliances. They tend to worry about flow charts with their myriad functional paths. In a functional solution to the nachos problem, the flow of control would pass through my finger to the front panel and then to the internals of the microwave. Pretty soon, flow would be wiggling around through complex logic paths about how long to turn on the microwave tube and whether to sound the "come and get it" tone.

In a world like this, it's difficult to think in terms of levels of abstraction. There are no objects, no abstractions behind which to hide inherent complexity.

Preparing object-oriented nachos

In an object-oriented approach to making nachos, I would first identify the types of objects in the problem: chips, beans, cheese, and an oven. Then I would begin the task of modeling these objects in software, without regard to the details of how they will be used in the final program.

While I am doing this, I'm said to be working (and thinking) at the level of the basic objects. I need to think about making a useful oven, but I don't have to think about the logical process of making nachos yet. After all, the microwave designers didn't think about the specific problem of my making a snack. Rather, they set about the problem of designing and building a useful microwave.

After the objects I need have been successfully coded and tested, I can ratchet up to the next level of abstraction. I can start thinking at the nacho-making level, rather than the microwave-making level. At this point, I can pretty much translate my son's instructions directly into C++ code.

Classifying Microwave Ovens

Critical to the concept of abstraction is that of classification. If I were to ask my son, "What's a microwave?" he would probably say, "It's an oven that . . ." If I then asked, "What's an oven?" he might reply, "It's a kitchen appliance that . . ." (If I then asked, "What's a kitchen appliance?" he would probably say, "Why are you asking so many stupid questions?")

The answers my son gave to my questions stem from his understanding of our particular microwave as an example of the type of things called microwave ovens. In addition, my son sees microwave ovens as just a special type of oven, which itself is just a special type of kitchen appliance.

In object-oriented computerese, my microwave is an *instance* of the class microwave. The class microwave is a subclass of the class oven, and the class oven is a subclass of the class kitchen appliances.

Humans classify. Everything about our world is ordered into taxonomies. We do this to reduce the number of things we have to remember. Take, for example, the first time you saw an SUV. The advertisement probably called the SUV "revolutionary, the likes of which have never been seen." But you and I know that that just isn't so. I like the looks of some SUVs (others need to go back to take another crack at it), but, hey, an SUV is a car. As such, it shares all of (or at least most of) the properties of other cars. It has a steering wheel, seats, a motor, brakes, and so on. I bet I could even drive one without first reading the owner's manual.

I don't have to clutter my limited storage with all the things that an SUV has in common with other cars. All I have to remember is "an SUV is a car that . . ." and tack on those few things that are unique to an SUV (like the price tag). I can go further. Cars are a subclass of wheeled vehicles along with other members, such as trucks and pickups. Maybe wheeled vehicles are a subclass of vehicles, which includes boats and planes. And on and on and on.

Why Classify?

Why do we classify? It sounds like a lot of trouble. Besides, people have been using the functional approach for so long, why change now?

It may seem easier to design and build a microwave oven specifically for this one problem, rather than build a separate, more generic oven object. Suppose, for example, that I want to build a microwave to cook nachos and nachos only. I wouldn't need to put a front panel on it, other than a START button. I always cook nachos the same amount of time, so I could dispense with all that DEFROST and TEMP COOK nonsense. My nachos-only microwave needs to hold only one flat little plate. Three cubic feet of space would be wasted on nachos.

For that matter, I can dispense with the concept of "microwave oven" altogether. All I really need is the guts of the oven. Then, in the recipe, I put the instructions to make it work: "Put nachos in the box. Connect the red wire to the black wire. Bring the radar tube up to about 3,000 volts. Notice a slight hum. Try not to stand too close if you intend to have children." Stuff like that.

But the functional approach has some problems:

- ✔ **Too complex.** I don't want the details of oven building mixed into the details of nacho building. If I can't define the objects and pull them out of the morass of details to deal with separately, I must deal with all the complexities of the problem at the same time.

- ✔ **Not flexible.** Someday I may need to replace the microwave oven with some other type of oven. I should be able to do so as long as its interface is the same. Without being clearly delineated and developed separately, it becomes impossible to cleanly remove an object type and replace it with another.

- ✔ **Not reusable.** Ovens are used to make lots of different dishes. I don't want to create a new oven every time I encounter a new recipe. Having solved a problem once, it would be nice to be able to reuse the solution in future programs.

The remaining chapters in this Part demonstrate how object-oriented language features address these problems.

Chapter 12

Adding Class to C++

. . . .

In This Chapter

▶ Grouping data into classes

▶ Declaring and defining class members

▶ Accessing class members

. . . .

*P*rograms often deal with groups of data: a person's name, rank, and serial number, stuff like that. Any one of these values is not sufficient to describe a person — only in the aggregate do the values make any sense. A simple structure such as an array is great for holding stand-alone values; however, it doesn't work very well for data groups. This makes good ol' arrays inadequate for storing complex data (such as personal credit records that the Web companies maintain so they can lose them to hackers).

For reasons that will become clear shortly, I'll call such a grouping of data an *object*. A microwave oven is an object (see Chapter 11 if that doesn't make sense). You are an object. Your name, rank, and credit card number in a database are objects.

Introducing the Class

What you need is a structure that can hold all the different types of data necessary to describe a single object. In my simple example, a single object can hold both a first name and a last name along with a credit card number.

C++ calls the structure that combines multiples pieces of data into a single object a *class*.

The Format of a Class

A class used to describe a name and credit card grouping might appear as follows:

```
// the dataset class
class NameDataSet
{
    public:
      char firstName[128];
      char lastName [128];
      int  creditCard;
};

// a single instance of a dataset
NameDataSet nds;
```

A class definition starts with the keyword `class` followed by the name of the class and an open-close brace pair.

The statement after the open brace is the keyword `public`. (Hold off asking about the meaning of the `public` keyword. I'll make its meaning public a little later. Later chapters describe options to `public`, such as `private`. Thus, the *public* must stay private until I can make the *private* public.)

The alternative keyword `struct` can be used. The keywords `struct` and `class` are identical except that the *public* declaration is assumed in the *struct* and can be omitted. You should stick with `class` for most programs for reasons that will become clear later in this chapter.

Following the `public` keyword are the entries it takes to describe the object. The `NameDataSet` class contains the first and last name entries along with the credit card number. As you would expect, the first and last names are both character arrays — the credit card number is shown here as a simple integer ("the better to steal you with, my dear").

A class declaration includes the data necessary to describe a single object.

The last line of the snippet declares the variable `nds` to be a single entry of class `NameDataSet`. Thus, `nds` might be an entry that describes a single person.

We say that `nds` is an *instance* of the class `NameDataSet`. You *instantiate* the class `NameDataSet` to create `nds`. Finally, we say that `firstName` and the others are *members* or *properties* of the class. We say a whole lot of silly things.

Accessing the Members of a Class

The following syntax is used to access the property of a particular object:

```
NameDataSet nds;
nds.creditCard = 10;
cin >> nds.firstName;
cin >> nds.lastName;
```

Here, nds is an instance of the class NameDataSet (for example, a particular NameDataSet object). The integer nds.creditCard is a property of the nds object. The type of nds.creditCard is int, whereas that of nds.firstName is char[].

Okay, that's computerspeak. What has actually happened here? The program snippet declares an object nds, which it will use to describe a customer. For some reason, the program assigns the person the credit card number 10 (obviously bogus, but it's not like I'm going to include one of my credit card numbers).

Next, the program reads the person's first and last names from the default input.

I am using an array of characters rather than the class string to handle the name.

From now on, the program can refer to the single object nds without dealing with the separate parts (the first name, last name, and credit card number) until it needs to.

The following program demonstrates the NameDataSet class:

```
// DataSet - store associated data in
//           an array of objects
#include <cstdio>
#include <cstdlib>
#include <iostream>
#include <string.h>
using namespace std;

// NameDataSet - store name and credit card
//               information
class NameDataSet
{
  public:
    char firstName[128];
    char lastName [128];
    int  creditCard;
};
```

```cpp
// function prototypes:
bool getData(NameDataSet& nds);
void displayData(NameDataSet& nds);

int main(int nNumberofArgs, char* pszArgs[])
{
    // allocate space for 25 name data sets
    const int MAX = 25;
    NameDataSet nds[MAX];

    // load first names, last names and social
    // security numbers
    cout << "Read name/credit card information\n"
         << "Enter 'exit' to quit"
         << endl;
    int index = 0;
    while (getData(nds[index]) && index < MAX)
    {
        index++;
    }

    // display the names and numbers entered
    cout << "\nEntries:" << endl;
    for (int i = 0; i < index; i++)
    {
        displayData(nds[i]);
    }

    // wait until user is ready before terminating program
    // to allow the user to see the program results
    system("PAUSE");
    return 0;
}

// getData - populate a NameDataSet object
bool getData(NameDataSet& nds)
{
    cout << "\nEnter first name:";
    cin >> nds.firstName;

    // compare the name input irrespective of case
    if (stricmp(nds.firstName, "exit") == 0)
    {
        return false;
    }

    cout << "Enter last name:";
    cin >> nds.lastName;

    cout << "Enter credit card number:";
    cin >> nds.creditCard;

    return true;
```

```
}

// displayData - display a data set
void displayData(NameDataSet& nds)
{
    cout << nds.firstName
         << " "
         << nds.lastName
         << "/"
         << nds.creditCard
         << endl;
}
```

The `main()` function allocates 25 objects of class `NameDataSet`. `main()`, prompts the user as to what is expected of her, and then enters a loop in which entries are read from the keyboard using the function `getData()`. The loop terminates when either `getData()` returns a `false` or the maximum number of objects (25) have been created. The same objects read are next passed to `displayData(NameDataSet)` for display.

The `getData()` function accepts a `NameDataSet` object as its input argument, which it assigns the name `nds`.

Ignore the ampersand for now — I explain it in Chapter 14.

`getData()` then reads a string from standard input into the entry `firstName`. If the `stricmp()` function can find no difference between the name entered and "exit," the function returns a `false` to `main()` indicating that it's time to quit. (The function `stricmp()` compares two strings without regard to their case. This function considers "exit" and "EXIT" plus any other combination of uppercase and lowercase letters to be identical.) Otherwise, the function pushes on, reading the last name and the credit card number into the object `nds`.

The `displayData()` function outputs each of the members of the `NameDataSet` object `nds` separated by delimiters.

A simple run of this program appears as follows:

```
Read name/credit card information
Enter 'exit' for first name to exit

Enter first name:Stephen
Enter last name:Davis
Enter credit card number:123456

Enter first name:Marshall
Enter last name:Smith
Enter credit card number:567890

Enter first name:exit
```

```
Entries:
Stephen Davis/123456
Marshall Smith/567890
Press any key to continue
```

The program begins with an explanatory banner. I enter my own glorious name at the first prompt (I'm modest that way). Because the name entered does not rhyme with "exit," the program continues, and I add a last name and a pretend credit card number. On the next pass, I tack on the name Marshall Smith and his real credit card number (have fun, Marshall). On the final path, I enter "exit", which terminated the input loop. The program does nothing more than spit back at me the names I just entered.

Chapter 13

Making Classes Work

*P*rogrammers use classes to group related data elements into a single object. The following `Savings` class associates an account balance with a unique account number:

```
class Savings
{
    public:
        unsigned accountNumber;
        float balance;
};
```

Every instance of `Savings` contains the same two data elements:

```
void fn(void)
{
    Savings a;
    Savings b;
    a.accountNumber = 1; // this is not the same as...
    b.accountNumber = 2; // ...this one
}
```

The variable `a.accountNumber` is different from the variable `b.accountNumber`, just as the balance in my bank account is different from the balance in yours, even though they're both called balance (or, in the case of my account, lack of balance).

Activating Our Objects

You use classes to simulate real-world objects. The Savings class tries to represent a savings account. This allows you to think in terms of objects rather than simply lines of code. The closer C++ objects are to the real world, the easier it is to deal with them in programs. This sounds simple enough. However, the Savings class doesn't do a very good job of simulating a savings account.

Simulating real-world objects

Real-world objects have data-type properties such as account numbers and balances, the same as the Savings class. This makes Savings a good starting point for describing a real object. But real-world objects do things. Ovens cook. Savings accounts accumulate interest, CDs charge a substantial penalty for early withdrawal — stuff like that.

Functional programs "do things" via functions. A C++ program might call strcmp() to compare two strings or max() to return the maximum of two values. In fact, Chapter 24 explains that even stream I/O (cin >> and cout <<) is a special form of function call.

The Savings class needs active properties of its own if its to do a good job of representing a real concept:

```
class Savings
{
    public:
        float deposit(float amount)
        {
            balance += amount;
            return balance;
        }

        unsigned int accountNumber;
        float  balance;
};
```

In addition to the account number and balance, this version of Savings includes the function deposit(). This gives Savings the ability to control its own future. A class MicrowaveOven has the function cook(), the class Savings has the function accumulateInterest(), and the class CD has the function penalizeForEarlyWithdrawal().

Functions defined in a class are called *member functions*.

Why bother with member functions?

Why should you bother with member functions? What's wrong with the good ol' days:

```
class Savings
{
    public:
        unsigned accountNumber;
        float   balance;
};
float deposit(Savings& s, unsigned amount)
{
    s.balance += amount;
    return s.balance;
}
```

Here, deposit() implements the "deposit into savings account" function. This functional solution relies on an outside function, deposit(), to implement an activity that savings accounts perform but that Savings lacks. This gets the job done, but it does so by breaking the object-oriented (OO) rules.

The microwave oven has internal components that it "knows" how to use to cook, defrost, and burn to a crisp. Class data members are similar to the parts of a microwave — the member functions of a class perform cook-like functions.

When I make nachos, I don't have to start hooking up the internal components of the oven in a certain way to make it work. Nor do I rely on some external device to reach into a mess of wiring for me. I want my classes to work the same way my microwave does (and, no, I don't mean "not very well"). I want my classes to know how to manipulate their internals without outside intervention.

Member functions of Savings such as deposit() can be written as external functions. I can put all of the functions necessary to make a savings account work in one place. Microwave ovens can be made to work by soldering and cutting wires. I don't want my classes or my microwave ovens to work that way. I want a Savings class that I can use in my banking program without considering how it might work on the inside.

Adding a Member Function

There are two aspects to adding a member function to a class: creating the member function and naming it (sounds silly, doesn't it?).

Creating a member function

To demonstrate member functions, start by defining a class `Student`. One possible representation of such a class follows (taken from the program CallMemberFunction):

```
class Student
{
    public:
        // add a completed course to the record
        float addCourse(int hours, float grade)
        {
            // calculate the sum of all courses times
            // the average grade
            float weightedGPA;
            weightedGPA = semesterHours * gpa;

            // now add in the new course
            semesterHours += hours;
            weightedGPA += grade * hours;
            gpa = weightedGPA / semesterHours;

            // return the new gpa
            return gpa;
        }

        int  semesterHours;
        float gpa;
};
```

The function `addCourse(int, float)` is called a member function of the class `Student`. In principle, it's a property of the class like the data members `semesterHours` and `gpa`.

There isn't a special name for functions or data that are not members of a class, but I'll refer to them as *non-members*.

The member functions do not have to precede the data members as in this example. The members of a class can be listed in any order — I just prefer to put the functions first.

For historical reasons, member functions are also called *methods*. This term originated in one of the original object-oriented languages. The name made sense there, but it makes no sense in C++. Nevertheless, the term has gained popularity in OO circles because it's easier to say than "member function." (The fact that it sounds more impressive probably doesn't hurt either.) So, if your friends start spouting off at a dinner party about "methods of the class," just replace methods with member functions and reparse anything they say.

Naming class members

A member function is a lot like a member of a family. The full name of the function addCourse(int, float) is Student::addCourse(int, float), just as my full name is Stephen Davis. The short name of the function is addCourse(int, float), just as my short name is Stephen. The class name at the beginning of the full name indicates that the function is a member of the class Student. (The :: between the class name and the function name is simply a separator.) The name Davis on the end of my name indicates that I am a member of the Davis family.

Another name for a full name is *extended name*.

You can define an addCourse(int, float) function that has nothing to do with Student — there are Stephens out there who have nothing to do with my family. (I mean this literally: I know several Stephens who want *nothing* to do with my family.)

You could have a function Teacher::addCourse(int, float) or even Golf::addCourse(). A function addCourse(int, float) without a class name is just a plain ol' conventional non-member function.

The extended name for the non-member function is ::addCourse(int, float). (Note the colon without a family name in front.)

Calling a Member Function

Before you look at how to call a member function, remember how to access a data member:

```
class Student
{
  public:
    int  semesterHours;
    float gpa;
};

Student s;
void fn(void)
{
    // access data members of s
    s.semesterHours = 10;
    s.gpa       = 3.0;
}
```

Notice that you have to specify an object along with the member name. In other words, the following makes no sense:

```
Student s;
void fn(void)
{
    // neither of these is legal
    semesterHours = 10;   // member of what object of what
                          // class?
    Student::semesterHours = 10; // okay, I know the class
                                 // but I still don't know
                                 // the object
}
```

Accessing a member function

Remember that member functions function like data members functionally. The following CallMemberFunction shows how to invoke the member function addCourse():

```
//
//   CallMemberFunction - define and invoke a function that's
//                        a member of the class Student
//
#include <cstdio>
#include <cstdlib>
#include <iostream>
using namespace std;

class Student
{
    public:
        // add a completed course to the record
        float addCourse(int hours, float grade)
        {
            // calculate the sum of all courses times
            // the average grade
            float weightedGPA;
            weightedGPA = semesterHours * gpa;

            // now add in the new course
            semesterHours += hours;
            weightedGPA += grade * hours;
            gpa = weightedGPA / semesterHours;

            // return the new gpa
            return gpa;
```

```
        }

        int  semesterHours;
        float gpa;

};

int main(int nNumberofArgs, char* pszArgs[])
{
    Student s;
    s.semesterHours = 10;
    s.gpa        = 3.0;

    // the values before the call
    cout << "Before: s = (" << s.semesterHours
         << ", "     << s. gpa
         << endl;

    // the following subjects the data members of the s
    // object to the member function addCourse()
    s.addCourse(3, 4.0); // call the member function

    // the values are now changed
    cout << "After: s = (" << s.semesterHours
         << ", "     << s. gpa
         << ")"     << endl;

    // access another object just for the heck of it
    Student t;
    t.semesterHours = 6;
    t.gpa        = 1.0;    // not doing so good
    t.addCourse(3, 1.5); // things aren't getting any better


    // wait until user is ready before terminating program
    // to allow the user to see the program results
    system("PAUSE");
    return 0;
}
```

The syntax for calling a member function looks like a cross between the syntax for accessing a data member and that used for calling a function. The right side of the dot looks like a conventional function call, but an object is on the left of the dot.

We say that "addCourse() operates on the object s" or, said another way, *s* is the student to which the course is to be added. You can't fetch the number of semester hours without knowing from which student — you can't add a student to a course without knowing which student to add. Calling a member function without an object makes no more sense than referencing a data member without an object.

Accessing other members from a member function

I can see it clearly: You repeat to yourself, "Accessing a member without an object makes no sense. Accessing a member without an object. Accessing . . ." Just about the time you've accepted this, you look at the member function `Student::addCourse()` and *Wham!* It hits you: `addCourse()` accesses other class members without reference to an object. Just like the TV show: "How Do They Do That?"

Okay, which is it, can you or can't you? Believe me, you can't. When you reference a member of `Student` from `addCourse()`, that reference is against the `Student` object with which the call to `addCourse()` was made. Huh? Go back to the CallMemberFunction example. The critical subsections appear here:

```
int main(int nNumberofArgs, char* pszArgs[])
{
    Student s;
    s.semesterHours = 10;
    s.gpa       = 3.0;
    s.addCourse(3, 4.0); // call the member function

    Student t;
    t.semesterHours = 6;
    t.gpa       = 1.0;    // not doing so good
    t.addCourse(3, 1.5); // things aren't getting any better

    system("PAUSE");
    return 0;
}
```

When `addCourse()` is invoked with the object s, all of the otherwise unqualified member references in `addCourse()` refer to s as well. Thus, the reference to `semesterHours` in `addCourse()` refers to `s.semesterHours`, and `gpa` refers to `s.gpa`. But when `addCourse()` is invoked with the `Student t` object, these same references are to `t.semesterHours` and `t.gpa` instead.

The object with which the member function was invoked is the "current" object, and all unqualified references to class members refer to this object. Put another way, unqualified references to class members made from a member function are always against the current object.

TECHNICAL STUFF

Naming the current object

How does the member function know what the current object is? It's not magic — the address of the object is passed to the member function as an implicit and hidden first argument. In other words, the following conversion is taking place:

```
s.addCourse(3, 2.5)
is like
Student::addCourse(&s, 3, 2.5)
```

(Note that you can't actually use the syntax on the right; this is just the way C++ sees it.)

Inside the function, this implicit pointer to the current object has a name, in case you need to refer to it. It is called this, as in "Which object? *This* object." Get it? The type of this is always a pointer to an object of the appropriate class.

Anytime a member function refers to another member of the same class without providing an object explicitly, C++ assumes "this." You also can refer to this explicitly, if you like. You could have written Student::addCourse() as follows:

```
float Student::addCourse(int
    hours, float grade)
{
    float weightedGPA;
    weightedGPA = this-
>semesterHours * this->gpa;

    // now add in the new
course
    this->semesterHours +=
hours;
    weightedGPA += hours *
grade;
    this->gpa = weightedGPA /
this->semesterHours;
    return this->gpa;
}
```

The effect is the same whether you explicitly include "this," as in the preceding example, or leave it implicit, as you did before.

Scope Resolution (And I Don't Mean How Well Your Microscope Works)

The :: between a member and its class name is called the *scope resolution operator* because it indicates the scope to which class a member belongs. The class name before the colon is like the family last name, while the function name after the colons is like the first name — the order is similar to an oriental name, family name first.

You use the :: operator to describe a non-member function by using a null class name. The non-member function addCourse, for example, can be referred to as ::addCourse(int, float), if you prefer. This is like a function without a home.

Normally the :: operator is optional, but there are a few occasions when this is not so, as illustrated here:

```
// addCourse - combine the hours and grade into
//              a weighted grade
float addCourse(int hours, float grade)
{
    return hours * grade;
}

class Student
{
  public:
    int  semesterHours;
    float gpa;

    // add a completed course to the record
    float addCourse(int hours, float grade)
    {
        // call some external function to calculate the
        // weighted grade
        float weightedGPA = addCourse(semesterHours, gpa);

        // now add in the new course
        semesterHours += hours;

        // use the same function to calculate the weighted
        // grade of this new course
        weightedGPA += addCourse(hours, grade);
        gpa = weightedGPA / semesterHours;

        // return the new gpa
        return gpa;
    }
};
```

Here, I want the member function Student::addCourse() to call the non-member function ::addCourse(). Without the :: operator, however, a call to addCourse() from Student refers to Student::addCourse().

One member of the family can use the short name when referring to another member of the same family. The family . . . I mean class name . . . is understood.

Not indicating the class name in this case results in the function calling itself, which is generally not a good thing. Adding the :: operator to the front directs the call to the global version, as desired:

```
class Student
{
  public:
    int  semesterHours;
    float gpa;
    // add a completed course to the record
    float addCourse(int hours, float grade)
    {
        // call some external function to calculate the
        // weighted grade
        float weightedGPA = ::addCourse(semesterHours, gpa);

        // now add in the new course
        semesterHours += hours;

        // use the same function to calculate the
        // weighted grade of this new course
        weightedGPA += ::addCourse(hours, grade);
        gpa = weightedGPA / semesterHours;

        // return the new gpa
        return gpa;
    }
};
```

This is just like when I call out the name "Stephen" in my own home; every-one assumes that I mean me — they default the Davis onto my name. If I mean some other Stephen out there outside my family, I need to say "Stephen Smith," or "Stephen Jones," or whatever. That's what the scope resolution operator does.

The extended name of a function includes its arguments. Now you've added the class name to which the function belongs.

Defining a Member Function in the Class

A member function can be defined either in the class or separately. When defined in the class definition, the function looks like the following contained in the include file Savings.h.

```
// Savings - define a class that includes the ability
//            to make a deposit
class Savings
{
  public:
```

```
        // declare but don't define member function
        float deposit(float amount);
        unsigned int accountNumber;
        float  balance;
};
```

Using an include like this is pretty slick. Now a program can include the class definition (along with the definition for the member function), as follows in the venerable SavingsClass_inline program:

```
//
//   SavingsClassInline - invoke a member function that's
//                        both declared and defined within
//                        the class Student
//
#include <cstdio>
#include <cstdlib>
#include <iostream>

using namespace std;
#include "Savings.h"

int main(int nNumberofArgs, char* pszArgs[])
{
    Savings s;
    s.accountNumber = 123456;
    s.balance = 0.0;

    // now add something to the account
    cout << "Depositing 10 to account " << s.accountNumber <<
            endl;
    s.deposit(10);
    cout << "Balance is " << s.balance << endl;

    // wait until user is ready before terminating program
    // to allow the user to see the program results
    system("PAUSE");
    return 0;
}
```

This is cool because everyone other than the programmer of the Savings class can concentrate on the act of performing a deposit rather the details of banking. These have been neatly tucked away in their own include files.

The #include directive inserts the contents of the file during the compilation process. The C++ compiler actually "sees" your source file with the Savings.h file included.

TECHNICAL STUFF

Inlining member functions

Member functions defined in the class default to inline (unless they have been specifically outlined by a compiler switch or because they contain a loop). Mostly, this is because a member function defined in the class is usually very small, and small functions are prime candidates for inlining.

The content of an inline function is inserted wherever it is invoked. An inline function executes faster because the processor doesn't have to jump over to where the function is defined — inline functions take up more memory because they are copied into every call instead of being defined just once.

There is another good but more technical reason to inline member functions defined within a class. Remember that C structures are normally defined in include files, which are then included in the .C source files that need them. Such include files should not contain data or functions because these files are compiled multiple times. Including an inline function is okay, however, because it (like a macro) expands in place in the source file. The same applies to C++ classes. By defaulting member functions defined in classes inline, the preceding problem is avoided.

Keeping a Member Function After Class

For larger functions, putting the code directly in the class definition can lead to some very large, unwieldy class definitions. To prevent this, C++ lets you define member functions outside the class.

TIP

A function that is defined outside the class is said to be an outline function. This term is meant to be the opposite of an inline function that has been defined within the class.

When written outside the class declaration, the Savings.h file declares the deposit() function without defining it as follows:

```
// Savings - define a class that includes the ability
//           to make a deposit
class Savings
{
  public:
    // declare but don't define member function
    float deposit(float amount);
    unsigned int accountNumber;
    float  balance;
};
```

The definition of the deposit() function must be included in one of the source files that make up the program. For simplicity, I define the functions within the same SavingsClassOutline.cpp file that contains main().

You would not normally combine the member function definition with the rest of your program. It is more convenient to collect the outlined member function definitions into a source file with an appropriate name (like Savings.cpp). This source file is combined with other source files as part of building the executable program. I describe this in Chapter 22.

```
//
// SavingsClassOutline - invoke a member function that's
//                        declared within a class but defined
//                        in a separate file
//
#include <cstdio>
#include <cstdlib>
#include <iostream>

using namespace std;
#include "Savings.h"

// define the member function Savings::deposit()
// (normally this is contained in a separate file that is
// then combined with a different file that is combined)
float Savings::deposit(float amount)
{
    balance += amount;
    return balance;
}

// the main program
int main(int nNumberofArgs, char* pszArgs[])
{
    Savings s;
    s.accountNumber = 123456;
    s.balance = 0.0;

    // now add something to the account
    cout << "Depositing 10 to account " << s.accountNumber <<
            endl;
    s.deposit(10);
    cout << "Balance is " << s.balance << endl;

    // wait until user is ready before terminating program
    // to allow the user to see the program results
    system("PAUSE");
    return 0;
}
```

This class definition contains nothing more than a prototype declaration for the function `deposit()`. The function definition appears separately. The member function prototype declaration in the structure is analogous to any other prototype declaration and, like all prototype declarations, is required.

Notice how the function nickname `deposit()` was good enough when the function was defined within the class. When defined outside the class, however, the function requires its extended name.

Overloading Member Functions

Member functions can be overloaded in the same way that conventional functions are overloaded (see Chapter 6 if you don't remember what that means). Remember, however, that the class name is part of the extended name. Thus, the following functions are all legal:

```
class Student
{
  public:
    // grade -- return the current grade point average
    float grade();
    // grade -- set the grade and return previous value
    float grade(float newGPA);
    // ...data members and other stuff...
};
class Slope
{
  public:
    // grade -- return the percentage grade of the slope
    float grade();
    // ...stuff goes here too...
};

// grade -- return the letter equivalent of a numerical grade
char grade(float value);

int main(int argcs, char* pArgs[])
{
    Student s;
    s.grade(3.5);        // Student::grade(float)
    float v = s.grade(); // Student::grade()

    char c = grade(v);   // ::grade(float)

    Slope o;
    float m = o.grade(); // Slope::grade()
    return 0;
}
```

Each call made from `main()` is noted in the comments with the extended name of the function called.

When calling overloaded functions, not only the arguments of the function but also the type of the object (if any) with which the function is invoked are used to disambiguate the call. (The term *disambiguate* is object-oriented talk for "decide at compile time which overloaded function to call." A mere mortal might say "differentiate.")

In the example, the first two calls to the member functions, `Student::grade(float)` and `Student::grade()`, are differentiated by their argument lists and the type of object used. The call to `s.grade()` calls `Student::grade()` because `s` is of type `Student`.

The third call has no object, so it unambiguously denotes the non-member function `::grade(float)`.

The final call is made with an object of type `Slope`; it must refer to the member function `Slope::grade()`.

Chapter 14

Point and Stare at Objects

C++ programmers are forever generating arrays of things — arrays of `int`s, arrays of `float`s, so why not arrays of students? Students stand in line all the time — a lot more than they care to. The concept of `Student` objects all lined up quietly awaiting their name to jump up to perform some mundane task is just too attractive to pass up.

Defining Arrays of and Pointers to Simple Things

An array is a sequence of identical objects much like the identical houses on a street that make up one of those starter neighborhoods. Each element in the array carries an index, which corresponds to the number of elements from the beginning of the array — the first element in the array carries an offset of 0.

C++ arrays are declared by using the bracket symbols containing the number of elements in the array:

```
int array[10];        // declare an array of 10 elements
```

The individual elements of the array can be accessed by counting the offset from the beginning of the array:

```
array[0] = 10;        // assign 10 to the first element
array[9] = 20;        // assign 20 to the last element
```

The program first assigns the value 10 to the first element in the array — the element at the beginning of the array. The program then assigns 20 to the last element in the array — element at offset nine from the beginning.

Always remember that C++ indices start at 0 and go through the size of the array minus 1.

I like to use the analogy of a street with houses. The array name represents the name of the street, and the house number in that street represents the array index. Similarly, variables can be identified by their unique address in computer memory. These addresses can be calculated and stored for later use.

```
int variable;                 // declare an int object
int* pVariable = &variable;   // store its address
                              // in pVariable
*pVariable = 10;              // assign 10 into the int
                              // pointed at by pVariable
```

The pointer pVariable is declared to contain the address of variable. The assignment stores 10 into the int pointed at by pVariable.

If you apply the house analogy one last time (I promise):

- variable is a house.
- pVariable is like a piece of paper containing the address of the house.
- The final assignment delivers the message 10 to the house whose address is written on pVariable just like a postman might (except unlike my postman, computers don't deliver mail to the wrong address).

Chapter 7 goes into the care and feeding of arrays of simple (intrinsic) variables, and Chapter 8 and Chapter 9 describe simple pointers in detail.

Declaring Arrays of Objects

Arrays of objects work the same way arrays of simple variables work. Take, for example, the following snippet from ArrayOfStudents.cpp:

```
// ArrayOfStudents - define an array of Student objects
//                   and access an element in it. This
//                   program doesn't do anything
class Student
{
  public:
    int   semesterHours;
    float gpa;
    float addCourse(int hours, float grade);
};
```

```
void someFn()
{
    // declare an array of 10 students
    Student s[10];

    // assign the 5th student a gpa of 5.0 (lucky guy)
    s[4].gpa = 5.0;

    // add another course to the 5th student;
    // this time he failed - serves him right
    s[4].addCourse(3, 0.0);
}
```

Here s is an array of Student objects. s[4] refers to the fifth Student object in the array. By extension, s[4].gpa refers to the GPA of the 5th student. Further, s[4].addCourse() adds a course to the 5th Student object.

Declaring Pointers to Objects

Pointers to objects work like pointers to simple types, as you can see in the example program ObjPtr:

```
// ObjPtr - define and use a pointer to a Student object
#include <cstdio>
#include <cstdlib>
#include <iostream>
using namespace std;

class Student
{
  public:
    int   semesterHours;
    float gpa;
    float addCourse(int hours, float grade){return 0.0;};
};

int main(int argc, char* pArgs[])
{
    // create a Student object
    Student s;
    s.gpa = 3.0;

    // now create a pointer to a Student object
    Student* pS;

    // make the Student pointer point to our Student object
    pS = &s;
    cout << "s.gpa   = " << s.gpa   << "\n"
         << "pS->gpa = " << pS->gpa << endl;
```

```
    // wait until user is ready before terminating program
    // to allow the user to see the program results
    system("PAUSE");
    return 0;
}
```

The program declares a variable s of type Student. It then goes on to declare a pointer variable pS of type pointer to a Student object, also written as Student*. The program initializes the value of one of the data members in s. It then precedes to assign the address of s to the variable pS. Finally, it refers to the same Student object, first using the object's name, s, and then using the pointer to the object, pS. I explain the strange notation pS->gpa; in the next section of this chapter.

Dereferencing an object pointer

By analogy of pointers to simple variables, you might think that the following refers to the GPA of student s:

```
int main(int argc, char* pArgs[])
{
    // the following is incorrect
    Student s;
    Student* pS = &s; // create a pointer to s

    // access the gpa member of the object pointed at by pS
    // (this doesn't work)
    *pS.gpa = 3.5;

    return 0;
}
```

As the comments indicate, this doesn't work. The problem is that the dot operator (.) is evaluated before the pointer (*).

Note: The * operator is often referred to as the *splat* operator — not a popular term with insects.

C++ programmers use parentheses to override the order in which operations are performed. For example, the parentheses force addition to be performed before multiplication in the following expression:

```
int i = 2 * (1 + 3);  // addition performed
                      // before multiplication
```

Parentheses have the same effect when applied to pointer variables:

```
int main(int argc, char* pArgs[])
{
```

```
    Student s;
    Student* pS = &s; // create a pointer to s

    // access the gpa member of the object pointed at by pS
    // (this works as expected)
    (*pS).gpa = 3.5;

    return 0;
}
```

The `*pS` evaluates to the pointer's `Student` object pointed at by `pS`. The
`.gpa` refers to the `gpa` member of that object.

Pointing toward arrow pointers

Using the splat operator together with parentheses works just fine for dereferencing pointers to objects; however, even the most hardened techies would
admit that this mixing of asterisks and parentheses is a bit tortured.

C++ offers a more convenient operator for accessing members of an object to
avoid clumsy object pointer expressions. The `->` operator is defined as follows:

```
ps->gpa is equivalent to(*pS).gpa
```

This leads to the following:

```
int main(int argc, char* pArgs[])
{
    Student s;
    Student* pS = &s; // create a pointer to s

    // access the gpa member of the object pointed at by pS
    pS->gpa = 3.5;

    return 0;
}
```

The arrow operator is used almost exclusively because it is easier to read;
however, the two forms are completely equivalent.

Passing Objects to Functions

Passing pointers to functions is just one of the ways to entertain yourself
with pointer variables.

Calling a function with an object value

As you know, C++ passes arguments to functions by reference when the argument type is flagged with the squiggly '&' property (see Chapter 8). However, by default, C++ passes arguments to functions by value (you can check Chapter 6, on this one, if you insist).

Complex, user-defined class objects are passed the same as simple `int` values as shown in the following PassObjVal program:

```
// PassObjVal - attempts to change the value of an object
//               in a function fail when the object is
//               passed by value
#include <cstdio>
#include <cstdlib>
#include <iostream>
using namespace std;

class Student
{
  public:
    int   semesterHours;
    float gpa;
};

void someFn(Student copyS)
{
    copyS.semesterHours = 10;
    copyS.gpa           = 3.0;
    cout << "The value of copyS.gpa = "
         << copyS.gpa << "\n";
}

int main(int argc, char* pArgs[])
{
    Student s;
    s.gpa = 0.0;

    // display the value of s.gpa before calling someFn()
    cout << "The value of s.gpa = " << s.gpa << "\n";

    // pass the address of the existing object
    cout << "Calling someFn(Student)\n";
    someFn(s);
    cout << "Returned from someFn(Student)\n";

    // the value of s.gpa remains 0
    cout << "The value of s.gpa = " << s.gpa << "\n";
```

```
    // wait until user is ready before terminating program
    // to allow the user to see the program results
    system("PAUSE");
    return 0;
}
```

The function `main()` creates an object *s* and then passes *s* to the function
`someFn()`.

It is not the object *s* itself that is passed, but a copy of *s*.

The object `copyS` in `someFn()` begins life as an exact copy of the variable *s* in
`main()`. Any change to `copyS` made within `someFn()` has no effect on *s* back
in `main()`. Executing this program generates the following understandable
but disappointing response:

```
The value of s.gpa = 0
Calling someFn(Student)
The value of copyS.gpa = 3
Returned from someFn(Student)
The value of s.gpa = 0
Press any key to continue . . .
```

Calling a function with an object pointer

Most of the time, the programmer wants any changes made in the function to
be reflected in the calling function as well. For this, the C++ programmer must
pass either the address of an object or a reference to the object rather than
the object itself. The following PassObjPtr program uses the address
approach.

```
// PassObjPtr - change the contents of an object in
//              a function by passing a pointer to the
#include <cstdio>
#include <cstdlib>
#include <iostream>
using namespace std;

class Student
{
  public:
    int   semesterHours;
    float gpa;
};
```

```
void someFn(Student* pS)
{
    pS->semesterHours = 10;
    pS->gpa           = 3.0;
    cout << "The value of pS->gpa = "
         << pS->gpa << "\n";
}

int main(int nNumberofArgs, char* pszArgs[])
{
    Student s;
    s.gpa = 0.0;

    // display the value of s.gpa before calling someFn()
    cout << "The value of s.gpa = " << s.gpa << "\n";

    // pass the address of the existing object
    cout << "Calling someFn(Student*)\n";
    someFn(&s);
    cout << "Returned from someFn(Student*)\n";

    // the value of s.gpa is now 3.0
    cout << "The value of s.gpa = " << s.gpa << "\n";

    // wait until user is ready before terminating program
    // to allow the user to see the program results
    system("PAUSE");
    return 0;
}
```

The type of the argument to someFn() is a pointer to a Student object (otherwise known as Student*). This is reflected in the way that the program calls someFn(), passing the address of *s* rather than the value of *s*. Giving someFn() the address of s allows him to modify whatever value that is stored there. Conceptually, this is akin to writing down the address of the house *s* on the piece of paper pS and then passing that paper to someFn(). The function someFn() uses the arrow syntax for dereferencing the pS pointer.

The output from PassObjPtr is much more satisfying (to me anyway):

```
The value of s.gpa = 0
Calling someFn(Student*)
The value of pS->gpa = 3
Returned from someFn(Student*)
The value of s.gpa = 3
Press any key to continue . . .
```

Calling a function by using the reference operator

The reference operator described in Chapter 9 works for user-defined objects. The following PassObjRef demonstrates references to user-defined objects:

```
// PassObjRef - change the contents of an object in
//              a function by using a reference
#include <cstdio>
#include <cstdlib>
#include <iostream>
using namespace std;

class Student
{
  public:
    int   semesterHours;
    float gpa;
};

// same as before, but this time using references
void someFn(Student& refS)
{
    refS.semesterHours = 10;
    refS.gpa        = 3.0;
    cout << "The value of refS.gpa = "
         << refS.gpa << "\n";
}

int main(int nNumberofArgs, char* pszArgs[])
{
    Student s;
    s.gpa = 0.0;

    // display the value of s.gpa before calling someFn()
    cout << "The value of s.gpa = " << s.gpa << "\n";

    // pass the address of the existing object
    cout << "Calling someFn(Student*)\n";
    someFn(s);
    cout << "Returned from someFn(Student&)\n";

    // the value of s.gpa is now 3.0
    cout << "The value of s.gpa = " << s.gpa << "\n";

    // wait until user is ready before terminating program
    // to allow the user to see the program results
```

```
        system("PAUSE");
        return 0;
}
```

In this example, C++ passes a reference to *s* rather than a copy. Changes made in `someFn()` are retained in `main()`.

Passing by reference is just another way of passing the address of the object. C++ keeps track of the address of a reference, whereas you manipulate the address in a pointer.

Why Bother with Either Pointers or References?

Okay, so both pointers and references provide relative advantages, but why bother with either one? Why not just always pass the object?

I discussed one obvious answer earlier in this chapter: You can't modify the object from a function that gets nothing but a copy of the structure object.

Here's a second reason: Some objects are large — I mean *really* large. Passing such an object by value means copying the entire thing into the function's memory.

The area used to pass arguments to a function is called the *call stack*.

The object will need to be copied again should that function call another, and so on. After a while, you can end up with dozens of copies of this object. That consumes memory, and copying all the objects can make execution of your program slower than booting up Windows.

The problem of copying objects actually gets worse. You see in Chapter 18 that making a copy of an object can be even more painful than simply copying some memory around.

Returning to the Heap

The problems that exist for simple types of pointers plague class object pointers as well. In particular, you must make sure that the pointer you're using actually points to a valid object. For example, don't return a reference to an object defined local to the function:

```
MyClass* myFunc()
{
    // the following does not work
    MyClass  mc;
    MyClass* pMC = &mc;
    return pMC;
}
```

Upon return from myFunc(), the mc object goes out of scope. The pointer returned by myFunc() is not valid in the calling function.

The problem of returning memory that's about to go out of scope is discussed in Chapter 9.

Allocating the object off the heap solves the problem:

```
MyClass* myFunc()
{
    MyClass* pMC = new MyClass;
    return pMC;
}
```

The heap is used to allocate objects in a number of different situations.

Comparing Pointers to References

I hate to keep referencing pointers and pointing to references, but new programmers often wonder why both are needed.

Actually, you could argue that you don't need both. C# and most other languages don't use pointers. However, pointer variables are an ingrained part of good ol' standard non-Visual Studio.NET–specific C++.

Why Not Use References Rather Than Pointers?

The syntax for manipulating a reference is similar to that used with normal objects. So why not just stick with references and never look back at pointers?

Objects and their addresses aren't the same thing. Many times, the syntax for a reference actually becomes more complicated than that for pointers. Consider the following examples:

```
class Student
{
  public:
    int semesterHours;
    float gpa;
    Student  valFriend;
    Student& refFriend;
    Student* ptrFriend;
};

int main(int nNumberofArgs, char* pszArgs[])
{
    // the following declares a reference off of the heap
    // (simple enough)
    Student& student = *new Student;
    student.gpa = 10;

    // ditto
    Student& studentFriend = *new Student;
    studentFriend.gpa = 20;

    // the following copies the value of one Student
    // object into the second
    student.valFriend = studentFriend;

    // this doesn't work at all
    Student& refFriend;
    refFriend = studentFriend;

    // this does work
    student.pFriend = &studentFriend;

    return 0;
}
```

As you can see, I modified that Student class so that one Student can reference her best buddy. I tried to use the reference variable type to do so. I created two students in main() in an attempt to link the one student object to its studentFriend.

The first assignment in the body of the program copies the contents of the friend into the data member — Student object contains a body double. The second assignment doesn't work at all — C++ can't differentiate assigning an object to a reference variable from assignment to an object itself. Only the third assignment works. The student object points to the address of the studentFriend, which is exactly what you want.

Linking Up with Linked Lists

The second most common structure after the array is called a *list*. Lists come in different sizes and types; however, the most common one is the *linked list*. In the linked list, each object points to the next member in a sort of chain that extends through memory. The program can simply point the last element in the list to an object to add it to the list. This means that the user doesn't have to declare the size of the linked list at the beginning of the program — you can cause the linked list to grow (and shrink) as necessary by adding (and removing) objects.

The cost of such flexibility is speed of access. You can't just reach in and grab the tenth element, for example, like you would in the case of an array. Now, you have to start at the beginning of the list and link ten times from one object to the next.

A linked list has one other feature besides its run-time expandability (that's good) and its difficulty in accessing an object at random (that's bad) — a linked list makes significant use of pointers. This makes linked lists a great tool for giving you experience in manipulating pointer variables.

Not every class can be used to create a linked list. You declare a linkable class as follows:

```
class LinkableClass
{
    public:
        LinkableClass* pNext;

        // other members of the class
};
```

The key is using the pNext pointer to an object of class LinkableClass. At first blush, this seems odd indeed — a class contains a pointer to itself? Actually, this says that the class Linkable contains a pointer to another object also of class Linkable.

The pNext pointer is similar to the appendage used to form a chain of children crossing the street. The list of children consists of a number of objects, all of type child. Each child holds onto another child.

The head pointer is simply a pointer of type LinkableClass*: To keep torturing the child chain analogy, the teacher points to an object of class child. (It's interesting to note that the teacher is not a child — the head pointer is not of type LinkableClass*.)

```
LinkableClass* pHead = (LinkableClass*)0;
```

Always initialize any pointer to 0. Zero, generally known as null when used in the context of pointers, is universally known as the *non-pointer.* In any case, referring to address 0 always causes the program to halt immediately. The cast from the int 0 to LinkableClass* is not necessary. C++ understands 0 to be of all types, sort of the "universal pointer." However, I find the use of explicit casts a good practice.

The pointer to the first member in a linked list is called the *head pointer.* The pointer to the last member, if there is one, is called the *tail pointer* — hence, the name pHead in this example. (I also like the name because it sounds like you're insulting someone by calling them a "pea head." Don't even get me started on a pointer to a pHead.)

To see how linked lists work in practice, consider the following function, which adds the argument passed it to the beginning of a list:

```
void addHead(LinkableClass* pLC)
{
    pLC->pNext = pHead;
    pHead = pLC;
}
```

Here, the pNext pointer of the object is set to point to the first member of the list. This is akin to grabbing the hand of the first kid in the chain. The second line points the head pointer to the object, sort of like having the teacher let go of the kid we're holding onto and grabbing us. That makes us the first kid in the chain.

Performing other operations on a linked list

Adding an object to the head of a list is the simplest operation on a linked list. Moving through the elements in a list gives you a better idea about how a linked list works:

```
// navigate through a linked list
LinkableClass* pL = pHead;
while(pL)
{
    // perform some operation here

    // get the next entry
    pL = pL->pNext;
}
```

The program initializes the pL pointer to the first object of a list of LinkableClass objects through the pointer pHead. (Grab the first kid's hand.)

The program then enters the `while` loop. If the `pL` pointer is not null, it points to some `LinkableClass` object. Control enters the loop, where the program can then perform whatever operations it wants on the object pointed at by `pL`.

The assignment `pL = pL->pNext` "moves" the `pL` pointer over to the next kid in the list of objects. The program checks to see if `pL` is null, meaning that we've exhausted the list . . . I mean run out of kids, not exhausted all the kids in the list.

Hooking up with a LinkedListData program

The LinkedListData program shown here implements a linked list of objects containing a person's name. The program could easily contain whatever other data you might like, such as social security number, grade point average, height, weight, and bank account balance. I've limited the information to just a name to keep the program as simple as possible.

```cpp
// LinkedListData - store data in a linked list of objects
#include <cstdio>
#include <cstdlib>
#include <iostream>
#include <string.h>
using namespace std;

// NameDataSet - stores a person's name (these objects
//               could easily store any other information
//               desired).
class NameDataSet
{
  public:
    char szName[128];

    // the link to the next entry in the list
    NameDataSet* pNext;
};

// the pointer to the first entry in the list
NameDataSet* pHead = 0;

// add - add a new member to the linked list
void add(NameDataSet* pNDS)
{
    // point the current entry to the beginning of
    // the list...
    pNDS->pNext = pHead;

    // point the head pointer to the current entry
    pHead = pNDS;
```

```
}

// getData - read a name and social security
//           number; return null if no more to
//           read
NameDataSet* getData()
{
    // read the first name
    char nameBuffer[128];
    cout << "\nEnter name:";
    cin  >> nameBuffer;

    // if the name entered is 'exit'...
    if ((stricmp(nameBuffer, "exit") == 0))
    {
        // ...return a null to terminate input
        return 0;
    }

    // get a new entry to fill
    NameDataSet* pNDS = new NameDataSet;

    // fill in the name and zero the link pointer
    strncpy(pNDS->szName, nameBuffer, 128);
    pNDS->szName[127] = '\0';  // ensure string is terminated
    pNDS->pNext = 0;

    // return the address of the object created
    return pNDS;
}

int main(int nNumberofArgs, char* pszArgs[])
{
    cout << "Read names of people\n"
         << "Enter 'exit' for first name to exit\n";

    // create (another) NameDataSet object
    NameDataSet* pNDS;
    while (pNDS = getData())
    {
        // add it onto the end of the list of
        // NameDataSet objects
        add(pNDS);
    }

    // to display the objects, iterate through the
    // list (stop when the next address is NULL)
    cout << "Entries:\n";
    pNDS = pHead;
    while(pNDS)
    {
        // display current entry
        cout << pNDS->szName << "\n";
```

```
        // get the next entry
        pNDS = pNDS->pNext;
    }

    // wait until user is ready before terminating program
    // to allow the user to see the program results
    system("PAUSE");
    return 0;
}
```

Although somewhat lengthy, the LinkedListData program is simple if you take it in parts. The NameDataSet structure has room for a person's name and a link to the next NameDataSet object in a linked list. I mentioned earlier that this class would have other members in a real-world application.

The main() function starts looping, calling getData() on each iteration to fetch another NameDataSet entry from the user. The program exits the loop if getData() returns a null, the "non-address," for an address.

The getData() function prompts the user for a name and reads in whatever the user enters. The program just hopes that the number of characters is less than 128, since it makes no checks. If the string entered is equal to exit, the function returns a null to the caller, thereby exiting the while loop. The stricmp() compares two strings without regard to case. If the string entered is not exit, the program creates a new NameDataSet object, populates the name, and zeroes out the pNext pointer.

Never leave link pointers uninitialized. Use the old programmer's wives' tale: "When in doubt, zero it out." (I mean "old tale," not "tale of an old wife.")

Finally, getData() returns the object's address to main().

main() adds each object returned from getData() to the beginning of the linked list pointed at by the global variable pHead. Control exits the initial while loop when the getData() returns a null. main() then enters a second section that iterates through the completed list, displaying each object. The second while loop terminates when it reaches the last object, the object with a pNext pointer whose value is null.

The program outputs the names entered in the opposite order. This is because each new object is added to the beginning of the list. Alternatively, the program could have added each object to the end of the list — doing so just takes a little more code.

A Ray of Hope: A List of Containers Linked to the C++ Library

I believe everyone should walk before they run, should figure out how to perform arithmetic in their head before using a calculator, and should write a linked list program before using a list class written by someone else. That being said, in Chapter 27, I describe other list classes provided by the C++ environment. These classes are known more generically as *container classes* because they contain other objects — array and linked list are just two examples of container classes.

Chapter 15

Protecting Members: Do Not Disturb

C hapter 12 introduces the concept of the class. That chapter describes the `public` keyword as though it were part of the class declaration — just something you do. In this chapter, you find out about an alternative to `public`.

Protecting Members

The members of a class can be marked protected, which makes them inaccessible outside the class. The alternative is to make the members public. Public members are accessible to all.

Please understand the term "inaccessible" in a weak sense. Any programmer can go into the source code, remove the `protected` keyword and do whatever she wants. Further, any hacker worth his salt can code into a protected section of code. The `protected` keyword is designed to protect a programmer from herself by preventing inadvertent access.

Why you need protected members

To understand the role of protected, think about the goals of object-oriented programming:

- ✔ To protect the internals of the class from outside functions. Suppose, for example, that you have a plan to build a software microwave (or whatever), provide it with a simple interface to the outside world, and then put a box around it to keep others from messing with the insides. The protected keyword is that box.

- ✔ To make the class responsible for maintaining its internal state. It's not fair to ask the class to be responsible if others can reach in and manipulate its internals (any more than it's fair to ask a microwave designer to be responsible for the consequences of my mucking with a microwave's internal wiring).

- ✔ To limit the interface of the class to the outside world. It's easier to figure out and use a class that has a limited interface (the public members). Protected members are hidden from the user and need not be learned. The interface becomes the class; this is called *abstraction* (see Chapter 11 for more on abstraction).

- ✔ To reduce the level of interconnection between the class and other code. By limiting interconnection, you can more easily replace one class with another or use the class in other programs.

Now, I know what you functional types out there are saying: "You don't need some fancy feature to do all that. Just make a rule that says certain members are publicly accessible, and others are not."

Although that is true in theory, it doesn't work. People start out with all kinds of good intentions, but as long as the language doesn't at least discourage direct access of protected members, these good intentions get crushed under the pressure to get the product out the door.

Discovering how protected members work

Adding the keyword `public` to a class makes subsequent members public, which means that they are accessible by non-member functions. Adding the keyword `protected` makes subsequent members of the class protected, which means they are not accessible by non-members of the class. You can switch between public and protected as often as you like.

Suppose you have a class named `Student`. In this example, the following capabilities are all that a fully functional, upstanding `Student` needs (notice the absence of `spendMoney()` and `drinkBeer()` — this is a highly stylized student):

`addCourse(int hours, float grade)` — adds a course

`grade()` — returns the current grade point average

`hours()` — returns the number of hours earned toward graduation

The remaining members of Student can be declared protected to keep other functions' prying expressions out of Student's business.

```
class Student
{
  public:
    // grade - return the current grade point average
    float grade()
    {
        return gpa;
    }

    // hours - return the number of semester hours
    int hours()
    {
        return semesterHours;
    }
    // addCourse - add another course to the student's record
    float addCourse(int hours, float grade);

    // the following members are off-limits to others
  protected:
    int  semesterHours; // hours earned toward graduation
    float gpa;          // grade point average
};
```

Now the members semester hours and gpa are accessible only to other members of Student. Thus, the following doesn't work:

```
Student s;
int main(int argcs, char* pArgs[])
{
  // raise my grade (don't make it too high; otherwise, no
  // one would believe it)
  s.gpa = 3.5;            // <- generates compiler error
  float gpa = s.grade(); // <- this public function reads
                         // a copy of the value, but you
                         // can't change it from here

  return 0;
}
```

The application's attempt to change the value of gpa is flagged with a compiler error.

It's considered good form not to rely on the default and specify either public or private at the beginning of the class. Most of the time, people start with the public members because they make up the interface of the class. Protected members are saved until later.

A class member can also be protected by declaring it `private`. In this book, I use the `protected` keyword exclusively since it expresses the more generic concept.

Making an Argument for Using Protected Members

Now that you know a little more about how to use protected members in an actual class, I can replay the arguments for using protected members.

Protecting the internal state of the class

Making the `gpa` member protected precludes the application from setting the grade point average to some arbitrary value. The application can add courses, but it can't change the grade point average.

If the application has a legitimate need to set the grade point average directly, the class can provide a member function for that purpose, as follows:

```
class Student
{
  public:
    // same as before
    float grade()
    {
        return gpa;
    }
    // here we allow the grade to be changed
    float grade(float newGPA)
    {
        float oldGPA = gpa;
        // only if the new value is valid
        if (newGPA > 0 && newGPA <= 4.0)
        {
            gpa = newGPA;
        }
        return oldGPA;
    }
    // ...other stuff is the same including the data members:
  protected:
    int  semesterHours; // hours earned toward graduation
    float gpa;
};
```

The addition of the member function `grade(float)` allows the application to set the `gpa`. Notice, however, that the class still hasn't given up control completely. The application can't set `gpa` to any old value; only a `gpa` in the legal range of values (from 0 through 4.0) is accepted.

Thus, `Student` class has provided access to an internal data member without abdicating its responsibility to make sure that the internal state of the class is valid.

Using a class with a limited interface

A class provides a limited interface. To use a class, all you need (or want) to know are its public members, what they do, and what their arguments are. This can drastically reduce the number of things you need to master — and remember to use the class.

As conditions change or as bugs are found, you want to be able to change the internal workings of a class. Changes to those details are less likely to require changes in the external application code if you can hide the internal workings of the class.

A second, perhaps more important reason, lies in the limited ability of humans (I can't speak for dogs and cats) to keep a large number of things in their minds at any given instant. Using a strictly defined class interface allows the programmer to forget the details that go on behind it. Likewise, a programmer building the class need not concentrate to quite the same degree on exactly how each of the functions is being used.

Giving Non-Member Functions Access to Protected Members

Occasionally, you want a non-member function to have access to the protected members of a class. You do so by declaring the function to be a friend of the class by using the keyword `friend`.

Sometimes, an external function can use direct access to a data member. I know this appears to break the strictly defined, well-sealed-off class interface position that I've been advocating, but just consider the following. First, including a friend function is, in effect, adding that function to the interface (that's why a class shouldn't have too many friends). You're okay as long as you attempt to treat this function as a normal function that, oh yeah, happens to have direct access. Second, providing a public access method that acts as a thin veil over a data member doesn't do anything to abstract away class details. Such a thin veneer function fulfills the letter of the law, but not the spirit.

The friend declaration appears in the class that contains the protected member. The friend declaration is like a prototype declaration in that it includes the extended name and the return type. In the following example, the function `initialize()` can now access anything it wants in `Student`:

```
class Student
{
    friend void initialize(Student*);
  public:
    // same public members as before...
  protected:
    int  semesterHours; // hours earned toward graduation
    float gpa;
};
// the following function is a friend of Student
// so it can access the protected members
void initialize(Student *pS)
{
    pS->gpa = 0;         // this is now legal...
    pS->semesterHours = 0;  // ...when it wasn't before
}
```

A single function can be declared a friend of two classes at the same time. Although this can be convenient, it tends to bind the two classes together. This binding of classes is normally considered bad because it makes one class dependent on the other. If the two classes naturally belong together, however, it's not all bad, as shown here:

```
class Student;    // forward declaration
class Teacher
{
    friend void registration(Teacher& t, Student& s);
  public:
    void assignGrades();
  protected:
    int   noStudents;
    Student *pList[100];
};
class Student
{
    friend void registration(Teacher& t, Student& s);
  public:
    // same public members as before...
  protected:
    Teacher *pT;
    int  semesterHours; // hours earned toward graduation
    float gpa;
};
```

```
void registration(Teacher& t, Student& s)
{
    // initialize the Student object
    s.semesterHours = 0;
    s.gpa = 0;

    // if there's room...
    if (t.noStudents < 100)
    {
        // ...add it onto the end of the list
        t.pList[t.noStudents] = &s;
        t.noStudents++;
    }
}
```

In this example, the registration() function can reach into both the Student and Teacher classes to tie them together at registration time, without being a member function of either one.

The first line in the example declares the class Student, but none of its members. This is called a *forward declaration* and just defines the name of the class so that other classes, such as Teacher, can define a pointer to it. Forward references are necessary when two classes refer to each other.

A member function of one class may be declared a friend of another class, as shown here:

```
class Teacher
{
    // ...other members as well...
  public:
    void assignGrades();
};
class Student
{
    friend void Teacher::assignGrades();
  public:
    // same public members as before...
  protected:
    int  semesterHours; // hours earned toward graduation
    float gpa;
};
void Teacher::assignGrades()
{
    // can access protected members of Teacher from here
}
```

Unlike in the non-member example, the member function assignGrades() must be declared before the class Student can declare it to be a friend.

An entire class can be named a friend of another. This has the effect of making every member function of the class a friend:

```
class Student;   // forward declaration
class Teacher
{
 protected:
   int   noStudents;
   Student *pList[100];
 public:
   void assignGrades();
};
class Student
{
   friend class Teacher; // make entire class a friend
 public:
   // same public members as before...
 protected:
   int  semesterHours; // hours earned toward graduation
   float gpa;
};
```

Now, any member function of Teacher has access to the protected members of Student. Declaring one class a friend of the other inseparably binds the two classes together.

Chapter 16

"Why Do You Build Me Up, Just to Tear Me Down, Baby?"

In This Chapter

▶ Creating and destroying objects

▶ Declaring constructors and destructors

▶ Invoking constructors and destructors

O bjects in programs are built and scrapped just like objects in the real world. If the class is to be responsible for its well-being, it must have some control over this process. As luck would have it (I suppose some pre-planning was involved as well), C++ provides just the right mechanism. But, first, a discussion of what it means to create an object.

Creating Objects

Some people get a little sloppy in using the terms *class* and *object*. What's the difference? What's the relationship?

I can create a class Dog that describes the relevant properties of man's best friend. At my house, we have two dogs. Thus, my class Dog has two instances, Trude (pronounced "Troo-duh") and Scooter (well, I think there are two instances — I haven't seen Scooter in a few days).

A class describes a type of thing. An object is one of those things. An object is an instance of a class. There is only one class Dog, no matter how many dogs I have.

Objects are created and destroyed, but classes simply exist. My pets, Trude and Scooter, come and go, but the class Dog (evolution aside) is perpetual.

Different types of objects are created at different times. *Global objects* are created when the program first begins execution. *Local objects* are created when the program encounters their declaration.

A global object is one that is declared outside of a function. A local object is one that is declared within a function and is, therefore, local to the function. In the following example, the variable me is global, and the variable notMe is local to the function pickOne():

```
int me = 0;
void pickOne()
{
    int notMe;
}
```

According to the rules, global objects are initialized to all zeros when the program starts executing. Objects declared local to a function have no particular initial value. Having all data members have a random state may not be a valid condition for all classes.

C++ allows the class to define a special member function that is invoked automatically when an object of that class is created. This member function, called the *constructor,* must initialize the object to a valid initial state. In addition, the class can define a destructor to handle the destruction of the object. These two functions are the topics of this chapter.

Using Constructors

The constructor is a member function that is called automatically when an object is created. Its primary job is to initialize the object to a legal initial value for the class. (It's the job of the remaining member functions to ensure that the state of the object stays legal.)

Why you need constructors

You could initialize an object as part of the declaration — that's the way the C programmer would do it — for example:

```
struct Student
{
    int   semesterHours;
    float gpa;
};
```

```
void fn()
{
    Student s1 = {0, 0.0};

    // or
    Student s2;

    s2.semesterHours = 0;
    s2.gpa = 0.0;

    // ...function continues...
}
```

You could outfit the class with an initialization function that the application calls as soon as the object is created. Because this initialization function is a member of the class, it would have access to the protected members. This solution appears as follows:

```
class Student
{
  public:
    void init()
    {
        semesterHours = 0;
        gpa = 0.0;
    }
    // ...other public members...
  protected:
    int   semesterHours;
    float gpa;
};
void fn()
{
    Student s;      // create the object...
    s.init();       // ...then initialize it
    // ...function continues...
}
```

The only problem with this solution is that it abrogates the responsibility of the class to look after its own data members. In other words, the class must rely on the application to call the init() function. If it does not, the object is full of garbage, and who knows what might happen.

What is needed is a way to take the responsibility for calling the init() function away from the application code and give it to the compiler. Every time an object is created, the compiler can insert a call to the special init() function to initialize it. That's a constructor!

Making constructors work

The constructor is a special member function that's called automatically when an object is created. It carries the same name as the class to differentiate it from the other members of the class. The designers of C++ could have made up a different rule, such as: "The constructor must be called `init()`." It wouldn't have made any difference, as long as the compiler could recognize the constructor. In addition, the constructor has no return type, not even `void`, because it is only called automatically — if the constructor did return something, there would be no place to put it. A constructor cannot be invoked manually.

Constructing a single object

With a constructor, the class `Student` appears as follows:

```
//
//   Constructor - example that invokes a constructor
//
#include <cstdio>
#include <cstdlib>
#include <iostream>
using namespace std;

class Student
{
  public:
    Student()
    {
        cout << "constructing student" << endl;
        semesterHours = 0;
        gpa = 0.0;
    }
  protected:
    int   semesterHours;
    float gpa;
};

int main(int nNumberofArgs, char* pszArgs[])
{
    cout << "Creating a new Student object" << endl;
    Student s;

    cout << "Creating a new object off the heap" << endl;
    Student* pS = new Student;

    // wait until user is ready before terminating program
    // to allow the user to see the program results
    system("PAUSE");
    return 0;
}
```

At the point of the declaration of s, the compiler inserts a call to the constructor Student::Student(). Allocating a new Student object from the heap has the same effect as demonstrated by the output from the program:

```
Creating a new Student object
constructing student
Creating a new object off the heap
constructing student
Press any key to continue . . .
```

This simple constructor was written as an inline member function. Constructors can be written also as outline functions, as shown here:

```
class Student
{
  public:
    Student();
    // ...other public members...
  protected:
    int  semesterHours;
    float gpa;
};
Student::Student()
{
    cout << "constructing student" << endl;
    semesterHours = 0;
    gpa = 0.0;
}
```

The output from this program can "prove" to you that constructors work as advertised, but to get the real effect, you really should single-step this simple program in your debugger. (See Chapter 10 for instructions on using the debugger.)

Single-step through this example until control comes to rest at the Student's declaration. Select Step Into and control magically jumps to Student::Student(). Continue single-stepping through the constructor. When the function has finished, control returns to the statement after the declaration.

In some cases, Step Into will actually execute the entire constructor without stopping. You may have to set a breakpoint in the constructor to get the effect. Setting a breakpoint always works.

Constructing multiple objects

Each element of an array must be constructed on its own. Making the following simple change to the Constructor program contained in ConstructArray:

```
//
//   ConstructArray - example that invokes a constructor
//                    on an array of objects
//
#include <cstdio>
#include <cstdlib>
#include <iostream>
using namespace std;

class Student
{
  public:
    Student()

    {
        cout << "constructing student" << endl;
        semesterHours = 0;
        gpa = 0.0;
    }
    // ...other public members...
  protected:
    int  semesterHours;
    float gpa;
};

int main(int nNumberofArgs, char* pszArgs[])
{
    cout << "Creating an array of 5 Student objects" << endl;
    Student s[5];

    // wait until user is ready before terminating program
    // to allow the user to see the program results
    system("PAUSE");
    return 0;
}
```

generates the following output:

```
Creating an array of 5 Student objects
constructing student
constructing student
constructing student
constructing student
constructing student
Press any key to continue . . .
```

Constructing a duplex

If a class contains a data member that is an object of another class, the constructor for that class is called automatically as well. Consider the following
ConstructMembers example program. I added output statements so that you
can see the order in which the objects are invoked.

```
//
//   ConstructMembers - the member objects of a class
//                      are each constructed before the
//                      container class constructor gets
//                      a shot at it
//
#include <cstdio>
#include <cstdlib>
#include <iostream>
using namespace std;

class Course
{
  public:
    Course()
    {
        cout << "constructing course" << endl;
    }
};

class Student
{
  public:
    Student()
    {
        cout << "constructing student" << endl;
        semesterHours = 0;
        gpa = 0.0;
    }
  protected:
    int  semesterHours;
    float gpa;
};
class Teacher
{
  public:
    Teacher()
    {
        cout << "constructing teacher" << endl;
    }
  protected:
    Course c;
};
class TutorPair
{
  public:
    TutorPair()
    {
        cout << "constructing tutorpair" << endl;
        noMeetings = 0;
    }
```

```
    protected:
      Student student;
      Teacher teacher;
      int    noMeetings;
};

int main(int nNumberofArgs, char* pszArgs[])
{
    cout << "Creating TutorPair object" << endl;
    TutorPair tp;

    // wait until user is ready before terminating program
    // to allow the user to see the program results
    system("PAUSE");
    return 0;
}
```

Executing this program generates the following output:

```
Creating TutorPair object
constructing student
constructing course
constructing teacher
constructing tutorpair
Press any key to continue . . .
```

Creating the object tp in main automatically invokes the constructor for TutorPair. Before control passes into the body of the TutorPair constructor, however, the constructors for the two-member objects, student and teacher, are invoked.

The constructor for Student is called first because it is declared first. Then the constructor for Teacher is called.

The member Teacher.c of class Course is constructed as part of building the Teacher object. The Course constructor gets a shot first. Each object within a class must construct itself before the class constructor can be invoked. Otherwise, the main constructor would not know the state of its data members.

After all member data objects have been constructed, control returns to the open brace, and the constructor for TutorPair is allowed to construct the remainder of the object.

It would not do for TutorPair to be responsible for initializing Student and Teacher. Each class is responsible for initializing its own objects.

Dissecting a Destructor

Just as objects are created, so are they destroyed (ashes to ashes, dust to dust). If a class can have a constructor to set things up, it should also have a special member function to take the object apart. This member is called the *destructor*.

Why you need the destructor

A class may allocate resources in the constructor; these resources need to be deallocated before the object ceases to exist. For example, if the constructor opens a file, the file needs to be closed before leaving that class or the program. Or, if the constructor allocates memory from the heap, this memory must be freed before the object goes away. The destructor allows the class to do these cleanup tasks automatically without relying on the application to call the proper member functions.

Working with destructors

The destructor member has the same name as the class, but with a tilde (~) added at the front. (C++ is being cute again — the tilde is the symbol for the logical NOT operator. Get it? A destructor is a "not constructor." *Très* clever.) Like a constructor, the destructor has no return type. For example, the class Student with a destructor added appears as follows:

```
class Student
{
  public:
    Student()
    {
        semesterHours = 0;
        gpa = 0.0;
    }
    ~Student()
    {
        // ...whatever assets are returned here...
    }
  protected:
    int   semesterHours;
    float gpa;
};
```

The destructor is invoked automatically when an object is destroyed, or in C++ parlance, when an object is *destructed*. That sounds sort of circular ("the destructor is invoked when an object is destructed"), so I've avoided the term until now. For non-heap memory, you can also say, "when the object goes out of scope." A local object goes out of scope when the function returns. A global or static object goes out of scope when the program terminates.

But what about heap memory? A pointer may go out of scope, but heap memory doesn't. By definition, it's memory that is not part of a given function. An object that has been allocated off the heap is destructed when it's returned to the heap using the delete command. This is demonstrated in the following DestructMembers program:

```
//
// DestructMembers - this program both constructs and
//                   destructs a set of data members
//
#include <cstdio>
#include <cstdlib>
#include <iostream>
using namespace std;

class Course
{
  public:
    Course() { cout << "constructing course" << endl; }
    ~Course() { cout << "destructing course" << endl;  }
};

class Student
{
  public:
    Student()
    {
        cout << "constructing student" << endl;
        semesterHours = 0;
        gpa = 0.0;
    }
    ~Student() { cout << "destructing student" << endl; }
  protected:
    int  semesterHours;
    float gpa;
};
class Teacher
{
  public:
    Teacher()
    {
        cout << "constructing teacher" << endl;
        pC = new Course;
```

```
    }
    ~Teacher()
    {
        cout << " destructing teacher" << endl;
        delete pC;
    }
  protected:
    Course* pC;
};
class TutorPair
{
  public:
    TutorPair()
    {
        cout << "constructing tutorpair" << endl;
        noMeetings = 0;
    }
    ~TutorPair() { cout << " destructing tutorpair" << endl;
            }
  protected:
    Student student;
    Teacher teacher;
    int   noMeetings;
};

TutorPair* fn()
{
    cout << "Creating TutorPair object in function fn()"
        << endl;
    TutorPair tp;

    cout << "Allocating TutorPair off the heap" << endl;
    TutorPair*  pTP = new TutorPair;

    cout << "Returning from fn()" << endl;
    return pTP;
}

int main(int nNumberofArgs, char* pszArgs[])
{
    // call function fn() and then return the
    // TutorPair object returned to the heap
    TutorPair* pTPReturned = fn();
    cout << "Return heap object to the heap" << endl;
    delete pTPReturned;

    // wait until user is ready before terminating program
    // to allow the user to see the program results
    system("PAUSE");
    return 0;
}
```

The function main() invokes a function fn() that defines the object tp — this is to allow you to watch the variable go out of scope when control exits the function. fn() also allocates heap memory that it returns to main() where the memory is returned to the heap.

If you execute this program, it generates the following output:

```
Creating TutorPair object in function fn()
constructing student
constructing teacher
constructing course
constructing tutorpair
Allocating TutorPair off the heap
constructing student
constructing teacher
constructing course
constructing tutorpair
Returning from fn()
destructing tutorpair
destructing teacher
destructing course
destructing student
Return heap object to the heap
destructing tutorpair
destructing teacher
destructing course
destructing student
Press any key to continue . . .
```

Each constructor is called in turn as the TutorPair object is built up, starting from the smallest data member and working its way up to the TutorPair ::TutorPair() constructor function.

Two TutorPair objects are created. The first, tp, is defined locally to the function fn(), the second, pTP, is allocated off the heap. tp goes out of scope and is destructed when control passes out of the function. The heap memory whose address is returned from fn() is not destructed until main() deletes it.

The sequence of destructors invoked when an object is destructed is invoked in the reverse order in which the constructors were called.

Chapter 17

Making Constructive Arguments

A class represents a type of object in the real world. For example, in earlier chapters, I use the class Student to represent the properties of a student. Just like students, classes are autonomous. Unlike a student, a class is responsible for its own care and feeding — a class must keep itself in a valid state at all times.

The default constructor presented in Chapter 16 isn't always enough. For example, a default constructor can initialize the student ID to zero so that it doesn't contain a random value; however, a Student ID of 0 is probably not valid. It's up to the class to make sure that the ID is initialized to a legal value when the object is created.

C++ programmers require a constructor that accepts some type of argument in order to initialize an object to other than its default value. This chapter examines constructors with arguments.

Outfitting Constructors with Arguments

C++ enables programmers to define a constructor with arguments, as shown here:

```
class Student
{
  public:
    Student(char *pName);

    // ...class continues...
};
```

Justifying constructors

Something as straightforward as adding arguments to the constructor shouldn't require much justification, but let me take a shot at it anyway. First, allowing arguments to constructors is convenient. It's a bit silly to make programmers construct a default object and then immediately call an initialization function to store data in it. A constructor with arguments is like one-stop shopping — sort of a full-service constructor.

Another more important reason to provide arguments to constructors is that it may not be possible to construct a reasonable default object. Remember that a constructor's job is to construct a legal object (legal as defined by the class). If some default object is not legal, the constructor isn't doing its job.

For example, a bank account without an account number is probably not legal. (C++ doesn't care one way or the other, but the bank might get snippy.) You could construct a numberless BankAccount object and then require that the application use some other member function to initialize the account number before it's used. This "create now/initialize later" approach breaks the rules, however, because it forces the class to rely on the application for initialization.

Using a constructor

Conceptually, the idea of adding an argument is simple. A constructor is a member function, and member functions can have arguments. Therefore, constructors can have arguments.

Remember, though, that you don't call the constructor like a normal function. Therefore, the only time to pass arguments to the constructor is when the object is created. For example, the following program creates an object s of the class Student by calling the Student(char*) constructor. The object s is destructed when the function main() returns.

```
//
//  ConstructorWArg - provide a constructor with arguments
//
#include <cstdio>
#include <cstdlib>
#include <iostream>
using namespace std;
const int MAXNAMESIZE = 40;
class Student
{
  public:
    Student(char* pName)
    {
        strncpy(name, pName, MAXNAMESIZE);
        name[MAXNAMESIZE - 1]  = '\0';
```

```
        semesterHours = 0;
        gpa = 0.0;
    }

  // ...other public members...
  protected:
    char  name[MAXNAMESIZE];
    int   semesterHours;
    float gpa;
};

int main(int argcs, char* pArgs[])
{
    Student s("O. Danny Boy");
    Student* pS = new Student("E. Z. Rider");

    // wait until user is ready before terminating program
    // to allow the user to see the program results
    system("PAUSE");
    return 0;
}
```

The constructor looks like the constructors shown in Chapter 16 except for the addition of the `char*` argument `pName`. The constructor initializes the data members to their empty start-up values, except for the data member `name`, which gets its initial value from `pName`.

The object `s` is created in `main()`. The argument to be passed to the constructor appears in the declaration of `s`, right next to the name of the object. Thus, the student `s` is given the name `Danny` in this declaration. The closed brace invokes the destructor on poor little `Danny`.

The arguments to the constructor appear next to the name of the class when the object is allocated off the heap.

Many of the constructors in this chapter violate the "functions with more than three lines shouldn't be inlined" rule. I decided to make them inline anyway because I think they're easier for you to read that way. Aren't I a nice guy?

Placing Too Many Demands on the Carpenter: Overloading the Constructor

I can draw one more parallel between constructors and other, more normal member functions in this chapter: Constructors can be overloaded.

Overloading a function means to define two functions with the same short name but with different types of arguments. See Chapter 6 for the latest news on function overloading.

C++ chooses the proper constructor based on the arguments in the declaration of the object. For example, the class Student can have all three constructors shown in the following snippet at the same time:

```
//
//  OverloadConstructor - provide the class multiple
//                        ways to create objects by
//                        overloading the constructor
//
#include <cstdio>
#include <cstdlib>
#include <iostream>
#include <strings.h>

using namespace std;
const int MAXNAMESIZE = 40;
class Student
{
  public:
    Student()
    {
        cout << "constructing student no name" << endl;
        semesterHours = 0;
        gpa = 0.0;
        name[0] = '\0';
    }
    Student(char *pName)
    {
        cout << "constructing student " << pName << endl;
        strncpy(name, pName, MAXNAMESIZE);
        name[MAXNAMESIZE - 1] = '\0';
        semesterHours = 0;
        gpa = 0;
    }
    Student(char *pName, int xfrHours, float xfrGPA)
    {
        cout << "constructing student " << pName << endl;
        strncpy(name, pName, MAXNAMESIZE);
        name[MAXNAMESIZE - 1] = '\0';
        semesterHours = xfrHours;
        gpa = xfrGPA;
    }
    ~Student()
    {
        cout << "destructing student" << endl;
    }
```

```
  protected:
    char   name[40];
    int    semesterHours;
    float gpa;
};

int main(int argcs, char* pArgs[])
{
    // the following invokes three different constructors
    Student noName;
    Student freshman("Marian Haste");
    Student xferStudent("Pikumup Andropov", 80, 2.5);

    // wait until user is ready before terminating program
    // to allow the user to see the program results
    system("PAUSE");
    return 0;
}
```

Because the object `noName` appears with no arguments, it's constructed using the constructor `Student::Student()`. This constructor is called the *default*, or *void,* constructor. (I prefer the latter name, but the former is the more common one, so I use it in this book — I'm a slave to fashion.) The `freshMan` is constructed using the constructor that has only a `char*` argument, and the `xferStudent` uses the constructor with three arguments.

Notice how similar all three constructors are. The number of semester hours and the GPA default to zero if only the name is provided. Otherwise, there is no difference between the two constructors. You wouldn't need both constructors if you could just specify a default value for the two arguments.

C++ enables you to specify a default value for a function argument in the declaration to be used in the event that the argument is not present. By adding defaults to the last constructor, all three constructors can be combined into one. For example, the following class combines all three constructors into a single, clever constructor:

```
//
//  ConstructorWDefaults - multiple constructors can often
//                         be combined with the definition
//                         of default arguments
//
#include <cstdio>
#include <cstdlib>
#include <iostream>
#include <strings.h>
using namespace std;
```

```
const int MAXNAMESIZE = 40;
class Student

{
  public:
    Student(char *pName  = "no name",
            int xfrHours = 0,
            float xfrGPA = 0.0)
    {
        cout << "constructing student " << pName << endl;
        strncpy(name, pName, MAXNAMESIZE);
        name[MAXNAMESIZE - 1] = '\0';
        semesterHours = xfrHours;
        gpa = xfrGPA;
    }
    ~Student()
    {
        cout << "destructing student " << endl;
    }

  // ...other public members...
  protected:
    char  name[MAXNAMESIZE];
    int   semesterHours;
    float gpa;
};

int main(int argcs, char* pArgs[])
{
    // the following invokes three different constructors
    Student noName;
    Student freshman("Marian Haste");
    Student xferStudent("Pikumup Andropov", 80, 2.5);

    // wait until user is ready before terminating program
    // to allow the user to see the program results
    system("PAUSE");
    return 0;
}
```

Now all three objects are constructed using the same constructor; defaults are provided for nonexistent arguments in noName and freshMan.

In earlier versions of C++, you couldn't create a default constructor by providing defaults for all the arguments. The default constructor had to be a separate explicit constructor. Although this restriction was lifted in the standard (it seems to have had no good basis), some older compilers may still impose it.

Defaulting Default Constructors

As far as C++ is concerned, every class must have a constructor; otherwise, you can't create objects of that class. If you don't provide a constructor for your class, C++ should probably just generate an error, but it doesn't. To provide compatibility with existing C code, which knows nothing about constructors, C++ automatically provides a default constructor (sort of a default default constructor) that sets all the data members of the object to binary zero. Sometimes I call this a Miranda constructor — you know, "if you cannot afford a constructor, a constructor will be provided for you."

If you define a constructor for your class, any constructor, C++ doesn't provide the automatic default constructor. (Having tipped your hand that this isn't a C program, C++ doesn't feel obliged to do any extra work to ensure compatibility.)

The result is that if you define a constructor for your class but you also want a default constructor, you must define it yourself. Some code snippets help demonstrate this point. The following is legal:

```
class Student
{
    // ...all the same stuff as before but no constructors
};

int main(int argcs, char* pArgs[])
{
    Student noName;
    return 0;
}
```

The following code snippet does not compile properly:

```
class Student
{
  public:
    Student(char *pName);
};

int main(int argcs, char* pArgs[])
{
    Student noName;
    return 0;
}
```

The seemingly innocuous addition of the Student(char*) constructor precludes C++ from automatically providing a Student() constructor with which to build object noName.

Avoiding the "object declaration trap"

Look again at the way the `Student` objects were declared in the ConstructorWDefaults example:

```
Student noName;
Student freshMan("Smell E. Fish");
Student xfer("Upp R. Classman", 80, 2.5);
```

All `Student` objects except `noName` are declared with parentheses surrounding the arguments to the constructor. Why is `noName` declared without parentheses?

To be neat and consistent, you may think you could have declared `noName` as follows:

```
Student noName();
```

Unfortunately, C++ allows a declaration with only an open and close parentheses. However, it doesn't mean what you think it does at all. Instead of declaring an object `noName` of class `Student` to be constructed with the default constructor, it declares a function that returns an object of class `Student` by value. Surprise!

The following two declarations demonstrate how similar the new C++ format for declaring an object is to that of declaring a function. (I think this was a mistake, but what do I know?) The only difference is that the function declaration contains types in the parentheses, whereas the object declaration contains objects:

```
Student thisIsAFunc(int);
Student thisIsAnObject(10);
```

If the parentheses are empty, nothing can differentiate between an object and a function. To retain compatibility with C, C++ chose to make a declaration with empty parentheses a function. (A safer alternative would have been to force the keyword `void` in the function case, but that would not have been compatible with existing C programs.)

Constructing Class Members

In the preceding examples, all data members are of simple types, such as `int` and `float`. With simple types, it's sufficient to assign a value to the variable within the constructor. Problems arise when initializing certain types of data members, however.

Constructing a complex data member

Members of a class have the same problems as any other variable. It makes no sense for a `Student` object to have some default ID of zero. This is true even if the object is a member of a class. Consider the following example:

```
//
//   ConstructingMembers - a class may pass along arguments
//                          to the members' constructors
//
#include <cstdio>
#include <cstdlib>
```

```
#include <iostream>
#include <strings.h>
using namespace std;
const int MAXNAMESIZE = 40;

int nextStudentId = 0;
class StudentId
{
  public:
    StudentId()
    {
        value = ++nextStudentId;
        cout << "Assigning student id " << value << endl;
    }
  protected:
    int value;
};

class Student
{
  public:
    Student(char* pName)
    {
        strncpy(name, pName, MAXNAMESIZE);
        name[MAXNAMESIZE - 1]  = '\0';
        semesterHours = 0;
        gpa = 0.0;
    }

  // ...other public members...
  protected:
    char  name[MAXNAMESIZE];
    int   semesterHours;
    float gpa;
    StudentId id;
};

int main(int argcs, char* pArgs[])
{
    Student s("Chester");

    // wait until user is ready before terminating program
    // to allow the user to see the program results
    system("PAUSE");
    return 0;
}
```

A student ID is assigned to each student as the student object is constructed. In this example, IDs are handed out sequentially using the global variable nextStudentId to keep track.

This Student class contains a member id of class StudentId. The constructor for Student can't assign a value to this id member because Student does not have access to the protected members of StudentId. You could make Student a friend of StudentId, but that violates the "you take care of your business, I'll take care of mine" philosophy. Somehow, you need to invoke the constructor for StudentId when Student is constructed.

C++ does this for you automatically in this case, invoking the default constructor StudentId::StudentId() on id. This occurs after the Student constructor is called, but before control passes to the first statement in the constructor. (Single-step the preceding program in the debugger to see what I mean. As always, be sure that inline functions are forced outline.) Following is the output that results from executing this program:

```
assigning student id 1
constructing Student Chester
Press any key to continue . . .
```

Notice that the message from the StudentId constructor appears before the output from the Student constructor. (By the way, with all these constructors performing output, you may think that constructors must output something. Most constructors don't output a bloody thing.)

If the programmer does not provide a constructor, the default constructor provided by C++ automatically invokes the default constructors for data members. The same is true come harvesting time. The destructor for the class automatically invokes the destructor for data members that have destructors. The C++-provided destructor does the same.

Okay, this is all great for the default constructor. But what if you want to invoke a constructor other than the default? Where do you put the object? For example, assume that a student ID is provided to the Student constructor, which passes the ID to the constructor for class StudentId.

Let me first show you what doesn't work. Consider the following program segment (only the relevant parts are included here — the entire program, ConstructSeparateID, is on the CD-ROM that accompanies this book):

```
class Student
{
  public:
    Student(char *pName  = "no name", int ssId = 0)
    {
        cout << "constructing student " << pName << endl;
        strncpy(name, pName, MAXNAMESIZE);
        name[MAXNAMESIZE - 1] = '\0';
        // don't try this at home kids. It doesn't work
        StudentId id(ssId);    // construct a student id
    }
  protected:
    char  name[MAXNAMESIZE];
    StudentId id;
};
```

The constructor for StudentId has been changed to accept a value externally (the default value is necessary to get the example to compile, for reasons that will become clear shortly). Within the constructor for Student, the programmer (that's me) has (cleverly) attempted to construct a StudentId object named id.

If you look at the output from this program, you notice a problem:

```
assigning student id 0
constructing student Chester
assigning student id 1234
This message from main
Press any key to continue . . .
```

The first problem is that the constructor for StudentId appears to be invoked twice, once with zero and a second time with the expected 1234. Then you can see that the 1234 object is destructed before the output string in main(). Apparently the StudentId object is destructed within the Student constructor.

The explanation for this rather bizarre behavior is clear. The data member id already exists by the time the body of the constructor is entered. Instead of constructing the existing data member id, the declaration provided in the constructor creates a local object of the same name. This local object is destructed upon returning from the constructor.

Somehow, you need a different mechanism to indicate "construct the existing member; don't create a new one." This mechanism needs to appear before the open brace, before the data members are declared. C++ provides a construct for this, as shown in the following ConstructDataMembers program:

```
//
//   ConstructDataMember - construct a data member
//                         to a value other than the default
//
#include <cstdio>
#include <cstdlib>
#include <iostream>
#include <strings.h>

using namespace std;
const int MAXNAMESIZE = 40;
class StudentId
{
  public:
    StudentId(int id = 0)
    {
        value = id;
        cout << "assigning student id " << value << endl;
    }
```

```
     protected:
        int value;
};

class Student
{
   public:
      Student(char *pName  = "no name", int ssId = 0)
        : id(ssId)
      {
          cout << "constructing student " << pName << endl;
          strncpy(name, pName, MAXNAMESIZE);
          name[MAXNAMESIZE - 1]  = '\0';
      }
   protected:
      char  name[40];
      StudentId id;
};

int main(int argcs, char* pArgs[])
{
    Student s("Chester", 1234);
    cout << "This message from main" << endl;

    // wait until user is ready before terminating program
    // to allow the user to see the program results
    system("PAUSE");
    return 0;
}
```

Notice in particular the first line of the constructor. Here's something you
haven't seen before. The : means that what follows are calls to the constructors of data members of the current class. To the C++ compiler, this line
reads: "Construct the member id using the argument ssId of the Student
constructor. Whatever data members are not called out in this fashion are
constructed using the default constructor."

This new program generates the expected result:

```
assigning student id 1234
constructing student Chester
This message from main
Press any key to continue . . .
```

Constructing a constant data member

A problem also arises when initializing a member that has been declared const.
Remember that a const variable is initialized when it is declared and cannot

be changed thereafter. How can the constructor assign a `const` data member a value? The problem is solved with the same "colon syntax" used to initialize complex objects.

```
class Mammal
{
  public:
    Mammal(int nof) : numberOfFeet(nof) {}
  protected:
    const int numberOfFeet;
};
```

Ostensibly, a given `Mammal` has a fixed number of feet (barring amputation). The number of feet can, and should, be declared `const`. This declaration assigns a value to the variable `numberOfFeet` when the object is created. The `numberOfFeet` cannot be modified once it's been declared and initialized.

Programmers commonly use the "colon syntax" to initialize even non-`const` data members. Doing so isn't necessary, but it's common practice.

Constructing the Order of Construction

When there are multiple objects, all with constructors, programmers usually don't care about the order in which things are built. If one or more of the constructors has side effects, however, the order can make a difference.

The rules for the order of construction are as follows:

- ✔ Local and static objects are constructed in the order in which their declarations are invoked.
- ✔ Static objects are constructed only once.
- ✔ All global objects are constructed before `main()`.
- ✔ Global objects are constructed in no particular order.
- ✔ Members are constructed in the order in which they are declared in the class.
- ✔ Destructors are invoked in the reverse order from constructors.

A *static variable* is a variable that is local to a function but retains its value from one function invocation to the next. A *global variable* is a variable declared outside a function.

Now, consider each of the preceding rules in turn.

Local objects construct in order

Local objects are constructed in the order in which the program encounters their declaration. Normally, this is the same as the order in which the objects appear in the function, unless the function jumps around particular declarations. (By the way, jumping around declarations is a bad thing. It confuses the reader and the compiler.)

Static objects construct only once

Static objects are similar to local variables, except that they are constructed only once. C++ must wait until the first time control passes through the static's before constructing the object. Consider the following trivial ConstructStatic program:

```
//
//   ConstructStatic - demonstrate that statics are only
//                     constructed once
//
#include <cstdio>
#include <cstdlib>
#include <iostream>
using namespace std;

class DoNothing
{
  public:
    DoNothing(int initial)
    {
        cout << "DoNothing constructed with a value of "
             << initial
             << endl;
    }
};
void fn(int i)
{
    cout << "Function fn passed a value of " << i << endl;
    static DoNothing dn(i);
}

int main(int argcs, char* pArgs[])
{
    fn(10);
    fn(20);
    system("PAUSE");
    return 0;
}
```

Executing this program generates the following results:

```
Function fn passed a value of 10
DoNothing constructed with a value of 10
Function fn passed a value of 20
Press any key to continue . . .
```

Notice that the message from the function fn( ) appears twice, but the message from the constructor for DoNothing appears only the first time fn( ) is called. This indicates that the object is constructed the first time that fn( ) is called, but not thereafter.

All global objects construct before main ( )

All global variables go into scope as soon as the program starts. Thus, all global objects are constructed before control is passed to main( ).

Initializing global variables can cause real debugging headaches. Some debuggers try to execute up to main( ) as soon as the program is loaded and before they hand over control to the user. This can be a problem because the constructor code for all global objects has already been executed by the time you can wrest control of your program. If one of these constructors has a fatal bug, you never even get a chance to find the problem. In this case, the program appears to die before it even starts!

You can approach this problem in several ways. One is to test each constructor on local objects before using it on globals. If that doesn't solve the problem, you can try adding output statements to the beginning of all suspected constructors. The last output statement you see probably came from the flawed constructor.

Global objects construct in no particular order

Figuring out the order of construction of local objects is easy. An order is implied by the flow of control. With globals, no such flow is available to give order. All globals go into scope simultaneously — remember? Okay, you argue, why can't the compiler just start at the top of the file and work its way down the list of global objects?

That would work fine for a single file (and I presume that's what most compilers do). Unfortunately, most programs in the real world consist of several files that are compiled separately and then linked. Because the compiler has no control over the order in which these files are linked, it cannot affect the order in which global objects are constructed from file to file.

Most of the time, the order of global construction is pretty ho-hum stuff. Once in a while, though, global variables generate bugs that are extremely difficult to track down. (It happens just often enough to make it worth mentioning in a book.)

Consider the following example:

```
class Student
{
  public:
    Student (int id) : studentId(id) {}
    const int studentId;
};
class Tutor
{
  public:
    Tutor(Student& s) : tutoredId(s.studentId) {}
    int tutoredId;
};

// set up a student
Student randy(1234);

// assign that student a tutor
Tutor    jenny(randy);
```

Here the constructor for `Student` assigns a student ID. The constructor for `Tutor` records the ID of the student to help. The program declares a student `randy` and then assigns that student a tutor `jenny`.

The problem is that the program makes the implicit assumption that `randy` is constructed before `jenny`. Suppose that it were the other way around. Then `jenny` would be constructed with a block of memory that had not yet been turned into a `Student` object and, therefore, had garbage for a student ID.

The preceding example is not too difficult to figure out and more than a little contrived. Nevertheless, problems deriving from global objects being constructed in no particular order can appear in subtle ways. To avoid this problem, don't allow the constructor for one global object to refer to the contents of another global object.

Members construct in the order in which they are declared

Members of a class are constructed according to the order in which they're declared within the class. This isn't quite as obvious as it may sound. Consider the following example:

```
class Student
{
  public:
    Student (int id, int age) : sAge(age), sId(id){}
    const int sId;
    const int sAge;
};
```

In this example, sId is constructed before sAge, even though sId appears second in the constructor's initialization list. The only time you might detect a difference in the construction order is when both data members are an instance of a class that has a constructor that has some mutual side effect.

Destructors destruct in the reverse order of the constructors

Finally, no matter in what order the constructors kick off, you can be assured that the destructors are invoked in the reverse order. (It's nice to know that at least one rule in C++ has no ifs, ands, or buts.)

Chapter 18

Copying the Copy Copy Copy Constructor

*T*he constructor is a special function that C++ invokes automatically when an object is created to allow the object to initialize itself. Chapter 16 introduces the concept of the constructor, whereas Chapter 17 describes other types of constructors. This chapter examines a particular variation of the constructor known as the *copy constructor*.

Copying an Object

A copy constructor is the constructor that C++ uses to make copies of objects. It carries the name $X::X(X\&)$, where X is the name of the class. That is, it's the constructor of class X, which takes as its argument a reference to an object of class X. Now, I know that this sounds really useless, but just give me a chance to explain why C++ needs such a beastie.

Why you need the copy constructor

Think for a moment about what happens when you call a function like the following:

```
void fn(Student fs)
{
    // ...same scenario; different argument...
```

```
}
int main(int argcs, char* pArgs[])
{
    Student ms;
    fn(ms);
    return 0;
}
```

In the call to fn( ), C++ passes a copy of the object ms and not the object itself.

C++ passes arguments to functions by value.

Now consider what it means to create a copy of an object. First, it takes a constructor to create an object, even a copy of an existing object. C++ could copy the object into the new object one at a time. That's what older languages like C would have done. But what if you don't want a simple copy of the object? What if something else is required? (Ignore the "why?" for a little while.) You need to be able to specify how the copy should be constructed.

Thus, the copy constructor is necessary in the preceding example to create a copy of the object ms on the stack during the call of function fn( ). This particular copy constructor would be Student::Student(Student&) — say that three times quickly.

Using the copy constructor

The best way to understand how the copy constructor works is to see one in action. Consider the following CopyConstructor program:

```
//
//  CopyConstructor - demonstrate an example copy constructor
//
#include <cstdio>
#include <cstdlib>
#include <iostream>
using namespace std;

const int MAXNAMESIZE = 40;
class Student
{
  public:
    // conventional constructor
    Student(char *pName = "no name", int ssId = 0)
    {
        strcpy(name, pName);
        id = ssId;
        cout << "constructed "  << name << endl;
    }
```

```
    // copy constructor
    Student(Student& s)
    {
        strcpy(name, "Copy of ");
        strcat(name, s.name);
        id = s.id;
        cout << "constructed " << name << endl;
    }

    ~Student()
    {
        cout << "destructing " << name << endl;
    }

  protected:
    char name[MAXNAMESIZE];
    int  id;
};

// fn - receives its argument by value
void fn(Student copy)
{
    cout << "In function fn()" << endl;
}

int main(int nNumberofArgs, char* pszArgs[])
{
    Student chester("Chester", 1234);
    cout << "Calling fn()" << endl;
    fn(chester);
    cout << "Returned from fn()" << endl;

    // wait until user is ready before terminating program
    // to allow the user to see the program results
    system("PAUSE");
    return 0;
}
```

The output from executing this program follows:

```
constructed Chester
Calling fn()
constructed Copy of Chester
In function fn()
destructing Copy of Chester
Returned from fn()
Press any key to continue . . .
```

The normal constructor generates the first message from the declaration on the first line of main(). main() then ouputs the calling... message before calling fn(). As part of the function call process, C++ invokes the copy constructor to make a copy of chester to pass to fn(). The function fn() outputs the In function... message. The copied Student object copy is destructed at the return from fn(). The original object, randy, is destructed at the end of main().

The copy constructor here is flagged with comments to allow you to see the process. This copy constructor first copies the string Copy of into its name field. It then copies the name string from the source object s into the current object. The constructor outputs the resulting name field before returning.

The first line of output shows the chester object being created. The third line demonstrates the copy Student being generated from the copy constructor. Once within the function, it does nothing more than output a message. The copy is destructed as part of the return, which generates the destructing... message.

The Automatic Copy Constructor

Like the default constructor, the copy constructor is important, important enough that C++ thinks no class should be without one. If you don't provide your own copy constructor, C++ generates one for you. (This differs from the default constructor that C++ provides unless your class has constructors defined for it.)

The copy constructor provided by C++ performs a member-by-member copy of each data member. The copy constructor that early versions of C++ provided performed a bit-wise copy. The difference is that a member-by-member copy invokes all copy constructors that might exist for the members of the class, whereas a bit-wise copy does not. You can see the effects of this difference in the following DefaultCopyConstructor sample program. (I left out the definition of the Student class to save space — it's identical to that shown in the CopyConstructor program. The entire DefaultCopyConstructor program is included on this book's CD-ROM.)

```
//
//  DefaultCopyConstructor - demonstrate that the default
//                           copy constructor invokes the
//                           copy constructor for any member
//
#include <cstdio>
#include <cstdlib>
#include <iostream>
using namespace std;

class Tutor
{
  public:
    Tutor(Student& s) : student(s) // invoke copy
    {                  // constructor on member student
```

```
            cout << "constructing Tutor object" << endl;
            id = 0;
      }
  protected:
      Student student;
      int id;
};

void fn(Tutor tutor)
{
      cout << "In function fn()" << endl;
}

int main(int argcs, char* pArgs[])
{
      Student chester("Chester");
      Tutor tutor(chester);
      cout << "Calling fn()" << endl;
      fn(tutor);
      cout << "Returned from fn()" << endl;

      // wait until user is ready before terminating program
      // to allow the user to see the program results
      system("PAUSE");
      return 0;
}
```

Executing this program generates the following output:

```
constructed Chester
constructed Copy of Chester
constructing Tutor object
Calling fn()
constructed Copy of Copy of Chester
In function fn()
destructing Copy of Copy of Chester
Returned from fn()
Press any key to continue . . .
```

Constructing the chester object generates the first output message from the "plain Jane" constructor. The constructor for the tutor object invokes the Student copy constructor in order to generate its own student data member. This accounts for the next two lines of output.

The program then passes a copy of the Tutor object to the function fn() (pronounced "fun," by the way). Because the Tutor class does not define a copy constructor, the program invokes the default copy constructor to make a copy to pass to fn().

The default Tutor copy constructor invokes the copy constructor for each data member. The copy constructor for the int "class" does nothing more than copy the value. However, you've already seen how the Student copy constructor works. This is what generates the `constructed Copy of Copy of Chester` message. The destructor for the copy is invoked as part of the return from function `fn()`.

Creating Shallow Copies versus Deep Copies

Performing a member-by-member copy seems the obvious thing to do in a copy constructor. Other than adding the capability to tack on silly things such as "`Copy of `" to the front of students' names, when would you ever want to do anything but a member-by-member copy?

Consider what happens if the constructor allocates an asset, such as memory off the heap. If the copy constructor simply makes a copy of that asset without allocating its own, you end up with a troublesome situation: two objects thinking they have exclusive access to the same asset. This becomes nastier when the destructor is invoked for both objects and they both try to put the same asset back. To make this more concrete, consider the following example class:

```
//
//   ShallowCopy - performing a byte-by-byte (shallow) copy
//                 is not correct when the class holds assets
//
#include <cstdio>
#include <cstdlib>
#include <iostream>
#include <strings.h>
using namespace std;

class Person
{
  public:
    Person(char *pN)
    {
        cout << "constructing " << pN << endl;
        pName = new char[strlen(pN) + 1];
        if (pName != 0)
        {
            strcpy(pName, pN);
        }
    }
    ~Person()
    {
        cout << "destructing " << pName << endl;
        strcpy(pName, "already destructed memory");
        // delete pName;
    }
```

```
 protected:
    char *pName;
};

void fn()
{
    // create a new object
    Person p1("This_is_a_very_long_name");

    // copy the contents of p1 into p2
    Person p2(p1);
}

int main(int argcs, char* pArgs[])
{
    cout << "Calling fn()" << endl;
    fn();
    cout << "Returned from fn()" << endl;

    // wait until user is ready before terminating program
    // to allow the user to see the program results
    system("PAUSE");
    return 0;
}
```

This program generates the following output:

```
Calling fn()
constructing This_is_a_very_long_name
destructing This_is_a_very_long_name
destructing already destructed memory
Returned from fn()
Press any key to continue . . .
```

The constructor for `Person` allocates memory off the heap to store the person's name, rather than put up with some arbitrary limit imposed by a fixed-length array. However, the destructor copies a message into this memory buffer rather than put it back on the heap. The main program calls the function `fn()`, which creates one person, p1, and then makes a copy of that person, p2. Both objects are destructed automatically when the program returns from the function.

Only one constructor output message appears when this program is executed. That's not too surprising because the C++ provided copy constructor used to build p2 performs no output. As p1 and p2 go out of scope, you don't receive the two output messages that you might have expected. The first destructor outputs the expected `This_is_a_very_long_name`. However, the second destructor indicates that the memory has already been deleted.

If you really were to delete the name, the program would become unstable after the second delete and might not even complete properly without crashing.

The constructor is called once and allocates a block of memory off the heap to hold the person's name. The copy constructor provided by C++ copies that address into the new object without allocating a new block.

The problem is shown in Figure 18-1. The object p1 is copied into the new object p2, but the assets are not. Thus, p1 and p2 end up pointing to the same assets (in this case, heap memory). This is known as a shallow copy because it just "skims the surface," copying the members themselves.

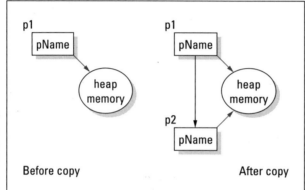

Figure 18-1:
Shallow
copy of
p1 to p2.

The solution to this problem is demonstrated visually in Figure 18-2. This figure represents a copy constructor that allocates its own assets to the new object. The following shows an appropriate copy constructor for class Person, the type you've seen up until now. (This class is embodied in the program DeepCopy, which is on this book's CD-ROM.)

```
class Person
{
  public:
    Person(char *pN)
    {
        cout << "constructing " << pN << endl;
        pName = new char[strlen(pN) + 1];
        if (pName != 0)
        {
            strcpy(pName, pN);
        }
    }
// copy constructor allocates a new heap block
    // from the heap
    Person(Person& p)
    {
        cout << "copying " << p.pName
             << " into its own block" << endl;
        pName = new char[strlen(p.pName) + 1];
```

```
            if (pName != 0)
            {
                strcpy(pName, p.pName);
            }
    }

    ~Person()
    {
        cout << "destructing " << pName << endl;
        strcpy(pName, "already destructed memory");
        // delete pName;
    }
  protected:
    char *pName;
};
```

Here you see that the copy constructor allocates its own memory block for the name and then copies the contents of the source object name into this new name block. This is a situation similar to that shown in Figure 18-2. *Deep copy* is so named because it reaches down and copies all the assets. (Okay, the analogy is pretty strained, but that's what they call it.)

The output from this program is as follows:

```
Calling fn()
constructing This_is_a_very_long_name
copying This_is_a_very_long_name into its own block
destructing This_is_a_very_long_name
destructing This_is_a_very_long_name
Returned from fn()
Press any key to continue . . .
```

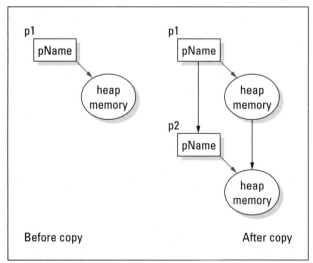

Figure 18-2:
Deep copy
of p1 to p2.

The destructor for Person now indicates that the string pointers in p1 and p2 don't point to common block of data. (Note, again, that the destructor outputs the most helpful "destructing..." message for debug purposes instead of actually doing anything.

It's a Long Way to Temporaries

C++ generates a copy of an object to pass to a function by value. (This is described in the earlier sections of this chapter.) This is the most obvious but not the only example. C++ creates a copy of an object under other conditions as well.

Consider a function that returns an object by value. In this case, C++ must create a copy using the copy constructor. This situation is demonstrated in the following code snippet:

```
Student fn();        // returns object by value
int main(int argcs, char* pArgs[])
{
    Student s;
    s = fn();            // call to fn() creates temporary

    // how long does the temporary returned by fn()last?
    return 0;
}
```

The function fn() returns an object by value. Eventually, the returned object is copied to s, but where does it reside until then?

C++ creates a temporary object into which it stuffs the returned object. "Okay," you say. "C++ creates the temporary, but how does it know when to destruct it?" Good question. In this example, it doesn't make much difference, because you'll be through with the temporary when the copy constructor copies it into s. But what if s is defined as a reference:

```
int main(int argcs, char* pArgs[])
{
    Student& refS = fn();
    // ...now what?...
    return 0;
}
```

It makes a big difference how long temporaries live because refS exists for the entire function. Temporaries created by the compiler are valid throughout the extended expression in which they were created and no further.

In the following function, I mark the point at which the temporary is no longer valid:

```
Student fn1();
int fn2(Student&);
int main(int argcs, char* pArgs[])
{
    int x;
    // create a Student object by calling fn1().
    // Pass that object to the function fn2().
    // fn2() returns an integer that is used in some
    // silly calculation.
    // All this time the temporary returned from fn1()
    // remains valid.
    x = 3 * fn2(fn1()) + 10;

    // the temporary returned from fn1() is now no longer
           valid
    // ...other stuff...
    return 0;
}
```

This makes the reference example invalid because the object may go away before refS does, leaving refS referring to a non-object.

Avoiding temporaries, permanently

It may have occurred to you that all this copying of objects hither and yon can be a bit time-consuming. What if you don't want to make copies of everything? The most straightforward solution is to pass objects to functions and return objects from functions by reference. Doing so avoids the majority of temporaries.

But what if you're still not convinced that C++ isn't out there craftily constructing temporaries that you know nothing about? Or what if your class allocates unique assets that you don't want copied? What do you do then?

You can add an output statement to your copy constructor. The presence of this message when you execute the program warns you that a copy has just been made.

A more crafty approach is to declare the copy constructor protected, as follows:

```
class Student
{
  protected:
    Student(Student&s){}

  public:
    // ...everything else normal...
};
```

This precludes any external functions, including C++, from constructing a copy of your Student objects. (This does not affect the capability of member functions to create copies.) If no one can invoke the copy constructor, no copies are being generated. Voilà.

Referring to the copy constructor's referential argument

The fact that the copy constructor is used to create temporaries and copies on the stack answers one pesky detail that may have occurred to you. Consider the following program:

```
class Student
{
  public:
    Student(Student s)
    {
        // ...whatever...
    }
};

void fn(Student fs) {}

void fn()
{
    Student ms;
    fn(ms);
}
```

Notice how the argument to the copy constructor is no longer referential. In fact, such a declaration isn't even legal. The Dev-C++ compiler generates a horrible list of meaningless error messages in this case. Another public domain C++ compiler generates the following, much more meaningful error message:

```
Error: invalid constructor; you probably meant 'Student
          (const Student&)'
```

Why must the argument to the copy constructor be referential? Consider the program carefully: When main() calls the function fn(), the C++ compiler uses the copy constructor to create a copy of the Student object on the stack. However, the copy constructor itself requires an object of class Student. No problem, the compiler can invoke the copy constructor to create a Student object for the copy constructor. But, of course, that requires another call to the copy constructor, and so it goes until eventually the compiler collapses in a confused heap of exhaustion.

Chapter 19

Static Members: Can Fabric Softener Help?

*B*y default, data members are allocated on a "per object" basis. For example, each person has his or her own name.

You can also declare a member to be shared by all objects of a class by declaring that member static. The term *static* applies to both data members and member functions, although the meaning is slightly different. This chapter describes these differences, beginning with static data members.

Defining a Static Member

The programmer can make a data member common to all objects of the class by adding the keyword *static* to the declaration. Such members are called *static data members* (I would be a little upset if they were called something else).

Why you need static members

Most properties are properties of the object. Using the well-worn (one might say, threadbare) student example, properties such as name, ID number, and courses are specific to the individual student. However, all students share some properties — for example, the number of students currently enrolled, the highest grade of all students, or a pointer to the first student in a linked list.

It's easy enough to store this type of information in a common, ordinary, garden-variety global variable. For example, you could use a lowly `int` variable to keep track of the number of `Student` objects. The problem with this solution is that global variables are outside the class. It's like putting the voltage regulator for my microwave outside the enclosure. Sure, it could be done, and it would probably work — the only problem is that I wouldn't be too happy if my dog got into the wires, and I had to peel him off the ceiling (the dog wouldn't be thrilled about it, either).

If a class is going to be held responsible for its own state, objects such as global variables must be brought inside the class, just as the voltage regulator must be inside the microwave lid, away from prying paws. This is the idea behind static members.

You may hear static members referred to as *class members;* this is because all objects in the class share them. By comparison, normal members are referred to as *instance members,* or *object members,* because each object receives its own copy of these members.

Using static members

A static data member is one that has been declared with the `static` storage class, as shown here:

```
class Student
{
  public:
    Student(char *pName = "no name") : name(pName)
    {
        noOfStudents++;
    }

    ~Student()
    {
        noOfStudents--;
    }

    static int noOfStudents;
    string name;
};

Student s1;
Student s2;
```

The data member `noOfStudents` is part of the class `Student` but is not part of either `s1` or `s2`. That is, for every object of class `Student`, there is a separate `name`, but there is only one `noOfStudents`, which all `Student`s must share.

"Well then," you ask, "if the space for noOfStudents is not allocated in any of the objects of class Student, where is it allocated?" The answer is, "It isn't." You have to specifically allocate space for it, as follows:

```
int Student::noOfStudents = 0;
```

This somewhat peculiar-looking syntax allocates space for the static data member and initializes it to zero. Static data members must be global — a static variable cannot be local to a function.

The name of the class is required for any member when it appears outside its class boundaries.

This business of allocating space manually is somewhat confusing until you consider that class definitions are designed to go into files that are included by multiple source code modules. C++ has to know in which of those .cpp source files to allocate space for the static variable. This is not a problem with non-static variables because space is allocated in each and every object created.

Referencing static data members

The access rules for static members are the same as the access rules for normal members. From within the class, static members are referenced like any other class member. Public static members can be referenced from outside the class, whereas well-protected static members can't. Both types of reference are shown in the following code snippet:

```
class Student
{
  public:
    Student()
    {
        noOfStudents++;  // reference from inside the class
        // ...other stuff...
    }

    static int noOfStudents;
    // ...other stuff like before...
};

void fn(Student& s1, Student& s2)
{
    // reference public static
    cout << "No of students "
         << s1.noOfStudents // reference from outside
         << endl;           // of the class
}
```

In fn(), noOfStudents is referenced using the object s1. But s1 and s2 share the same member noOfStudents. How did I know to choose s1? Why didn't I use s2 instead? It doesn't make any difference. You can reference a static member using any object of that class, as illustrated here:

```
// ...class defined the same as before...
void fn(Student& s1, Student& s2)
{
    // the following produce identical results
    cout << " Number of students "
         << s1.noOfStudents
         << endl;
    cout << " Number of students "
         << s2.noOfStudents
         << endl;
}
```

In fact, you don't need an object at all. You can use the class name directly instead, if you prefer, as in the following:

```
// ...class defined the same as before...
void fn(Student& s1, Student& s2)
{
  // the following produce identical results
  cout << "Number of students "
       << Student::noOfStudents
       << endl;
}
```

If you do use an object name when accessing a static member, C++ uses only the declared class of the object.

This is a minor technicality, but in the interest of full disclosure: the object used to reference a static member is not evaluated even if it's an expression. For example, consider the following case:

```
class Student
{
  public:
    static int noOfStudents;
    Student& nextStudent();
    // ...other stuff the same...
};

void fn(Student& s)
{
    cout << s.nextStudent().noOfStudents << "\n"
}
```

The member function nextStudent() is not actually called. All C++ needs to access noOfStudents is the return type, and it can get that without bothering to evaluate the expression. This is true even if nextStudent() should do other things, such as wash windows or shine your shoes. None of those things will be done. Although the example is obscure, it does happen. That's what you get for trying to cram too much stuff into one expression.

Uses for static data members

Static data members have umpteen uses, but let me touch on a few here. First, you can use static members to keep count of the number of objects floating about. In the Student class, for example, the count is initialized to zero, the constructor increments it, and the destructor decrements it. At any given instant, the static member contains the count of the number of existing Student objects. Remember, however, that this count reflects the number of Student objects (including any temporaries) and not necessarily the number of students.

A closely related use for a static member is as a flag to indicate whether a particular action has occurred. For example, a class Radio may need to initialize hardware before sending the first tune command but not before subsequent tunes. A flag indicating that this is the first tune is just the ticket. This includes flagging when an error has occurred.

Another common use is to provide space for the pointer to the first member of a list — the so-called head pointer (see Chapter 14 if this doesn't sound familiar). Static members can allocate bits of common data that all objects in all functions share (overuse of this common memory is a really bad idea because doing so makes tracking errors difficult).

Declaring Static Member Functions

Member functions can be declared static as well. Static member functions are useful when you want to associate an action to a class but you don't need to associate that action with a particular object. For example, the member function Duck::fly() is associated with a particular duck, whereas the rather more drastic member function Duck::goExtinct() is not.

Like static data members, static member functions are associated with a class and not with a particular object of that class. This means that, like a reference to a static data member, a reference to a static member function does not require an object. If an object is present, only its type is used.

Thus, both calls to the static member function number() in the following example are legal. This brings us to our first static program — I mean our first program using static members — CallStaticMember:

```
//
// CallStaticMember - demonstrate two ways to call a static
//                    member function
//
#include <cstdio>
#include <cstdlib>
#include <iostream>
using namespace std;

class Student
{
  public:
    Student(char* pN = "no name")
    {
        pName = new char[strlen(pN) + 1];
        if (pName)
        {
            strcpy(pName, pN);
        }
        noOfStudents++;
    }
    ~Student() { noOfStudents--; }
    static int number() { return noOfStudents; }

  // ...other stuff the same...
  protected:
    char* pName;
    static int noOfStudents;
};
int Student::noOfStudents = 0;

int main(int argcs, char* pArgs[])
{
    Student s1("Chester");
    Student s2("Scooter");
    cout << "Number of students is "
         << s1.number() << endl;
    cout << "Number of students is "
         << Student::number() << endl;

    // wait until user is ready before terminating program
    // to allow the user to see the program results
    system("PAUSE");
    return 0;
}
```

Notice how the static member function can access the static data member. On the other hand, a static member function is not directly associated with an object, so it doesn't have default access to non-static members. Thus, the following would not be legal:

```
class Student
{
  public:
    // the following is not legal
    static char* sName()
    {
        return pName;    // which pName? there's no object
    }

    // ...other stuff the same...
  protected:
    char* pName;
    static int noOfStudents;
};
```

That's not to say that static member functions have no access to non-static data members. Consider the following useful function `findName()` that finds a specific object in a linked list (see Chapter 14 for an explanation of how linked lists work). The majority of the code necessary to make the linked list work is left as an exercise for the reader. Don't you just hate that phrase? But, seriously, the linked list code is already in Chapter 14:

```
class Student
{
  public:
    Student(char *pName)
    {
        // ...construct the object and add it to a
        //    list of Student objects...
    }

    // findName - return student w/specified name
    static Student *findName(char *pName)
    {
        // ...starting from the first object in the list
        //    which is pointed at by pHead link through
        //    the list using pNext until the correct
        //    object is found...
    }

  protected:
    static Student *pHead;
    Student *pNext;
    char* pName;
};
Student* Student::pHead = 0;
```

The function `findName()` has access to pHead because all objects share it. Being a member of class `Student`, `findName()` also has access to pNext.

This access allows the function to navigate through the list until the matching object is found. The following shows how such static member functions might be used:

```
int main(int argcs, char* pArgs[])
{
  Student s1("Randy");
  Student s2("Jenny");
  Student s3("Kinsey");
  Student *pS = Student::findName("Jenny");
  return 0;
}
```

What Is This About, Anyway?

It's time to discuss the `this` keyword, just for grins. `this` is a pointer to the current object within a member function. It's used when no other object name is specified. In a normal member function, `this` is the implied first argument to the function, as illustrated here:

```
class SC
{
  public:
    void nFn(int a); // like SC::nFn(SC *this, int a)
    static void sFn(int a); // like SC::sFn(int a)
};

void fn(SC& s)
{
    s.nFn(10); // -converts to-> SC::nFn(&s, 10);
    s.sFn(10); // -converts to-> SC::sFn(10);
}
```

That is, the function `nFn()` is interpreted almost as though it were declared `void SC::nFn(SC *this, int a)`. The call to `nFn()` is converted by the compiler as shown, with the address of s passed as the first argument. (You can't actually write the call this way; this is only what the compiler is doing.)

References to other non-static members within `SC::nFn()` automatically use the `this` argument as the pointer to the current object. When `SC::sFn()` was called, no object address was passed. Thus, it has no `this` pointer to use when referencing non-static functions, which is why I say that a static member function is not associated with any current object.

Part IV
Inheritance

The 5th Wave   By Rich Tennant

In this part . . .

In the discussions of object-oriented philosophy in Part III, two main features of real-world solutions are seemingly not shared by functional programming solutions.

The first is the capability of treating objects separately. I present the example of using a microwave oven to whip up a snack. The microwave oven provides an interface (the front panel) that I use to control the oven, without worrying about its internal workings. This is true even if I know all about how the darn thing works (which I don't).

A second aspect of real-world solutions is the capability of categorizing like objects — recognizing and exploiting their similarities. If my recipe calls for an oven of any type, I should be okay because a microwave is an oven.

I already presented the mechanism that C++ uses to implement the first feature, the class. To support the second aspect of object-oriented programming, C++ uses a concept known as *inheritance,* which extends classes.

Inheritance is the central topic of this part and the central message of the BUDGET3 program on the enclosed CD-ROM.

Chapter 20

Inheriting a Class

*T*his chapter discusses *inheritance,* the ability of one class to inherit capabilities or properties from another class.

Inheritance is a common concept. I am a human (except when I first wake up in the morning). I inherit certain properties from the class Human, such as my ability to converse (more or less) intelligently and my dependence on air, water, and carbohydrate-based nourishment (a little too dependent on the latter, I'm afraid). These properties are not unique to humans. The class Human inherits the dependencies on air, water, and nourishment from the class Mammal, which inherited it from the class Animal.

The capability of passing down properties is a powerful one. It enables you to describe things in an economical way. For example, if my son asks, "What's a duck?" I can say, "It's a bird that goes quack." Despite what you may think, that answer conveys a considerable amount of information. He knows what a bird is, and now he knows all those same things about a duck plus the duck's additional property of "quackness." (Refer to Chapter 12 for a further discussion of this and other profound observations.)

Object-oriented (OO) languages express this inheritance relationship by allowing one class to inherit from another. Thus, OO languages can generate a model that's closer to the real world (remember that real-world stuff!) than the model generated by languages that don't support inheritance.

C++ allows one class to inherit another class as follows:

```
class Student
{
};
```

```
class GraduateStudent : public Student
{
};
```

Here, a `GraduateStudent` inherits all the members of `Student`. Thus, a `GraduateStudent` IS_A `Student`. (The capitalization of IS_A stresses the importance of this relationship.) Of course, `GraduateStudent` may also contain other members that are unique to a `GraduateStudent`.

Do I Need My Inheritance?

Inheritance was introduced into C++ for several reasons. Of course, the major reason is the capability of expressing the inheritance relationship. (I'll return to that in a moment.) A minor reason is to reduce the amount of typing. Suppose that you have a class `Student`, and you're asked to add a new class called `GraduateStudent`. Inheritance can drastically reduce the number of things you have to put in the class. All you really need in the class `GraduateStudent` are things that describe the differences between students and graduate students.

This IS_A-mazing

To make sense of our surroundings, humans build extensive taxonomies. Fido is a special case of dog, which is a special case of canine, which is a special case of mammal, and so it goes. This shapes our understanding of the world.

To use another example, a student is a (special type of) person. Having said this, I already know a lot of things about students (American students, anyway). I know they have social security numbers, they watch too much TV, and they daydream about the opposite sex (the male ones, anyway). I know all these things because these are properties of all people.

In C++, we say that the class `Student` inherits from the class `Person`. Also, we say that `Person` is a *base class* of `Student`, and `Student` is a *subclass* of `Person`. Finally, we say that a `Student` IS_A `Person` (using all caps is a common way of expressing this

unique relationship — I didn't make it up). C++ shares this terminology with other object-oriented languages.

Notice that although `Student` IS_A `Person`, the reverse is not true. A `Person` IS not a `Student`. (A statement like this always refers to the general case. It could be that a particular `Person` is, in fact, a `Student`.) A lot of people who are members of class `Person` are not members of class `Student`. In addition, class `Student` has properties it does not share with class `Person`. For example, `Student` has a grade point average, but `Person` does not.

The inheritance property is transitive. For example, if I define a new class `GraduateStudent` as a subclass of `Student`, `GraduateStudent` must also be `Person`. It has to be that way: If a `GraduateStudent` IS_A `Student` and a `Student` IS_A `Person`, a `GraduateStudent` IS_A `Person`.

Another minor side effect has to do with software modification. Suppose you inherit from some existing class. Later, you find that the base class doesn't do exactly what the subclass needs. Or, perhaps, the class has a bug. Modifying the base class might break any code that uses that base class. Creating and using a new subclass that overloads the incorrect feature solves your problem without causing someone else further problems.

How Does a Class Inherit?

Here's the `GraduateStudent` example filled out into a program InheritanceExample:

```
//
//   InheritanceExample - demonstrate an inheritance
//                 relationship in which the subclass
//                 constructor passes argument information
//                 to the constructor in the base class
//
#include <cstdio>
#include <cstdlib>
#include <iostream>
#include <strings.h>
using namespace std;

// Advisor - empty class
class Advisor {};

const int MAXNAMESIZE = 40;
class Student
{
  public:
    Student(char *pName = "no name")
       : average(0.0), semesterHours(0)
    {
        strncpy(name, pName, MAXNAMESIZE);
        name[MAXNAMESIZE - 1] = '\0';
        cout << "constructing student "
             << name
             << endl;
    }

    void addCourse(int hours, float grade)
    {
        cout << "adding grade to " << name << endl;
        average = (semesterHours * average + grade);
        semesterHours += hours;
        average = average / semesterHours;
    }
```

```
      int hours( ) { return semesterHours;}
      float gpa( ) { return average;}

  protected:
    char name[MAXNAMESIZE];
    int  semesterHours;
    float average;
};

class GraduateStudent : public Student
{
  public:
    GraduateStudent(char *pName, Advisor& adv, float qG =
           0.0)
        : Student(pName), advisor(adv), qualifierGrade(qG)
    {
        cout << "constructing graduate student "
             << pName
             << endl;
    }

    float qualifier( ) { return qualifierGrade; }

  protected:
    Advisor advisor;
    float qualifierGrade;
};

int main(int nNumberofArgs, char* pszArgs[])
{
    Advisor advisor;

    // create two Student types
    Student llu("Cy N Sense");
    GraduateStudent gs("Matt Madox", advisor, 1.5);

    // now add a grade to their grade point average
    llu.addCourse(3, 2.5);
    gs.addCourse(3, 3.0);

    // display the graduate student's qualifier grade
    cout << "Matt's qualifier grade = "
         << gs.qualifier()
         << endl;

    // wait until user is ready before terminating program
    // to allow the user to see the program results
    system("PAUSE");
    return 0;
}
```

This program demonstrates the creation and use of two objects, one of class Student and a second of GraduateStudent. The output of this program is as follows:

```
constructing student Cy N Sense
constructing student Matt Madox
constructing graduate student Matt Madox
adding grade to Cy N Sense
adding grade to Matt Madox
Matt's qualifier grade = 1.5
Press any key to continue . . .
```

Using a subclass

The class Student has been defined in the conventional fashion. The class GraduateStudent is a bit different, however; the colon followed by the phrase public Student at the beginning of the class definition declares GraduateStudent to be a subclass of Student.

The appearance of the keyword public implies that there is probably protected inheritance as well. All right, it's true, but *protected* inheritance is beyond the scope of this book.

Programmers love inventing new terms or giving new meaning to existing terms. Heck, programmers even invent new terms and then give them a second meaning. Here is a set of equivalent expressions that describes the same relationship:

- ✔ GraduateStudent is a subclass of Student.
- ✔ Student is the base class or is the parent class of GraduateStudent.
- ✔ GraduateStudent inherits from Student.
- ✔ GraduateStudent extends Student.

As a subclass of Student, GraduateStudent inherits all of its members. For example, a GraduateStudent has a name even though that member is declared up in the base class. However, a subclass can add its own members, for example qualifierGrade. After all, gs quite literally IS_A Student plus a little bit more than a Student.

The main() function declares two objects, llu of type Student and gs of type GraduateStudent. It then proceeds to access the addCourse() member function for both types of students. main() then accesses the qualifier() function that is only a member of the subclass.

Constructing a subclass

Even though a subclass has access to the protected members of the base class and could initialize them, each subclass is responsible for initializing itself.

Before control passes beyond the open brace of the constructor for GraduateStudent, control passes to the proper constructor of Student. If Student were based on another class, such as Person, the constructor for that class would be invoked before the Student constructor got control. Like a skyscraper, the object is constructed starting at the "base"-ment class and working its way up the class structure one story at a time.

Just as with member objects, you often need to be able to pass arguments to the base class constructor. The example program declares the subclass constructor as follows:

```
GraduateStudent(char *pName, Advisor& adv, float qG = 0.0)
        : Student(pName), advisor(adv), qualifierGrade(qG)
{
    // whatever construction code goes here
}
```

Here the constructor for GraduateStudent invokes the Student constructor, passing it the argument pName. C++ then initializes the members advisor and qualifierGrade before executing the statements within the constructor's open and close braces.

The default constructor for the base class is executed if the subclass makes no explicit reference to a different constructor. Thus, in the following code snippet the Pig base class is constructed before any members of LittlePig, even though LittlePig makes no explicit reference to that constructor:

```
class Pig
{
  public:
    Pig() : pHouse(null)
    {}
  protected:
    House* pHouse;
};
class LittlePig : public Pig
{
  public:
    LittlePig(float volStraw, int numSticks, int numBricks)
      : straw(volStraw), sticks(numSticks), bricks(numBricks)
    { }

  protected:
    float straw;
    int sticks;
    int bricks;
};
```

Similarly, the copy constructor for a base class is invoked automatically.

Destructing a subclass

Following the rule that destructors are invoked in the reverse order of the constructors, the destructor for `GraduateStudent` is given control first. After it's given its last full measure of devotion, control passes to the destructor for `Advisor` and then to the destructor for `Student`. If `Student` were based on a class `Person`, the destructor for `Person` would get control after `Student`.

This is logical. The blob of memory is first converted to a `Student` object. Only then is it the job of the `GraduateStudent` constructor to transform this simple `Student` into a `GraduateStudent`. The destructor simply reverses the process.

Having a HAS_A Relationship

Notice that the class `GraduateStudent` includes the members of class `Student` and `Advisor`, but in a different way. By defining a data member of class `Advisor`, you know that a `Student` has all the data members of an `Advisor` within it; however you can't say that a `GraduateStudent` is an `Advisor` — instead you say that a `GraduateStudent` HAS_A `Advisor`. What's the difference between this and inheritance?

Use a car as an example. You could logically define a car as being a subclass of vehicle, so it inherits the properties of other vehicles. At the same time, a car has a motor. If you buy a car, you can logically assume that you are buying a motor as well. (Unless you go to the used-car lot where I got my last junk heap.)

If friends ask you to show up at a rally on Saturday with your vehicle of choice and you go in your car, they can't complain (even if someone else shows up on a bicycle) because a car IS_A vehicle. But, if you appear on foot carrying a motor, your friends will have reason to laugh at you because a motor is not a vehicle. A motor is missing certain critical properties that vehicles share — such as electric clocks that don't work.

From a programming standpoint, the HAS_A relationship is just as straightforward. Consider the following:

```
class Vehicle {};
class Motor {};
class Car : public Vehicle
{
  public:
    Motor motor;
};
```

```
void VehicleFn(Vehicle& v);
void MotorFn(Motor& m);

int main(int nNumberofArgs, char* pszArgs[])
{
    Car car;
    VehicleFn(car);    // this is allowed
    MotorFn(car);      // this is not allowed
    MotorFn(car.motor);// this is, however
    return 0;
}
```

The call VehicleFn(c) is allowed because car IS_A vehicle. The call
MotorFn(car) is not because car is not a Motor, even though it contains a
Motor. If the intention was to pass the Motor portion of c to the function, this
must be expressed explicitly, as in the call MotorFn(car.motor).

Chapter 21

Examining Virtual Member Functions: Are They for Real?

*T*he number and type of a function's arguments are included in its full, or *extended,* name. This enables you to give two functions the same name as long as the extended name is different:

```
void someFn(int);
void someFn(char*);
void someFn(char*, double);
```

In all three cases the short name for these functions is someFn() (hey! this is some fun). The extended names for all three differ: someFn(int) versus someFn(char*), and so on. C++ is left to figure out which function is meant by the arguments during the call.

The return type is not part of the extended name, so you can't have two functions with the same extended name that differ only in the type of object they return.

Member functions can be overloaded. The number of arguments, the type of arguments and the class name are all part of the extended name.

Inheritance introduces a whole new wrinkle, however. What if a function in a base class has the same name as a function in the subclass? Consider, for example, the following simple code snippet:

```
class Student
{
  public:
    float calcTuition();
};
class GraduateStudent : public Student
{
  public:
    float calcTuition();
};

int main(int argcs, char* pArgs[])
{
    Student s;
    GraduateStudent gs;
    s.calcTuition(); // calls Student::calcTuition()
    gs.calcTuition();// calls GraduateStudent::calcTuition()
    return 0;
}
```

As with any overloading situation, when the programmer refers to
calcTuition(), C++ has to decide which calcTuition() is intended.
Obviously, if the two functions differed in the type of arguments, there's no
problem. Even if the arguments were the same, the class name should be sufficient to resolve the call, and this example is no different. The call
s.calcTuition() **refers to** Student::calcTuition() **because** s **is
declared locally as a** Student, **whereas** gs.calcTuition() **refers to**
GraduateStudent::calcTuition().

But what if the exact class of the object can't be determined at compile time?
To demonstrate how this can occur, change the preceding program in a seemingly trivial way:

```
//
//   OverloadOverride - demonstrate when a function is
//                      declare-time overloaded vs. runtime
//                      overridden
//
#include <cstdio>
#include <cstdlib>
#include <iostream>
using namespace std;

class Student
{
  public:
    float calcTuition()
    {
        cout << "We're in Student::calcTuition" << endl;
        return 0;
    }
};
```

```
class GraduateStudent : public Student
{
  public:
    float calcTuition()
    {
        cout << "We're in GraduateStudent::calcTuition"
             << endl;
        return 0;
    }
};

void fn(Student& x)
{
    x.calcTuition();    // to which calcTuition() does
                        // this refer?
}

int main(int nNumberofArgs, char* pszArgs[])
{
    // pass a base class object to function
    // (to match the declaration)
    Student s;
    fn(s);

    // pass a specialization of the base class instead
    GraduateStudent gs;
    fn(gs);

    // wait until user is ready before terminating program
    // to allow the user to see the program results
    system("PAUSE");
    return 0;
}
```

This program generates the following output:

```
We're in Student::calcTuition
We're in Student::calcTuition
Press any key to continue . . .
```

Instead of calling `calcTuition()` directly, the call is now made through an intermediate function, `fn()`. Depending on how `fn()` is called, x can be a `Student` or a `GraduateStudent`. A `GraduateStudent` IS_A `Student`.

Refer to Chapter 20 if you don't remember why a `GraduateStudent` IS_A `Student`.

The argument x passed to `fn()` is declared to be a reference to `Student`.

Passing an object by reference can be a lot more efficient than passing it by value. See Chapter 18 for a treatise on making copies of objects.

You might want `x.calcTuition()` to call `Student::calcTuition()` when x is a `Student` but to call `GraduateStudent::calcTuition()` when x is a `GraduateStudent`. It would be really cool if C++ were that smart.

Normally, the compiler decides which function a call refers to at compile time. When you click the button to tell the C++ compiler to rebuild your executable program, the compiler snoops around in your program to decide which function you mean with every call based on the arguments used.

In the case described here, the declared type of the argument to `fn()` is not completely descriptive. Although the argument is declared `Student`, it may actually be a `GraduateStudent`. A decision can't be made until you're actually executing the program (this is known as *runtime*). Only when the function is actually called can C++ look at the type of the argument and decide whether it's a plain old student or a graduate student.

The type that you've been accustomed to until now is called the *declared* or *compile-time* type. The declared type of x is `Student` in both cases because that's what the declaration in `fn()` says. The other kind is the runtime type. In the case of the example function `fn()`, the runtime type of x is `Student` when `fn()` is called with s and `GraduateStudent` when `fn()` is called with gs. Aren't we having fun?

The capability of deciding at runtime which of several overloaded member functions to call based on the runtime type is called *polymorphism,* or late binding. Deciding which overloaded to call at compile time is called *early binding* because that sounds like the opposite of late binding.

Overloading a base class function polymorphically is called *overriding the base class function.* This new name is used in order to differentiate this more complicated case from the normal overload case.

Why You Need Polymorphism

Polymorphism is key to the power of object-oriented programming. It's so important that languages that don't support polymorphism can't advertise themselves as OO languages. (I think it's an FDA regulation — you can't label a language that doesn't support OO unless you add a disclaimer from the Surgeon General, or something like that.)

Languages that support classes but not polymorphism are called object-based languages.

Without polymorphism, inheritance has little meaning. Let me spring yet another example on you to show why. Suppose that I had written a really fabulous program that used some class called, just to pick a name out of the air,

`Student`. After months of design, coding, and testing, I release this application to rave reviews from colleagues and critics alike. (There's even talk of starting a new Nobel Prize category for software, but I modestly brush such talk aside.)

Time passes and my boss asks me to add to this program the capability of handling graduate students who are similar but not identical to normal students. (The graduate students probably claim that they're not similar at all.) Now, my boss doesn't know or care that deep within the program, `someFunction()` calls the member function `calcTuition()`. (There's a lot that he doesn't know or care about, by the way, and that's a good thing if you ask me.)

```
void someFunction(Student& s)
{
    // ...whatever it might do...
    s.calcTuition();
    // ...continues on...
}
```

If C++ didn't support late binding, I would need to edit `someFunction()` to something like the following to add class `GraduateStudent`:

```
#define STUDENT 1
#define GRADUATESTUDENT 2
void someFunction(Student& s)
{
    // ...whatever it might do...
    // add some member type that indicates
    // the actual type of the object
    switch (s.type)
    {
      case STUDENT:
        s.Student::calcTuition();
        break;

      case GRADUATESTUDENT:
        s.GraduateStudent::calcTuition();
        break;
    }
    // ...continues on...
}
```

I would have to add the variable `type` to the class. I would then add the assignment `type = STUDENT` to the constructor for `Student` and `type = GRADUATESTUDENT` to the constructor for `GraduateStudent`. The value of `type` would then indicate the runtime type of `s`. I would then add the test shown in the preceding code snippet to every place where an overridden member function is called.

That doesn't seem so bad, except for three things. First, this is only one function. Suppose that `calcTuition()` is called from a lot of places and suppose that `calcTuition()` is not the only difference between the two classes. The chances are not good that I will find all the places that need to be changed.

Second, I must edit (read "break") code that was debugged and working, introducing opportunities for screwing up. Edits can be time-consuming and boring, which usually makes my attention drift. Any one of my edits may be wrong or may not fit in with the existing code. Who knows?

Finally, after I've finished editing, redebugging, and retesting everything, I now have two versions to keep track of (unless I can drop support for the original version). This means two sources to edit when bugs are found (perish the thought) and some type of accounting system to keep them straight.

Then what happens when my boss wants yet another class added? (My boss is like that.) Not only do I get to repeat the process, but I'll have three copies to keep track of.

With polymorphism, there's a good chance that all I need to do is add the new subclass and recompile. I may need to modify the base class itself, but at least it's all in one place. Modifications to the application code are minimized.

At some philosophical level, there's an even more important reason for polymorphism. Remember how I made nachos in the oven? In this sense, I was acting as the late binder. The recipe read: Heat the nachos in the oven. It didn't read: If the type of oven is microwave, do this; if the type of oven is conventional, do that; if the type of oven is convection, do this other thing. The recipe (the code) relied on me (the late binder) to decide what the action (member function) heat means when applied to the oven (the particular instance of class `Oven`) or any of its variations (subclasses), such as a microwave oven (`Microwave`). This is the way people think, and designing a language along the lines of the way people think allows the programming model to more accurately describe the real world.

How Polymorphism Works

Any given language could support early or late binding upon its whim. Older languages like C tend to support early binding alone. Recent languages like Java only support late binding. As a fence straddler between the two, C++ supports both early and late binding.

You may be surprised that the default for C++ is early binding. The reason is simple, if a little dated. First, C++ has to act as much like C as possible by default to retain upward compatibility with its predecessor. Second, polymorphism adds a small amount of overhead to each and every function call both in terms of data storage and code needed to perform the call. The founders of C++ were concerned that any additional overhead would be used as a reason not to adopt C++ as the system's language of choice, so they made the more efficient early binding the default.

One final reason is that it can be useful as a programmer of a given class to decide whether you want a given member function to be overridden at some time in the future. This argument is strong enough that Microsoft's new C# language also allows the programmer to flag a function as not overridable (however, the default is overridable).

To make a member function polymorphic, the programmer must flag the function with the C++ keyword `virtual`, as shown in the following modification to the declaration in the OverloadOveride program:

```
class Student
{
  public:
    virtual float calcTuition()
    {
        cout << "We're in Student::calcTuition" << endl;
        return 0;
    }
};
```

The keyword `virtual` that tells C++ that `calcTuition()` is a polymorphic member function. That is to say, declaring `calcTuition()` virtual means that calls to it will be bound late if there is any doubt as to the runtime type of the object with which `calcTuition()` is called.

In the example OverloadOverride program at the beginning of this chapter, `fn()` is called through the intermediate function `test()`. When `test()` is passed a `Base` class object, `b.fn()` calls `Base::fn()`. But when `test()` is passed a `SubClass` object, the same call invokes `SubClass::fn()`.

Executing the OverloadOveride program with `calcTuition()` declared virtual generates the following output:

```
We're in Student::calcTuition
We're in GraduateStudent::calcTuition
Press any key to continue . . .
```

If you're comfortable with the debugger that comes with your C++ environment, you really should single-step through this example.

You only need to declare the function virtual in the base class. The "virtualness" is carried down to the subclass automatically. In this book, however, I follow the coding standard of declaring the function virtual everywhere (virtually).

You can also review the program PolymorphicNachos on the enclosed CD-ROM for a further example of polymorphism.

When Is a Virtual Function Not?

Just because you think that a particular function call is bound late doesn't mean that it is. If not declared with the same arguments in the subclasses, the member functions are not overridden polymorphically, whether or not they are declared virtual.

One exception to the identical declaration rule is that if the member function in the base class returns a pointer or reference to a base class object, an overridden member function in a subclass may return a pointer or reference to an object of the subclass. In other words, the function makeACopy() is polymorphic even though the return type of the two functions have a different return type:

```
class Base
{
  public:
    // return a copy of the current object
    Base* makeACopy()
    {
        // ...do whatever it takes to make a copy
    }
};

class SubClass : public Base
{
  public:
    // return a copy of the current object
    SubClass* makeACopy()
    {
        // ...do whatever it takes to make a copy
    };
};

void fn(Base& bc)
{
    BaseClass* pCopy = bc.makeACopy();

    // proceed on...
}
```

In practice, this is quite natural. A makeACopy() function should return an object of type SubClass, even though it might override BaseClass::makeACopy().

Considering Virtual Considerations

You need to keep in mind a few things when using virtual functions.

First, static member functions cannot be declared virtual. Because static member functions are not called with an object, there is no runtime object upon which to base a binding decision.

Second, specifying the class name in the call forces a call to bind early, whether or not the function is virtual. For example, the following call is to `Base::fn()` because that's what the programmer indicated, even if `fn()` is declared virtual:

```
void test(Base& b)
{
  b.Base::fn();      // this call is not bound late
}
```

Finally, constructors cannot be virtual because there is no (completed) object to use to determine the type. At the time the constructor is called, the memory that the object occupies is just an amorphous mass. It's only after the constructor has finished that the object is a member of the class in good standing.

By comparison, the destructor should almost always be declared virtual. If not, you run the risk of improperly destructing the object, as in the following circumstance:

```
class Base
{
  public:
    ~Base();
};

class SubClass : public Base
{
  public:
    ~SubClass();
};

void finishWithObject(Base* pHeapObject)
{
    // ...work with object...
    // now return it to the heap
    delete pHeapObject; // this calls ~Base() no matter
}                       // the runtime type of
                        // pHeapObject
```

If the pointer passed to finishWithObject() really points to a SubClass, the SubClass destructor is not invoked properly — because the destructor has been not been declared virtual, it's always bound early. Declaring the destructor virtual solves the problem.

So when would you not want to declare the destructor virtual? There's only one case. Virtual functions introduce a "little" overhead. Let me be more specific. When the programmer defines the first virtual function in a class, C++ adds an additional, hidden pointer — not one pointer per virtual function, just one pointer if the class has any virtual functions. A class that has no virtual functions (and does not inherit any virtual functions from base classes) does not have this pointer.

Now, one pointer doesn't sound like much, and it isn't unless the following two conditions are true:

- ✔ The class doesn't have many data members (so that one pointer represents a lot compared to what's there already).
- ✔ You intend to create a lot of objects of this class (otherwise, the overhead doesn't make any difference).

If these two conditions are met and your class doesn't already have virtual member functions, you may not want to declare the destructor virtual.

Except for this one case, always declare destructors to be virtual, even if a class is not subclassed (yet) — you never know when someone will come along and use your class as the base class for her own. If you don't declare the destructor virtual, document it!

Chapter 22

Factoring Classes

• •

In This Chapter

▶ Factoring common properties into a base class

▶ Using abstract classes to hold factored information

▶ Declaring abstract classes

▶ Inheriting from an abstract class

▶ Dividing a program into multiple modules using a project file

• •

*T*he concept of inheritance allows one class to inherit the properties of a base class. Inheritance has a number of purposes, including paying for my son's college. It can save programming time by avoiding needless code repetition. Inheritance allows the program to reuse existing classes in new applications by overriding functions.

The main benefit of inheritance is the ability to point out the relationship between classes. This is the so-called IS_A relationship — a `MicrowaveOven` `IS_A Oven` and stuff like that.

Factoring is great stuff if you make the correct correlations. For example, the microwave versus conventional oven relationship seems natural. Claim that microwave is a special kind of toaster, and you're headed for trouble. True, they both make things hot, they both use electricity, and they're both found in the kitchen, but the similarity ends there — a microwave can't make toast.

Identifying the classes inherent in a problem and drawing the correct relationships among these classes is a process known as *factoring*. (The word is related to the arithmetic that you were forced to do in grade school: factoring out the Least Common Denominators; for example, 12 is equal to 2 times 2 times 3.)

Factoring

This section describes how you can use inheritance to simplify your programs using a simple bank account example.

Suppose that you were asked to a write a simple bank program that imple-mented the concept of a savings account and a checking account.

ON THE CD

Bonus Chapter 1 on the enclosed CD-ROM features the BUDGET programs, which implement just such a simple bank application.

I can talk until I'm blue in the face about these classes; however, object-oriented programmers have come up with a concise way to describe the salient points of a class in a drawing. The Checking and Savings classes are shown in Figure 22-1. (This is only one of several ways to graphically express the same thing.)

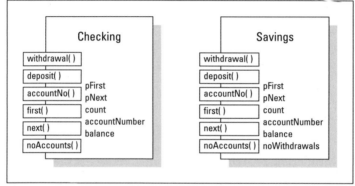

Figure 22-1: Independent classes Checking and Savings.

To read this figure and the other figures, remember the following:

- ✔ The big box is the class, with the class name at the top.
- ✔ The names in boxes are member functions.
- ✔ The names not in boxes are data members.
- ✔ The names that extend partway out of the boxes are publicly accessible members; that is, these members can be accessed by functions that are not part of the class or any of its descendents. Those members that are completely within the box are not accessible from outside the class.
- ✔ A thick arrow represents the IS_A relationship.
- ✔ A thin arrow represents the HAS_A relationship.

REMEMBER

A Car IS_A Vehicle, but a Car HAS_A Motor.

You can see in Figure 22-1 that the Checking and Savings classes have a lot in common. For example, both classes have a withdrawal() and deposit() member function. Because the two classes aren't identical, however, they must remain as separate classes. (In a real-life bank application, the two classes would be a good deal more different than in this example.) Still, there should be a way to avoid this repetition.

You could have one of these classes inherit from the other. Savings has more members than Checking, so you could let Savings inherit from Checking. This arrangement is shown in Figure 22-2. The Savings class inherits all the members. The class is completed with the addition of the data member noWithdrawals and by overriding the function withdrawal(). You have to override withdrawal() because the rules for withdrawing money from a savings account are different from those for withdrawing money from a checking account. (These rules don't apply to me because I don't have any money to withdraw anyway.)

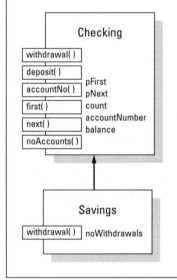

Figure 22-2:
Savings implemented as a subclass of checking.

Although letting Savings inherit from Checking is laborsaving, it's not completely satisfying. The main problem is that it, like the weight listed on my driver's license, misrepresents the truth. This inheritance relationship implies that a savings account is a special type of checking account, which it is not.

"So what?" you say. "Inheriting works, and it saves effort." True, but my reservations are more than stylistic trivialities — my reservations are at some of the best restaurants in town (at least that's what all the truckers say). Such misrepresentations are confusing to the programmer, both today's and tomorrow's.

Someday, a programmer unfamiliar with our programming tricks will have to read and understand what our code does. Misleading representations are difficult to reconcile and understand.

In addition, such misrepresentations can lead to problems down the road. Suppose, for example, that the bank changes its policies with respect to checking accounts. Say it decides to charge a service fee on checking accounts only if the minimum balance dips below a given value during the month.

A change like this can be easily handled with minimal changes to the class Checking. You'll have to add a new data member to the class Checking to keep track of the minimum balance during the month. Let's go out on a limb and call it minimumBalance.

But now you have a problem. Because Savings inherits from Checking, Savings gets this new data member as well. It has no use for this member because the minimum balance does not affect savings accounts, so it just sits there. Remember that every checking account object has this extra minimumBalance member. One extra data member may not be a big deal, but it adds further confusion.

Changes like this accumulate. Today it's an extra data member — tomorrow it's a changed member function. Eventually, the savings account class is carrying a lot of extra baggage that is applicable only to checking accounts.

Now the bank comes back and decides to change some savings account policy. This requires you to modify some function in Checking. Changes like this in the base class automatically propagate down to the subclass unless the function is already overridden in the subclass Savings. For example, suppose that the bank decides to give away toasters for every deposit into the checking account. (Hey — it could happen!) Without the bank (or its programmers) knowing it, deposits to checking accounts would automatically result in toaster donations. Unless you're very careful, changes to Checking may unexpectedly appear in Savings.

How can you avoid these problems? Claiming that Checking is a special case of Savings changes but doesn't solve our problem. What you need is a third class (call it Account, just for grins) that embodies the things that are common between Checking and Savings. This relationship is shown in Figure 22-3.

How does building a new account solve the problems? First, creating a new account is a more accurate description of the real world (whatever that is). In our concept of things (or at least in mine), there really is something known as an account. Savings accounts and checking accounts are special cases of this more fundamental concept.

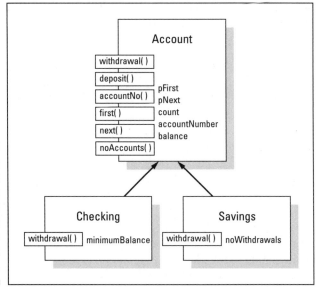

Figure 22-3:
Basing
Checking
and Savings
on a
common
Account
class.

In addition, the class Savings is insulated from changes to the class Checking (and vice versa). If the bank institutes a fundamental change to all accounts, you can modify Account, and all subclasses will automatically inherit the change. But, if the bank changes its policy only for checking accounts, you can modify just the checking account class without modifying Savings.

This process of culling out common properties from similar classes is called *factoring*.

Factoring is legitimate only if the inheritance relationship corresponds to reality. Factoring together a class Mouse and Joystick because they're both hardware pointing devices is legitimate. Factoring together a class Mouse and Display because they both make low-level operating system calls is not.

Factoring can and usually does result in multiple levels of abstraction. For example, a program written for a more developed bank may have a class structure such as that shown in Figure 22-4.

Here you see that another class has been inserted between Checking and Savings and the most general class Account. This class, called Conventional, incorporates features common to conventional accounts. Other account types, such as stock market accounts, are also foreseen.

Such multitiered class structures are common and desirable as long as the relationships they express correspond to reality. Note, however, that no one correct class hierarchy exists for any given set of classes.

Figure 22-4:
A more
developed
bank
account
hierarchy.

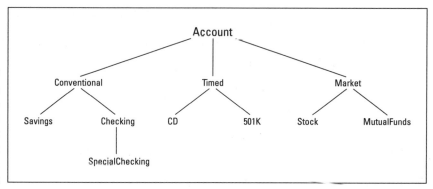

Suppose that the bank allows account holders to access checking and stock market accounts remotely. Withdrawals from other account types can be made only at the bank. Although the class structure in Figure 22-4 seems natural, the one shown in Figure 22-5 is also justifiable given this information. The programmer must decide which class structure best fits the data and leads to the cleanest, most natural implementation.

Figure 22-5:
An alternate
class
hierarchy to
the one in
Figure 22-4.

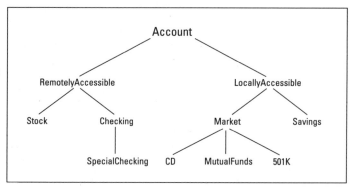

Implementing Abstract Classes

As intellectually satisfying as factoring is, it introduces a problem of its own. Return one more time to the bank account classes, specifically the common base class `Account`. Think for a minute about how you might go about defining the different member functions defined in `Account`.

Most `Account` member functions are no problem because both account types implement them in the same way. Implementing those common functions with `Account::withdrawal()` is different, however. The rules for withdrawing from a savings account are different than those for withdrawing from a checking account. You'll have to implement `Savings::withdrawal()` differently than you do `Checking::withdrawal()`. But how are you supposed to implement `Account::withdrawal()`?

Let's ask the bank manager for help. I imagine the conversation going something like the following:

"What are the rules for making a withdrawal from an account?" you ask expectantly.

"What type of account? Savings or checking?" comes the reply.

"From an account," you say. "Just an account."

Blank look. (One might say a "blank bank look" . . . then again, maybe not.)

The problem is that the question doesn't make sense. There's no such thing as "just an account." All accounts (in this example) are either checking accounts or savings accounts. The concept of an account is an abstract one that factors out properties common to the two concrete classes. It is incomplete because it lacks the critical property `withdrawal()`. (After you get further into the details, you may find other properties that a simple account lacks.)

An *abstract class* is one that only exists in subclasses. A *concrete class* is a class that is not abstract. Hardly an abstract concept.

Let me borrow an example from the animal kingdom. You can observe the different species of warm-blooded, baby-bearing animals and conclude that there is a concept called mammal. You can derive classes from mammal, such as canine, feline, and hominid. It is impossible, however, to find anywhere on earth a pure mammal, that is, a mammal that isn't a member of some subspecies of mammal. Mammal is a high-level concept that man has created — no instances of mammal exist.

Note that I can make this assertion confidently although time has passed since I first wrote this (it took you only a few seconds to get from there to here — I hope). Scientists discover new animals all the time. One scientist even discovered a new phylum in the 1990s (if you're a biologist, that's a big deal). Not once has a scientist come back and said, "This new thing is a mammal and nothing more . . . just a mammal." The problem with a statement like this is that this animal surely has properties that other mammals don't share and, even if doesn't, there's a distinct possibility that someone will find such a property in the future.

C++ supports a concept known as an abstract class to describe an incomplete concept such as mammal.

Describing the abstract class concept

An abstract class is a class with one or more pure virtual functions. Oh, great! That helps a lot.

Okay, a *pure virtual* function is a virtual member function that is marked as having no implementation. Most likely it has no implementation because no implementation is possible with the information provided in the class, including any base classes.

It doesn't make sense to ask exactly how to implement the `withdrawal()` function in the class `Account`. However, the concept of a withdrawal from an account does make sense. The C++ programmer can write a function `withdrawal()` that is impossible to implement. Such a function is called a pure virtual function. (Don't ask me how they came up with that name.)

The syntax for declaring a function pure virtual is demonstrated in the following class `Account`:

```
// Account - this class is an abstract class
class Account
{
  protected:
    Account(Account& c);  // avoid making any copies
  public:
    Account(unsigned accNo, float initialBalance = 0.0F);

    // access functions
    unsigned int accountNo( );
    float acntBalance( );
    static int noAccounts( );

    // transaction functions
    void deposit(float amount);

    // the following is a pure virtual function
    virtual void withdrawal(float amount) = 0;

  protected:
    // keep accounts in a linked list so there's no limit
    // to the number of accounts
    static int count;      // number of accounts
    unsigned  accountNumber;
    float    balance;
};
```

The `= 0` after the declaration of `withdrawal()` indicates that the programmer does not intend to define this function. The declaration is a placeholder for the subclasses. The subclasses of `Account` are expected to override this function with a concrete function. The programmer must provide an implementation for each member function not declared pure virtual.

I think this notation is silly, and I don't like it any more than you do. But it's here to stay, so you just have to learn to live with it. There is a reason, if not exactly a justification, for this notation. Every virtual function must have an entry in a special table. This entry contains the address of the function. The entry for a pure virtual function is zero. Some other languages define an abstract keyword — no, I mean a keyword abstract.

An abstract class cannot be instanced with an object; that is, you can't make an object out of an abstract class. For example, the following declaration is not legal:

```
void fn( )
{
    // declare an account with 100 dollars
    Account acnt(1234, 100.00);// this is not legal
    acnt.withdrawal(50);        // what would you expect
                                // this call to do?
}
```

If the declaration were allowed, the resulting object would be incomplete, lacking in some capability. For example, what should the preceding call do? Remember, there is no `Account::withdrawal()`.

Abstract classes serve as base classes for other classes. An `Account` contains all the properties associated with a generic bank account. You can create other types of bank accounts by inheriting from `Account`, but they can't be instanced with an object.

Making an honest class out of an abstract class

The subclass of an abstract class remains abstract until all pure virtual functions have been overridden. The class `Savings` is not abstract because it overrides the pure virtual function `withdrawal()` with a perfectly good definition. An object of class `Savings` knows how to perform `withdrawal()` when called on to do so. The same is true of class `Checking`. The class is not virtual because the function `withdrawal()` overrides the pure virtual function in the base class.

A subclass of an abstract class can remain abstract, however. Consider the following classes:

```
class Display
{
  public:
    virtual void initialize( ) = 0;
    virtual void write(char *pString) = 0;
};

class SVGA : public Display
{
  // override both member functions with "real" functions
  virtual void initialize( );
  virtual void write(char *pString);
};

class HWVGA : public Display
{
  // override the only function we know how to up until now
  virtual void write(char *pString);
};

class ThreedVGA : public HWVGA
{
  virtual void initialize( );
};

void fn( )
{
  SVGA mc;
  ThreedVGA  vga;
  // ...what the function chooses to do from here...
}
```

The class Display, intended to represent video PC displays, has two pure virtual functions: initialize() and write(). You can't implement either function for adapters in general. The different types of video cards do not initialize or write in the same way.

One of the subclasses, SVGA, is not abstract. This is a particular type of video adapter that the programmer knows how to program. Therefore, the class SVGA has overridden both initialize() and write() appropriately for this adapter.

HWVGA, another one of the subclasses, is also not abstract. Here again, the programmer knows how to program the accelerated VGA adapter hardware. In this case, however, a level of abstraction is between the generic Display and the specific case of the ThreedVGA display, which represents the special 3-D hardware display cards.

For this discussion, assume that all hardware-accelerated VGA cards are written to in the same way, but that each must be initialized in its own way. (This

isn't necessarily true, but assume that it is.) To express the common write()
property, introduce the class HWVGA to implement the write() function (along
with any other properties that all HWVGA have in common). Don't override
the member function initialize(), however, because the different HWVGAs
do not have this property in common.

Therefore, although the function write() has been overridden, the class
HWVGA is still abstract because the initialize() function has yet to be
overridden.

Because ThreedVGA inherits from HWVGA, it has to override only the one missing member function, initialize(), to complete the definition of Display
adapter. The function fn() is therefore free to instance and use a ThreedVGA
object.

Overriding the last pure virtual function with a normal member function
makes the class complete (that is, non-abstract). Only non-abstract classes
can be instanced with an object.

Passing abstract classes

Because you can't instance an abstract class, it may sound odd that it's possible to declare a pointer or a reference to an abstract class. With polymorphism, however, this isn't as crazy as it sounds. Consider the following code
snippet:

```
void fn(Account *pAccount);  // this is legal
void otherFn( )
{
    Savings s;
    Checking c;

    // this is legitimate because Savings IS_A Account
    fn(&s);
    // same here
    fn(&c);
}
```

Here, pAccount is declared as a pointer to an Account. However, it's understood that when the function is called, it will be passed the address of some
non-abstract subclass object such as Savings or Checking.

All objects received by fn() will be of either class Savings or class Checking
(or some future non-abstract subclass of Account). The function is assured
that you will never pass an actual object of class Account because you could
never create one to pass in the first place.

Declaring pure virtual functions — is it really necessary?

If withdrawal() can't be defined, why not leave it out? Why not declare the function in Savings and Checking where it can also be defined and keep it out of Account? In many object-oriented languages, you can do just that. But C++ wants to be able to check that you really know what you're doing.

Remember that declaring a function establishes its extended name including arguments, whereas a definition includes the code to execute when the function is called.

I can make the following minor changes to Account to demonstrate the problem:

```
class Account
{
    // just like before but without
    // the declaration of withdrawal()
};

class Savings : public Account
{
  public:
    virtual void withdrawal(float amnt);
};

void fn(Account *pAcc)
{
    // withdraw some money
    pAcc->withdrawal(100.00F);
                // this call is not allowed
                // withdrawal( ) is not a member
                // of class Account
};

int main( )
{
    Savings s;  // open an account
    fn(&s);

    // ...continues on...
}
```

Suppose that you open a savings account s. You then pass the address of that account to the function fn(), which attempts to make a withdrawal. Because the function withdrawal() is not a member of Account, however, the compiler generates an error.

See how pure virtual functions correct the problem. Here's the same situation with Account declared as an abstract class:

```
class Account
{
  public:
    // just like preceding
    // declare withdrawal pure virtual
    virtual void withdrawal(float amnt) = 0;
};

class Savings : public Account
{
  public:
    virtual void withdrawal(float amnt);
};

void fn(Account *pAcc)
{
    // withdraw some money
    pAcc->withdrawal(100.00F); // now it works
};

int main( )
{
    Savings s;  // open an account
    fn(&s);
    // ...same as before...
}
```

The situation is the same except the class Account includes the member function withdrawal(). Now when the compiler checks to see whether pAcc->withdrawal() is defined, it sees the definition of Account:: withdrawal() just as it expects. The compiler is happy. You're happy. That makes me happy, too. (Frankly, a football game and a cold beer are enough to make me happy.)

The pure virtual function is a placeholder in the base class for the subclass to override with its own implementation. Without that placeholder in the base class, there is no overriding.

Factoring C++ Source Code

Factoring a problem has a physical side. Classes that have been factored out of the jumble of separate concepts that make up a program should be moved into their own "space."

The programmer can divide a single program into separate files known as *modules*. These individual source files are compiled separately and then combined during the build process to generate a single program. Modules can then be allocated to separate groups known as *namespaces*.

The process of combining separately compiled modules into a single executable is called *linking*.

There are a number of reasons to divide programs into more manageable pieces. First, dividing a program into modules results in a higher level of encapsulation. Classes wall off their internal members in order to provide a certain degree of safety. Programs can wall off functions to do the same thing.

Encapsulation is one of the advantages of object-oriented programming.

Second, it is easier to comprehend and, therefore, easier to write and debug a program that consists of a number of well-thought-out modules than a single source file full of all of the classes and functions that the program uses.

Next comes reuse. I used the reuse argument to help sell object-based programming. It is extremely difficult to keep track of a single class reused among multiple programs when a separate copy of the class is kept in each program. It is much better if a single class module is automatically shared among programs.

Finally, there is the argument of time. A compiler such as Visual C++ or Dev-C++ doesn't need very long to build the examples contained in this book using a high-speed computer like yours. Commercial programs sometimes consist of millions of source lines of code. Rebuilding a program of that size can take more than 24 hours. A programmer would not tolerate rebuilding a program like that for every single change. However, the majority of the time is spent compiling source files that haven't changed. It is much faster to recompile just those modules that have changed and then quickly link all modules together.

Separate namespaces allow a further level of encapsulation. A namespace should consist of a set of modules that perform a single capability. For example, all of the mathematical functions might be combined into a Math namespace.

This lesson builds a simplistic program, called SeparateModules, that consists of a Student class, a GraduateStudent subclass, and a main() module to test both.

Dividing the program — Student

You begin by deciding what the logical divisions of SeparateModules should be. First, you notice that Student is an entity of its own. It does not depend on any other functions (besides C++ functions). Thus, it would make sense to put Student in a module by itself. Because the class will be used in several places, you break the declaration into a student.h file and a separate implementation file, Student.cpp. By convention, the include file carries the name of the primary class it defines, but in lowercase letters. Ideally, the include file defines only one class. This allows the user program to include just the files that it needs.

Historically, all include files carried the extension .h. This was changed in the current C++ standard. System include files such as iostream now have no extension at all. However, many programmers stick with the .h convention for include files they write. This allows such include files to be easily differentiated by the reader of the program.

The resulting student.h file appears as follows:

```
// Student - basic student
#ifndef _STUDENT_
#define _STUDENT_

namespace Schools
{
    class Student
    {
      public:
        Student(char* pszName, int nID);
        virtual char* display();
      protected:
        // student's name
        char* pszName;
        int   nID;
    };
}
#endif
```

The #ifndef is a preprocessor control much like #include. #ifndef _STUDENT_ says to include only the following lines if the argument _STUDENT_ is defined. The first time that student.h is included, _STUDENT_ is not defined. However, the #define immediately following the #ifndef then defines it. This has the effect that student.h is processed only once, no matter how many times it is included in a given file.

Defining a namespace

The second feature of the Student class is the creation of the Schools namespace.

A *namespace* is a collection of loosely coupled classes that are somehow logically similar. In this case, I intend to throw all classes that I create concerning students, graduate students, classes, course schedules, and so forth into the Schools namespace.

The classes that make up the Schools namespace are like members of a family. One class within a namespace may refer to other members of the same namespace directly. However, external classes must specify the namespace. You will see the ways of specifying a class's namespace in the following SeparatedMain application.

Another reason for dividing modules into namespaces is to avoid "name collision." For example, the class Grade within the namespace Schools does not interfere with the class Grade in the namespace FoodProduction.

Implementing Student

I put the implementation of the Student class in the file Student.cpp:

```
// Student - implement the methods of the Student class
#include <cstdio>
#include <cstdlib>
#include <iostream>
#include <string>
#include "student.h"

namespace Schools
{
    Student::Student(char* pszNameArg, int nIDArg)
        : nID(nIDArg)
    {
        pszName = new char[strlen(pszNameArg) + 1];
        strcpy(pszName, pszNameArg);
    }

    // display - return a description of student
    char* Student::display()
    {
        // copy the student's name into a block of heap
        // memory that we can return to the caller
        char* pReturn = new char[strlen(pszName) + 1];
        strcpy(pReturn, pszName);
        return pReturn;
    }
}
```

The constructor for Student copies off the name and id provided it. The virtual display() method returns a string that describes the Student object.

Compiling the `Student.cpp` file generates an intermediate file. This intermediate file can be combined quickly with other intermediate files to form a completed executable program.

For historical reasons, this intermediate file carries the extension `.o` (for "object file") in most C++ environments.

Dividing the program — GraduateStudent

The next module that seems quasi-independent is `GraduateStudent`. Logically, one could fold the `GraduateStudent` class into `Student.cpp`; however, some programs may want to deal with `Student` as an abstraction and not worry about students versus graduate students.

I made the `GraduateStudent` class as simple as possible. The `include` file appears as follows:

```
// GraduateStudent - a special type of Student
#ifndef _GRADUATE_STUDENT_
#define _GRADUATE_STUDENT_

#include "student.h"
namespace Schools
{
    class GraduateStudent : public Student
    {
      public:
        // trivial constructors
        GraduateStudent(char* pszName, int nID)
                 : Student(pszName, nID){}
        // demonstration virtual function
        virtual char* display();
    };
}

#endif
```

Notice that the `graduateStudent.h` file includes `student.h`. This is because the `GraduateStudent` class is dependent upon the definition of `Student`.

The resulting source file implements the `display()` method, the only member function that is yet to be implemented:

```
// GraduateStudent - a special type of Student
#include <cstdio>
#include <cstdlib>
#include <iostream>
#include "graduateStudent.h"
```

```
namespace Schools
{
    char* GraduateStudent::display()
    {
        // get description of basic student
        char* pFirst = Student::display();

        // we'll add this text
        char* pSecond = "-G";

        // get a new string and tack second onto first
        char* pName = new char[strlen(pFirst) +
                                    strlen(pSecond) + 1];
        strcpy(pName, pFirst);
        strcat(pName, pSecond);

        // don't forget to return the string returned by
        // Student::display() to the heap before passing
        // our new string to the caller
        delete pFirst;
        return pName;
    }
}
```

The GraduateStudent version of display() concatenates a "-G" onto the end of whatever Student returns. It begins by allocating a new character array that's large enough to handle the extra information.

Never assume that there's enough room in the original buffer for any extra characters to be tacked onto the end.

The program copies the contents of the original string into the newly allocated array. It then appends the "- G". The display() function must return the buffer allocated by Student::display() to the heap before continuing.

Forgetting to return buffers to the heap is known as a *memory leak*. A program with memory leaks executes properly at first; however, the program slows more and more as the available memory is lost to the leaks. The program eventually grinds to a halt. Memory leaks are very difficult to find.

Implementing an application

The two classes, Student and GraduateStudent, have been separated into independent source files and included in the Schools namespace. I wrote the following very simple application to invoke the two classes:

```
// SeparatedMain - demonstrated an application separated
//                  into two parts - the main() part
#include <cstdio>
#include <cstdlib>
#include <iostream>

#include "graduateStudent.h"
#include "student.h"

using namespace std;
//using namespace Schools;
using Schools::GraduateStudent;

int main(int nArgc, char* pszArgs[])
{
    Schools::Student s("Sophie Moore", 1234);
    cout << "Student = " << s.display() << endl;

    GraduateStudent gs("Greg U. Waite", 5678);
    cout << "Student = " << gs.display() << endl;

    // wait until user is ready before terminating program
    // to allow the user to see the program results
    system("PAUSE");
    return 0;
}
```

The application includes both the student.h and graduateStudent.h include files. This gives the application access to the definition of the two classes.

You might notice that including graduatestudent.h automatically includes student.h. However, you shouldn't take it for granted; include student.h if you access the Student class directly, whether or not you include graduateStudent.h. The #ifndef, which you installed in student.h, will make sure that the contents of student.h are not processed twice by the C++ compiler.

SeparatedMain is not a member of the Schools namespace. When main() refers to the Student class, C++ does not know whether the programmer intends to use the Student found in the Schools namespace or a similarly named class in some other namespace.

main() can completely specify a class without any possibility of ambiguity because Schools::Student refers specifically to the namespace and class. Alternatively, the programmer can specify her intentions at the beginning of the module: The phrase using Schools::GraduateStudent; tells C++ that any mention to GraduateStudent refers to the Schools namespace.

The programmer can gain access to all members of the Schools namespace by adding the command using namespace Schools. The following version of main() builds successfully:

```
using namespace Schools;

int main(int nArgc, char* pszArgs[])
{
    Student s("Sophie Moore", 1234);
    cout << "Student = " << s.display() << endl;

    GraduateStudent gs("Greg U. Waite", 5678);
    cout << "Student = " << gs.display() << endl;

    // wait until user is ready before terminating program
    // to allow the user to see the program results
    system("PAUSE");
    return 0;
}
```

You began using the using namespace std statement at the beginning of the book. The modules that make up the Standard C++ Library are members of the std namespace.

Project file

Full of expectation, I open the SeparatedMain.cpp file in the compiler and click Build. The module compiles properly, but an error occurs during the linking process. C++ does not know what a Student is. Somehow you have to tell C++ that the Student.cpp and GraduateStudent.cpp files need to be linked together with SeparatedMain.cpp to create the program. Most C++ environments, including both Dev-C++ and Visual C++.NET, combine multiple modules together via a *project file*.

Dev-C++ and Visual C++ use their own project file formats. The directions for creating a C++ console application project within Visual Studio.NET is provided on the enclosed CD-ROM in Bonus Chapter 2.

Creating a project file under Dev-C++

Execute the following steps to create a Dev-C++ project:

1. **Choose File➪New➪Project. Select Console Application and type the name** SeparateModules.

   You should see the window in Figure 22-6.

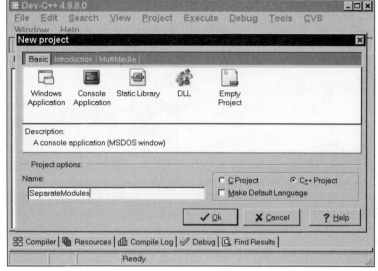

2. **Click OK.**

   Dev-C++ opens a file window.

3. **Select the directory into which to store the project.**

   I selected \CPP_Programs\Chap22. Dev-C++ creates a project with a default initial module main.cpp.

4. **Remove** main.cpp **from the project because you already have a** main() **module.**

5. **Choose Project➪Remove From Project.**

6. **Select** main.cpp **and click OK.**

7. **Copy the files** main.cpp, Student.cpp, GraduateStudent.cpp, student.h, **and** graduateStudent.h **to the Chap22 folder if they aren't there already.**

8. **Choose Project➪Add to Project.**

9. **Select the entire list of source modules and click OK.**

10. **Choose Execute➪Rebuild All to compile the modules in the project and create an executable program.**

11. **Click the Classes tab in the left window to see a detailed description of each class in the program, as shown in Figure 22-7.**

    Make sure that the class browser is enabled and configured properly.

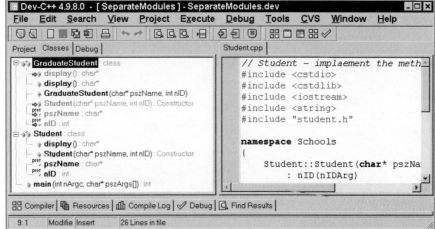

Figure 22-7:
The classes
tab displays
the
members of
each class.

12. **Choose Tools➪Editor options and click the Class browsing tab.**

13. **Click the Enable Class Browser browser and the options shown in Figure 22-8.**

    Notice how the class browser displays each member. Functions display with their argument types as well as the type of object returned. Notice also that the class browser shows two `display()` member functions under the `GraduateStudent` class.

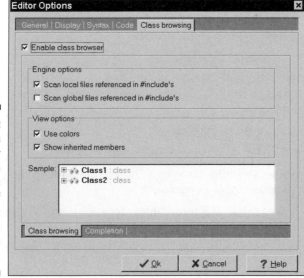

Figure 22-8:
The class
browser
options tab
determines
the type of
information
available in
the class
browser.

14. **Select the first** display() **entry in the list, the one with the small diamond in front of it.**

    This opens the Student.cpp file and places the cursor on the display() member function. Selecting the second display() entry in the class browser takes the editor to the GraduateStudent::display() member function.

    The properties of the project are initially set to the default. You can change the settings as follows.

15. **Select Project⇨Project Options.**

    For example, select the Linker options under the Compiler tab. Now make sure that Generate Debugging Information is set to Yes if you intend to use the Dev-C++ debugger.

I encourage you to break your programs into multiple source files. It simplifies the editing, modifying, and debugging process.

Part V
Optional Features

In this part . . .

The goal of this book is not to turn you into a C++ language lawyer; it's to give you a solid understanding of the fundamentals of C++ and object-oriented programming.

The earlier parts in this book cover the essential features you need to know to produce a well-written, object-oriented C++ program. C++, however, is a big language (it has a serious case of feature-itis, if you ask me), and I have yet to discuss many features such as file input/output and the Standard Template Library. Part V rights this wrong.

C++ programmers have increasingly come to exploit the features of this library in the past few years. The BUDGET4 and BUDGET5 programs on the enclosed CD-ROM demonstrate how.

Chapter 23

A New Assignment Operator, Should You Decide to Accept It

· ·

In This Chapter

▶ Introduction to the assignment operator

▶ Why and when the assignment operator is necessary

▶ Similarities between the assignment operator and the copy constructor

· ·

*T*he *intrinsic* data types are those that are built in the language, such as int, float, double, and so on, plus the various pointer types. Chapter 3 and Chapter 4 describe the operators that C++ defines for the intrinsic data types. C++ enables the programmer to define the operators for classes that the programmer has created in addition to these intrinsic operators. This is called *operator overloading*.

Normally, operator overloading is optional and not attempted by beginning C++ programmers. A lot of experienced C++ programmers (including me) don't think operator overloading is such a great idea either. However, you must figure out how to overload one operator: the assignment operator.

Comparing Operators with Functions

An operator is nothing more than a built-in function with a peculiar syntax. The following addition

```
a + b
```

could be understood as though it were written

```
operator+(a, b)
```

C++ gives each operator a function-style name. The functional name of an operator is the operator symbol preceded by the keyword `operator` and followed by the appropriate argument types. For example, the + operator that adds an `int` to an `int` generating an `int` is called `int operator+(int, int)`.

Any operator can be defined for a user-defined class. Thus, I could create a `Complex operator*(Complex&, Complex&)` that would allow me to multiply two objects of type `Complex`. The new operator may have the same semantics as the operator it overloads, but it doesn't have to. The following rules apply when overloading operators:

- The programmer cannot overload the ., ::, * (dereference), and & operators.

- The programmer cannot invent new operators. You cannot invent the operation x $ y.

- The format of the operators cannot be changed. Thus, you cannot define an operation %i because % is a binary operator.

- The operator precedence cannot change. A program cannot force `operator+` to be evaluated before `operator*`.

- The operators cannot be redefined when applied to intrinsic types — you can't change the meaning of 1 + 2. Existing operators can be overloaded only for newly defined types.

Overloading operators is one of those things that seems like a much better idea than it really is. In my experience, operator overloading introduces more problems than it solves, with two notable exceptions that are the subject of this chapter.

Inserting a New Operator

The insertion and extraction operators << and >> are nothing more than the left and right shift operators overloaded for a set of input/output classes. These definitions are found in the include file `iostream` (which is why every program includes that file). Thus, `cout << "some string"` becomes `operator<<(cout, "some string")`. Our old friends `cout` and `cin` are predefined objects that are tied to the console and keyboard, respectively. I discuss this relationship in Chapter 24.

Creating Shallow Copies Is a Deep Problem

No matter what anyone may think of operator overloading, you will need to overload the assignment operator for many classes that you generate. C++ provides a default definition for `operator=()` for all classes. This default definition performs a member-by-member copy. This works great for an intrinsic type like an `int`.

```
int i;
i = 10;   // "member by member" copy
```

This same default definition is applied to user-defined classes. In the following example, each member of `source` is copied over the corresponding member in `destination`.

```
void fn()
{
    MyStruct source, destination;
    destination = source;
}
```

The default assignment operator works for most classes; however, it is not correct for classes that allocate resources, such as heap memory. The programmer must overload `operator=()` to handle the transfer of resources.

The assignment operator is much like the copy constructor. In use, the two look almost identical:

```
void fn(MyClass &mc)
{
    MyClass newMC(mc);     // of course, this uses the
                           // copy constructor
    MyClass newerMC = mc;  // less obvious, this also invokes
                           // the copy constructor
    MyClass newestMC;      // this creates a default object
    newestMC = mc;         // and then overwrites it with
                           // the argument passed
}
```

The creation of `newMC` follows the standard pattern of creating a new object as a mirror image of the original using the copy constructor `MyClass(MyClass&)`. Not so obvious is that `newerMC` is also created using the copy constructor.

`MyClass a = b` is just another way of writing `MyClass a(b)` — in particular, this declaration does *not* involve the assignment operator despite its appearance. However, `newestMC` is created using the default (void) constructor and then overwritten by `mc` using the assignment operator.

Like the copy constructor, an assignment operator should be provided whenever a shallow copy is not appropriate. (Chapter 18 discusses shallow versus deep constructors.) A simple rule is to provide an assignment operator for classes that have a user-defined copy constructor.

The rule is this: The copy constructor is used when a new object is being created. The assignment operator is used if the left-hand object already exists.

Overloading the Assignment Operator

The `DemoAssignmentOperator` program demonstrates how to provide an assignment operator. The program also includes a copy constructor to provide a comparison.

```
//DemoAssignmentOperator - demonstrate the assignment
//                         operator on a user defined class
#include <cstdio>
#include <cstdlib>
#include <iostream>
#include <string>
using namespace std;

// Name - a generic class used to demonstrate
//        the assignment and copy constructor
//        operators
class Name
{
  public:
    Name(char *pszN = 0)
    {
        copyName(pszN, "");
    }
    Name(Name& s)
    {
        copyName(s.pszName, " (copy)");
    }
    ~Name()
    {
        deleteName();
    }

    //assignment operator
    Name& operator=(Name& s)
    {
```

```
            //delete existing stuff...
            deleteName();
            //...before replacing with new stuff
            copyName(s.pszName, " (replaced)");
            //return reference to existing object
            return *this;
        }

    // very simple access function
    char* out() { return pszName; }

  protected:
    void copyName(char* pszN, char* pszAdd);
    void deleteName();
    char *pszName;
};

//copyName() - allocate heap memory to store name
void Name::copyName(char* pszN, char* pszAdd)
{
    pszName = 0;
    if (pszN)
    {
        pszName = new char[strlen(pszN) +
                           strlen(pszAdd)  + 1];
        strcpy(pszName, pszN);
        strcat(pszName, pszAdd);
    }
}

//deleteName() - return heap memory
void Name::deleteName()
{
    if (pszName)
    {
        delete pszName;
        pszName = 0;
    }
}

int main(int nNumberofArgs, char* pszArgs[])
{
    // create two objects
    Name n1("Claudette");
    Name n2("Greg");
    cout << n1.out() << " and "
         << n2.out() << " are newly created objects"
         << endl;

    // now make a copy of an object
    Name n3(n1);
    cout << n3.out() << " is a copy of "
         << n1.out() << endl;
```

```
// create a new object using the "=" format
// for accessing the copy constructor
Name n4 = n1;
cout << n4.out() << " is also a copy of "
     << n1.out() << endl;

// overwrite n2 with n1
n2 = n1;
cout << n1.out() << " was assigned to "
     << n2.out() << endl;

// wait until user is ready before terminating program
// to allow the user to see the program results
system("PAUSE");
return 0;
}
```

The class `Name` contains a pointer to a person's name, which it allocates from the heap in the constructor. The constructors and destructor for class `Name` are similar to those presented in Chapters 17 and 18. The constructor `Name(char*)` copies the name given it to the `pszName` data member. This constructor also serves as the default constructor. The copy constructor `Name(&Name)` copies the name of the object passed to the name stored in the current object by calling `copyName()`. The destructor returns the `pszName` character string to the heap by calling `deleteName()`.

The assignment `operator=()` is a method of the class. It looks to all the world like a destructor immediately followed by a copy constructor. This is typical. Consider the assignment in the example `n2 = n1`. The object `n2` already has a name associated with it (`"Greg"`). In the assignment, the memory that the original name occupies must be returned to the heap by calling `deleteName()`, just like a destructor. The assignment operator then invokes `copyName()` to copy the new information into the object, much like a copy constructor.

The copy constructor did not need to call `deleteName()` because the object didn't already exist. Therefore, memory had not already been assigned to the object when the constructor was invoked. The destructor didn't perform the copy function.

There are two more details about the assignment operator. First, the return type of `operator=()` is `Name&`. Expressions involving the assignment operator have a value and a type, both of which are taken from the final value of the left-hand argument. In the following example, the value of `operator=()` is `2.0`, and the type is `double`.

```
double d1, d2;
void fn(double );
d1 = 2.0;                 // the value of this expression is 2.0
```

This is what enables the programmer to write the following:

```
d2 = d1 = 2.0
fn(d2 = 3.0);      // performs the assignment and passes the
                   // resulting value to fn()
```

The value of the assignment d1 = 2.0 (2.0) and the type (double) are passed to the assignment to d2. In the second example, the value of the assignment d2 = 3.0 is passed to the function fn().

The second detail is that operator=() was written as a member function. The left-hand argument is taken to be the current object (this). Unlike other operators, the assignment operator cannot be overloaded with a nonmember function.

Protecting the Escape Hatch

Providing your class with an assignment operator can add considerable flexibility to the application code. However, if this is too much work or if you don't want C++ to make copies of your object, overloading the assignment operator with a protected function will keep anyone from accidentally making an unauthorized member-by-member shallow copy, as illustrated here:

```
class Name
{
  //...just like before...
  protected:
    // copy constructor
    Name(Name&) {}
    //assignment operator
    Name& operator=(Name& s) { return *this; }
};
```

With this definition, assignments such as the following are precluded:

```
void fn(Name &n)
{
    Name newN;
    newN = n;        //generates a compiler error -
                     //function has no access to op=()
}
```

This copy protection for classes saves you the trouble of overloading the assignment operator but reduces the flexibility of your class.

If your class allocates resources such as memory off the heap, you *must* either write a satisfactory assignment operator and copy constructor or make both protected to preclude the default provided by C++ from being used.

Chapter 24

Using Stream I/O

*P*rograms appearing before this chapter read from the cin input object and output through the cout output object. Perhaps you haven't really thought about it much, but this input/output technique is a subset of what is known as *stream I/O*.

In this chapter, I describe stream I/O in more detail. I must warn you that stream I/O is too large a topic to be covered completely in a single chapter — entire books are devoted to this one topic. Fortunately for both of us, there isn't all that much that you need to know about stream I/O in order to write the vast majority of programs.

How Stream I/O Works

Stream I/O is based on overloaded versions of operator>>() and operator<<(). The declaration of these overloaded operators is found in the include file iostream, which are included in all the programs beginning in Chapter 1. The code for these functions is included in the standard library, which your C++ program links with.

The following code shows just a few of the prototypes appearing in iostream:

```
//for input we have:
istream& operator>>(istream& source, char *pDest);
istream& operator>>(istream& source, int  &dest);
istream& operator>>(istream& source, char &dest);
```

```
//...and so forth...

//for output we have:
ostream& operator<<(ostream& dest, char *pSource);
ostream& operator<<(ostream& dest, int   source);
ostream& operator<<(ostream& dest, char  source);
//...and so it goes...
```

When overloaded to perform I/O, operator>>() is called the *extractor,* and operator<<() is called the *inserter.* The class istream is the basic class for input from a file or a device like the keyboard. C++ opens the istream object cin when the program starts. Similarly, ostream is the basis for file output. cout is a default ostream object.

Take a detailed look at what happens when you write the following code, which is named DefaultStreamOutput and found on this book's CD-ROM:

```
// DefaultStreamOutput
#include <iostream>
using namespace std;

void fn(ostream& out)
{
    out << "My name is Stephen\n";
}
int main(int nNumberofArgs, char* pszArgs[])
{
    fn(cout);
    system("PAUSE");
    return 0;
}
```

The program passes cout to the function fn(). fn() applies the << operator, otherwise known as operator<<(). Thus, C++ determines that the best match is the operator<<(ostream&, char*) function. C++ generates a call to this function, the so-called char* inserter, passing the function the ostream object cout and the string "My name is Randy\n" as arguments. That is, it makes the call operator<<(cout, "My name is Randy\n"). The char* inserter function, which is part of the standard C++ library, performs the requested output.

The ostream and istream classes form the base of a set of classes that connects the application code with the outside world, including input from and output to the file system. How did the compiler know that cout is of class ostream? This and a few other global objects are also declared in iostream. h. A list is shown in Table 24-1. These objects are constructed automatically at program startup, before main() gets control. Subclasses of ostream and istream are used for input and output to files and internal buffers.

Table 24-1	Standard Stream I/O Objects	
Object	*Class*	*Purpose*
cin	istream	Standard input
cout	ostream	Standard output
cerr	ostream	Standard error output
clog	ostream	Standard printer output

The fstream Subclasses

The subclasses ofstream, ifstream, and fstream are defined in the include file fstream.h to perform stream input and output to a disk file. These three classes offer a large number of member functions. A complete list is provided with your compiler documentation, but let me get you started.

Class ofstream, which is used to perform file output, has several constructors, the most useful of which is the following:

```
ofstream::ofstream(char *pszFileName,
                   int mode = ios::out,
                   int prot = filebuff::openprot);
```

The first argument is a pointer to the name of the file to open. The second and third arguments specify how the file will be opened. The legal values for mode are listed in Table 24-2, and those for prot are in Table 24-3. These values are bit fields that are ORed together (the classes ios and filebuff are both parent classes of ostream). (See Chapter 4 for an explanation of the ORing of bit fields.)

The expression ios::out refers to a static data member of the class ios.

Table 24-2	Constants Defined in ios to Control How Files Are Opened
Flag	*Meaning*
ios::app	Append to the end of the line. Generate an error if the file doesn't already exist.
ios::ate	Append to the end of the file, if it exists.
ios::in	Open file for input (implied for istream).

(continued)

Table 24-2 (continued)

Flag	Meaning
ios::out	Open file for output (implied for ostream).
ios::trunc	Truncate file if it exists (default).
ios::noreplace	If file does exist, return error.
ios::binary	Open file in binary mode (alternative is text mode).

Table 24-3   Values for prot in the ofstream Constructor

Flag	Meaning
filebuf::openprot	Compatibility sharing mode
filebuf::sh_none	Exclusive; no sharing
filebuf::sh_read	Read sharing allowed
filebuf::sh_write	Write sharing allowed

For example, the following StreamOutput program opens the file `MyName.txt` and then writes some important and absolutely true information to that file:

```
// StreamOutput - simple output to a file
#include <fstream>
using namespace std;

int main(int nNumberofArgs, char* pszArgs[])
{
    ofstream my("MyName.txt");
    my << "Stephen Davis is suave and handsome\n"
       << "and definitely not balding prematurely"
       << endl;
    system("PAUSE");
    return 0;
}
```

The constructor `ofstream::ofstream(char*)` expects only a filename and provides defaults for the other file modes. If the file `MyName.txt` already exists, it is truncated; otherwise, `MyName.txt` is created. In addition, the file is opened in compatibility sharing mode.

Referring to Table 24-2, if I wanted to open the file in binary mode and append to the end of the file if the file already exists, I would create the ostream object as follows. (In binary mode, newlines are not converted to carriage returns and line feeds on output, nor are carriage returns and line feeds converted back to newlines on input.)

```
void fn()
{
    //open the binary file BINFILE for writing; if it
    //exists, append to end of whatever's already there

    ofstream bfile("BINFILE", ios::binary | ios::ate);
    //...continue on as before...
}
```

The stream objects maintain state information about the I/O process. The member function bad() returns a TRUE if something "bad" happens. That nebulous term means that the file couldn't be opened, some internal object was messed up, or things are just generally hosed. A lesser error fail() indicates that either something bad() happened or the last read failed — for example, if you try to read an int and all the program can find is a character that rates a fail() but not a bad(). The member function good() returns TRUE if both bad() and fail() are FALSE. The member function clear() zeros out the error flag to give you another chance. The following program adds basic error checking to the StreamOutput program:

```
// StreamOutputWithErrorChecking - simple output to a file
#include <fstream>
#include <iostream>
using namespace std;

int main(int nNumberofArgs, char* pszArgs[])
{
    const static char fileName[] = "MyName.txt";
    ofstream my(fileName);
    if (my.bad())           //if the open didn't work...
    {
        cerr << "Error opening file "
             << fileName
             << endl;
        return 0;           //...output error and quit
    }
    my << "Stephen Davis is suave and handsome\n"
       << "and definitely not balding prematurely"
       << endl;
    if (my.bad())
    {
        cerr << "Error writing to file "
             << fileName
             << endl;
    }
    system("PAUSE");
    return 0;
}
```

All attempts to output to an `ofstream` object that has an error have no effect if `my.bad()` is true.

This last paragraph is meant quite literally — no output is possible as long as the internal error state is non-zero. The program won't even try until you call `clear()` to clear the error flags.

The destructor for class `ofstream` automatically closes the file. In the preceding example, the file was closed when the function exited.

Class `ifstream` works much the same way for input, as the following example demonstrates:

```
// StreamInput - simple input from a file using fstream
#include <fstream>
#include <iostream>
using namespace std;

ifstream* openFile()
{
    ifstream* pFileStream = 0;
    for(;;)
    {
        // open the file specified by the user
        char fileName[80];
        cout << "Enter the name of a file with integers" <<
            endl;
        cin >> fileName;

        //open file for reading; don't create the file
        //if it isn't there
        pFileStream = new ifstream(fileName);
        if (pFileStream->good())
        {
            break;
        }
        cerr << "Couldn't open " << fileName << endl;
        delete pFileStream;
    }
    return pFileStream;
}

int main(int nNumberofArgs, char* pszArgs[])
{
    // get a file stream
    ifstream* pFileStream = openFile();

    // stop when no more data in file
    while (!pFileStream->eof())
    {
        // read a value
        int nValue = 0;
```

```
        (*pFileStream) >> nValue;

        // stop if the file read failed (probably because
        // we ran upon something that's not an int or
        // because we found a new line with nothing after it)
        if (pFileStream->fail())
        {
            break;
        }

        // output the value just read
        cout << nValue << endl;
    }

    system("PAUSE");
    return 0;
}
```

The function openFile() prompts the user for the name of a file to open. The function creates an ifstream() object with the specified name. Creating an ifstream object automatically opens the file for input. If the file is opened properly, the function returns a pointer to the ifstream object to use for reading. Otherwise, the program deletes the object and tries again. The only way to get out of the loop is to enter a valid filename or abort the program.

Don't forget to delete the pFileStream object if the open fails. These are the sneaky ways that memory leaks creep in.

The program reads integer values from the object pointed at by pFileStream until either fail() or the program reaches the End-Of-File as indicated by the member function eof(). An attempt to read an ifstream object that has the error flag set, indicating a previous error, returns immediately without reading anything.

Let me warn you one more time: Not only is nothing returned from reading an input stream that has an error, but also the buffer comes back unchanged. This program can easily come to the false conclusion that it has just read the same value it previously read. Furthermore, eof() will never return a true on an input stream that has an error.

The output from this program appears as follows (I added boldface to my input):

```
Enter the name of a file with integers
chicken
Couldn't open chicken
Enter the name of a file with integers
integers.txt
1
2
3
```

```
4
5
6
Press any key to continue . . .
```

Reading Directly from a Stream

The inserter and extracter operators provide a convenient mechanism for reading formatted input. However, there are times when you just want to say, "give it to me, I don't care what the format is." There are two methods that are useful in this context. The function getline() returns a string of characters up until some terminator — the default is a newline. getline() strips off the terminator but makes no other attempt to reformat or otherwise interpret the input.

The member function read() is even more fundamental. This function reads the number of characters that you specify, or less if the program encounters an end-of-file. The function gcount() always returns the actual number of characters read.

The following program uses both getLine() and read() to open a file with random contents and spit them out to the display.

```cpp
// FileInput - read blocks of data from a file
#include <fstream>
#include <iostream>
using namespace std;

ifstream* openFile(istream& input)
{
    for(;;)
    {
        // open the file specified by the user
        char fileName[80];
        cout << "Enter the name of a file" << endl;

        // read input from the user in such a way
        // that the input can't overflow the buffer
        input.getline(fileName, 80);

        //open file for reading; don't create the file
        //if it isn't there
        ifstream* pFileStream = new ifstream(fileName);
        if (pFileStream->good())
        {
            return pFileStream;
        }
        cerr << "Couldn't find " << fileName << endl;
    }
```

```
        return 0;
}

int main(int nNumberofArgs, char* pszArgs[])
{
    // get a file stream
    ifstream* pFileStream = openFile(cin);

    // read blocks of data 80 bytes at a time
    char buffer[80];
    while (!pFileStream->eof() && pFileStream->good())
    {
        // read a block - 80 is the max but gcount() returns
        // the actual number of bytes read
        pFileStream->read(buffer, 80);
        int noBytes = pFileStream->gcount();

        // do something with the block
        for(int i = 0; i < noBytes; i++)
        {
            cout << buffer[i];
        }
    }

    system("PAUSE");
    return 0;
}
```

The FileInput program first invokes openFile() to open a file. This version demonstrates two interesting aspects. First, the function reads from an istream object in the same way that it would read from cin. In fact, the main() function passes the cin object. However, a function that uses an arbitrary istream object can read from input files without modification.

The openFile() uses the getline() member function to read a string. One of the arguments to the function is the size of the buffer. getline() will not read beyond this point. Thus, getline(fileName, 80) reads up to the end of the line but not more than 80 characters and stores the result into the character buffer fileName.

Using the getline() function to read keyboard input is safer than using the extractor when reading into a simple character array — the extractor can read beyond the end of the array. The getline() function will not read more than the number of characters you specify.

The main() function reads 80 byte blocks from the file stream object returned from openFile(). The program checks the actual number of characters read using the gcount() function. The number returned from gcount() will never be more than the 80 bytes specified in the call to read() and will only be less when the program reaches the end-of-file. The program uses the conventional inserter to display the characters read.

The FileInput program simply outputs the contents of the file that you specify as shown in the following sample run:

```
Enter the name of a file
MyName.txt
Stephen Davis is suave and handsome
and definitely not balding prematurely
Press any key to continue . . .
```

What's Up with endl?

Most programs in this book terminate an output stream by inserting the object endl. However, some programs include a \n within the text to output a newline. What's the deal?

The \n is, in fact, the newline character. The expression cout << "First line\nSecond line; outputs two lines. The endl object outputs a newline, but continues one step further.

Disks are slow devices. Writing to disk more often than necessary will slow your program down considerably. To avoid this, the fstream class collects up output into an internal buffer. The class writes the contents to disk when the buffer is full (this is known as flushing the buffer). The endl object automatically flushes the output buffer. The member function flush() flushes the output buffer without tacking a newline onto the end.

Using the strstream Subclasses

The stream classes give the programmer mechanisms for easily breaking input among int, float, and char array variables (among others). A set of so-called "string stream" classes allow the program to "read" from an array of characters in memory. The classes istringstream and ostringstream are defined in the include file sstream.

The older versions of these are classes are istrstream and ostrstream defined in the include file strstream.

The string stream classes have the same semantics as the corresponding file based classes. This is demonstrated in the following StringStream program that parses account information from a file:

```
// StringStream - read and parse the contents of a file
#include <fstream>
#include <sstream>
#include <iostream>
```

```
using namespace std;

// parseAccountInfo - read a passed buffer as if it were
//                    an actual file - read the following
//                    format:
//                     name, account balance
//                    return true if all worked well
bool parseString(char* pString, char* pName, int arraySize,
                 long& accountNum, double& balance)
{
    // associate an istrstream object with the input
    // character string
    istringstream inp(pString);

    // read up to the comma separator
    inp.getline(pName, arraySize, ',');

    // now the account number
    inp >> accountNum;

    // and the balance
    inp >> balance;

    // return the error status
    return !inp.fail();
}

int main(int nNumberofArgs, char* pszArgs[])
{
    // get a file stream
    ifstream* pFileStream = new ifstream("Accounts.txt");
    if (!pFileStream->good())
    {
        cout << "Can't open Accounts.txt" << endl;
        return 0;
    }

    // read a line out of file, parse it and display results
    for(;;)
    {
        // add a divider
        cout << "===============================" << endl;
        // read a buffer
        char buffer[256];
        pFileStream->getline(buffer, 256);
        if (pFileStream->fail())
        {
            break;
        }

        // parse the individual fields
        char name[80];
        long accountNum;
```

```
        double balance;
        bool result = parseString(buffer, name, 80,
                                  accountNum, balance);

        // output the result
        cout << buffer << "\n";
        if (result == false)
        {
            cout << "Error parsing string\n";
            continue;
        }
        cout << "name = " << name << ","
             << "account = " << accountNum << ", "
             << "balance = " << balance << endl;

        // put the fields back together in a different
        // order (inserting the 'ends' makes sure the
        // buffer is null terminated
        ostringstream out;
        out << name << ", "
            << balance << " "
            << accountNum << ends;

        // output the result - istringstream also works with
        // the string class but I have been staying with
        // character arrays until the discussion of the
        //   templates
        string oString = out.str();
        cout << oString << "\n" << endl;
    }

    system("PAUSE");
    return 0;
}
```

This program begins by opening a file called `Accounts.txt` containing account information in the format of: *name, accountNumber, balance,\n*. Assuming that the file was opened successfully, the program enters a loop, reading lines until the contents of the file are exhausted. The call to `getline()` reads up to the default newline terminator. The program passes the line just read to the function `parseString()`.

`parseString()` associates an `istringstream` object with the character string. The program reads characters up to the `','` (or the end of the string buffer) using the `getline()` member function. The program then uses the conventional extractors to read `accountNum` and `balance`. The reads from `inp` will have worked if `inp.fail()` returns a `false`.

After the call to `parseString()`, `main()` outputs the buffer read from the file followed by the parsed values. It then uses the `ostringstream` class to reconstruct a `string` object with the same data but a different format.

The result from a sample execution appears as follows:

```
==============================
Chester, 12345 56.60
name = Chester,account = 12345, balance = 56.6
Chester, 56.6 12345

==============================
Arthur,  34567 67.50
name = Arthur,account = 34567, balance = 67.5
Arthur, 67.5 34567

==============================
Trudie,  56x78 78.90
Error parsing string
==============================
Valerie, 78901 89.10
name = Valerie,account = 78901, balance = 89.1
Valerie, 89.1 78901

==============================
Press any key to continue . . .
```

Reflect a second before continuing. Notice how the program was able to resynch itself after the error in the input file. Notice, also, the simplicity of the heart of the program, the parseString() function. Consider what this function would look like without the benefit of the istringstream class.

Manipulating Manipulators

You can use stream I/O to output numbers and character strings by using default formats. Usually the defaults are fine, but sometimes they don't cut it.

For example, I was less than tickled when the total from the result of a financial calculation from a recent program appeared as 249.600006 rather than 249.6 (or, better yet, 249.60). There must be a way to bend the defaults to my desires. True to form, C++ provides not one but two ways to control the format of output.

Depending on the default settings of your compiler, you may get 249.6 as your output. Nevertheless, you really want 249.60.

First, you can control the format by invoking a series of member functions on the stream object. For example, the number of significant digits to display is set by using the function precision() as follows:

```
#include <iostream.h>
void fn(float interest, float dollarAmount)
{
    cout << "Dollar amount = ";
    cout.precision(2);
    cout << dollarAmount;
    cout.precision(4);
    cout << interest
         << "\n";
}
```

In this example, the function precision() sets the precision to 2 immediately before outputting the value dollarAmount. This gives you a number such as 249.60, the type of result you want. It then sets the precision to 4 before outputting the interest.

A second approach uses what are called manipulators. (Sounds like someone behind the scenes of the New York Stock Exchange, doesn't it? Well, manipulators are every bit as sneaky.) *Manipulators* are objects defined in the include file iomanip.h to have the same effect as the member function calls. (You must include iomanip.h to have access to the manipulators.) The only advantage to manipulators is that the program can insert them directly into the stream rather than resort to a separate function call.

If you rewrite the preceding example to use manipulators, the program appears as follows:

```
#include <iostream.h>
#include <iomanip.h>
void fn(float interest, float dollarAmount)
{
    cout << "Dollar amount = "
         << setprecision(2) << dollarAmount
         << setprecision(4) << interest
         << "\n";
}
```

The most common manipulators and their corresponding meanings are shown in Table 24-4.

Table 24-4	Common Manipulators and Stream Format Control Functions	
Manipulator	**Member Function**	**Description**
dec	flags(10)	Set radix to 10
hex	flags(16)	Set radix to 16

Manipulator	Member Function	Description
oct	flags(8)	Set radix to 8
setfill(c)	fill(c)	Set the fill character to c
setprecision(c)	precision(c)	Set display precision to c
setw(n)	width(n)	Set width of field to n characters*

This returns to its default value after the next field is output.

Watch out for the width parameter (width() function and setw() manipulator). Most parameters retain their value until they are specifically reset by a subsequent call, but the width parameter does not. The width parameter is reset to its default value as soon as the next output is performed. For example, you might expect the following to produce two eight-character integers:

```
#include <iostream.h>
#include <iomanip.h>
void fn()
{
    cout << setw(8)     // width is 8...
         << 10          //...for the 10, but...
         << 20          //...default for the 20
         << "\n";
}
```

What you get, however, is an eight-character integer followed by a two-character integer. To get two eight-character output fields, the following is necessary:

```
#include <iostream.h>
#include <iomanip.h>
void fn()
{
    cout << setw(8)     // set the width...
         << 10
         << setw(8)     //...now reset it
         << 20
         << "\n";
}
```

Thus, if you have several objects to output and the default width is not good enough, you must include a setw() call for each object.

Which way is better, manipulators or member function calls? Member functions provide a bit more control because there are more of them. In addition, the member functions always return the previous setting so you know how to restore it (if you want to). Finally, a query version of each member function exists to enable you to just ask what the current setting is without changing it, as shown in the following example:

```
#include <iostream.h>
void fn(float value)
{
    int previousPrecision;
    // ...doing stuff here...
    // you can ask what the current precision is:
    previousPrecision = cout.precision();

    // or you can save the old value when you change it
    previousPrecision = cout.precision(2);
    cout << value;

    // now restore the precision to previous value
    cout.precision(previousPrecision);

    //...do more neat stuff...

}
```

Even with all these features, the manipulators are more common than member function calls, probably because they look neat. Use whatever you prefer, but be prepared to see both in other peoples' code.

Chapter 25

Handling Errors — Exceptions

• •

In This Chapter

▶ Introducing an exceptional way of handling program errors

▶ Finding what's wrong with good ol' error returns

▶ Examining throwing and catching exceptions

▶ Packing more heat into that throw

• •

1 know that it's hard to accept, but occasionally functions don't work properly — not even mine. The traditional means of reporting failure is to return some indication to the caller. C++ includes a new, improved mechanism for capturing and handling errors called *exceptions.* An exception is "a case in which a rule or principle does not apply." Exception is also defined as an objection to something. Either definition works: An exception is an unexpected (and presumably objectionable) condition that occurs during the execution of the program.

The exception mechanism is based on the keywords `try`, `catch`, and `throw` (that's right, more variable names that you can't use). In outline, it works like this: A function *try*s to get through a piece of code. If the code detects a problem, it *throw*s an error indication that the calling function must *catch*.

The following code snippet demonstrates how that works in 1s and 0s:

```
//
//  FactorialException - demonstrate exceptions using
//                       a factorial function
//
#include <cstdio>
#include <cstdlib>
#include <iostream>
using namespace std;

// factorial - compute factorial
int factorial(int n)
{
    // you can't handle negative values of n;
    // better check for that condition first
    if (n < 0)
```

```
    {
        throw string("Argument for factorial negative");
    }

    // go ahead and calculate factorial
    int accum = 1;
    while(n > 0)
    {
        accum *= n;
        n--;
    }
    return accum;
}

int main(int nNumberofArgs, char* pszArgs[])
{
    try
    {
        // this will work
        cout << "Factorial of 3 is " << factorial(3) << endl;

        // this will generate an exception
        cout << "Factorial of -1 is " << factorial(-1) <<
            endl;

        // control will never get here
        cout << "Factorial of 5 is " << factorial(5) << endl;
    }
    // control passes here
    catch(string error)
    {
        cout << "Error occurred: " << error << endl;

    }
    catch(...)
    {
        cout << "Default catch " << endl;
    }

    // wait until user is ready before terminating program
    // to allow the user to see the program results
    system("PAUSE");
    return 0;
}
```

main() starts out by creating a block outfitted with the try keyword. Within this block, it can proceed on the way it would if the block were not present. In this case, main() attempts to calculate the factorial of a negative number. Not to be hoodwinked, the clever factorial() function detects the bogus request and throws an error indication using the throw keyword. Control passes to the catch phrase, which immediately follows the closing brace of the try block. The second call to factorial() is not performed.

Justifying a New Error Mechanism?

What's wrong with error returns like FORTRAN used to make? Factorials cannot be negative, so I could have said something like "Okay, if `factorial()` detects an error, it returns a negative number. The actual value indicates the source of the problem." What's wrong with that? That's how it's been accomplished for ages.

Unfortunately, several problems arise. First, although it's true that the result of a factorial can't be negative, other functions aren't so lucky. For example, you can't take the log of a negative number either, but the negative return value trick won't work here — logarithms can be either negative or positive.

Second, there's just so much information that you can store in an integer. Maybe you can have –1 for "argument is negative" and –2 for "argument is too large." But, if the argument is too large, you want to know what the argument is, because that information might help you debug the problem. There's no place to store that type of information.

Third, the processing of error returns is optional. Suppose someone writes `factorial()` so that it dutifully checks the argument and returns a negative number if the argument is out of range. If a function that calls `factorial()` doesn't check the error return, returning an error value doesn't do any good. Sure, you can make all kinds of menacing threats, such as "You will check your error returns or else," and the programmer may have the best of intentions, but you all know that people get lazy and return to their old, non-error-checking ways.

Even if you do check the error return from `factorial()` or any other function, what can the function do with the error? It can probably do nothing more than output an error message of your own and return another error indication to the caller, which probably does the same. Pretty soon, all code begins to have the following appearance:

```
// call some function, check the error return, handle it,
// and return
errRtn = someFunc();
if (errRtn)
{
  errorOut("Error on call to someFunc()");
  return MY_ERROR_1;
}
errRtn = someOtherFunc();
if (errRtn)
{
  errorOut("Error on call to someOtherFunc()");
  return MY_ERROR_1;
}
```

This mechanism has several problems:

- ✔ It's highly repetitive.
- ✔ It forces the user to invent and keep track of numerous error return indications.
- ✔ It mixes the error-handling code into the normal code flow, thereby obscuring the normal, non-error path.

These problems don't seem so bad in this simple example, but they become increasingly worse as the calling code becomes more complex. The result is that error-handling code doesn't get written to handle all the conditions that it should.

The exception mechanism addresses these problems by removing the error path from the normal code path. Furthermore, exceptions make error handling obligatory. If your function doesn't handle the thrown exception, control passes up the chain of called functions until C++ finds a function to handle the error. This also gives you the flexibility to ignore errors that you can't do anything about anyway. Only the functions that can actually correct the problem need to catch the exception.

Examining the Exception Mechanism

Take a closer look at the steps that the code goes through to handle an exception. When the throw occurs, C++ first copies the thrown object to some neutral place. It then begins looking for the end of the current try block.

If a try block is not found in the current function, control passes to the calling function. A search is then made of that function. If no try block is found there, control passes to the function that called it, and so on up the stack of calling functions. This process is called *unwinding the stack*.

An important feature of stack unwinding is that as each stack is unwound, objects that go out of scope are destructed just as though the function had executed a return statement. This keeps the program from losing assets or leaving objects dangling.

When the encasing try block is found, the code searches the first catch phrase immediately following the closing brace of the catch block. If the object thrown matches the type of argument specified in the catch statement, control passes to that catch phrase. If not, a check is made of the next catch phrase. If no matching catch phrases are found, the code searches for the next higher level try block in an ever-outward spiral until an appropriate catch can be found. If no catch phrase is found, the program is terminated.

Consider the following example:

```
// CascadingException - note that the following program
//                      may generate warnings because the
//                      variables f, i and pMsg
//                      are not used for anything - the
//                      compiler is trying to give you a
//                      hint that maybe you don't
//                      need the arguments at all
#include <cstdio>
#include <cstdlib>
#include <iostream>
using namespace std;

class Obj
{
  public:
    Obj(char c)
    {
        label = c;
        cout << "Constructing object " << label << endl;
    }
    ~Obj()
    {
        cout << "Destructing object " << label << endl;
    }

  protected:
    char label;
};

void f1();
void f2();
int f3()
{
    Obj a('a');
    try
    {
        Obj b('b');
        f1();
    }
    catch(float f)
    {
        cout << "Float catch" << endl;
    }
    catch(int i)
    {
        cout << "Int catch" << endl;
    }
    catch(...)
    {
        cout << string("Generic catch") << endl;
    }
}
```

```
int main(int nNumberofArgs, char* pszArgs[])
{
    f3();

    // wait until user is ready before terminating program
    // to allow the user to see the program results
    system("PAUSE");
    return 0;
}

void f1()
{
    try
    {
        Obj c('c');
        f2();
    }
    catch(string msg)
    {
        cout << "String catch" << endl;
    }
}
void f2()
{
    Obj d('d');
    throw 10;
}
```

The output from executing this program appears as follows:

```
Constructing object a
Constructing object b
Constructing object c
Constructing object d
Destructing object d
Destructing object c
Destructing object b
Int catch
Destructing object a
Press any key to continue . . .
```

First, you see the four objects a, b, c, and d being constructed as control passes through each declaration before f2() throws the int 10. Because no try block is defined in f2(), C++ unwinds f2()'s stack, causing object d to be destructed. f1() defines a try block, but its only catch phrase is designed to handle char*, which doesn't match the int thrown. Therefore, C++ continues looking. This unwinds f1()'s stack, resulting in object c being destructed.

Back in f3(), C++ finds another try block. Exiting that block causes object b to go out of scope. The first catch phrase is designed to catch floats that don't match the int, so it's skipped. The next catch phrase matches the int exactly, so control stops there. The final catch phrase, which would catch any object thrown, is skipped because a matching catch phrase was already found.

What Kinds of Things Can I Throw?

The thing following the throw keyword is actually an expression that creates an object of some kind. In the examples so far, I've thrown an int and a string object, but throw can handle any type of object. This means that you can throw almost as much information as you want. Consider the following update to the factorial program, CustomExceptionClass:

```
//
//   CustomExceptionClass - demonstrate exceptions using
//                          a factorial function
//
#include <cstdio>
#include <cstdlib>
#include <iostream>
#include <sstream>
using namespace std;

// Exception - generic exception handling class
class Exception
{
  public:
    Exception(char* pMsg, int n, char* pFile, int nLine)
      : msg(pMsg), errorValue(n), file(pFile), lineNum(nLine)
    {}

    virtual string display()
    {
        ostringstream out;
        out << "Error <" << msg
            << " - value is " << errorValue
            << ">\n";
        out << " @" << file << "-" << lineNum << endl;
        return out.str();
    }
  protected:
    // error message
    string msg;
    int    errorValue;

    // file name and line number where error occurred
    string file;
    int lineNum;
};

// factorial - compute factorial
```

```
int factorial(int n)
{
    // you can't handle negative values of n;
    // better check for that condition first
    if (n < 0)
    {
        throw Exception("Argument for factorial negative",
                        n, __FILE__, __LINE__);
    }

    // go ahead and calculate factorial
    int accum = 1;
    while(n > 0)
    {
        accum *= n;
        n--;
    }
    return accum;
}

int main(int nNumberofArgs, char* pszArgs[])
{
    try
    {
        // this will work
        cout << "Factorial of 3 is " << factorial(3) << endl;

        // this will generate an exception
        cout << "Factorial of -1 is " << factorial(-1) <<
            endl;
    }
    // control passes here
    catch(Exception e)
    {
        cout << "Error occurred: \n" << e.display() << endl;
    }

    // wait until user is ready before terminating program
    // to allow the user to see the program results
    system("PAUSE");
    return 0;
}
```

This program appears much the same as the factorial program at the beginning of this chapter. The difference is the use of a user-defined Exception class that contains more information concerning the nature of the error than a simple string contains. The factorial program is able to throw the error message, the illegal value, and the exact location where the error occurred.

__FILE__ and __LINE__ are intrinsic *#defines* that are set to the name of the source file and the current line number in that file, respectively.

The catch snags the `Exception` object and then uses the built-in `display()` member function to display the error message. The output from this program appears as follows:

```
Factorial of 3 is 6
Error occurred:
Error <Argument for factorial negative - value is -1>
 @//cpp_programs/Chap25/CustomExceptionClass.cpp-46

Press any key to continue . . .
```

The `Exception` class represents a generic error-reporting class. However, you can inherit from this class to provide further detail for a particular type of error. For example, I can define an `InvalidArgumentException` class that stores the value of the invalid argument in addition to the message and location of the error:

```cpp
class InvalidArgumentException : public Exception
{
  public:
    InvalidArgumentException(int arg,
                             char* pFile,
                             int nLine)
          : Exception("Invalid argument", pFile, nLine)
    {
        invArg = arg;
    }

    virtual void display(ostream& out)
    {
        Exception::display(out);
        out << "Argument was " << invArg << endl;
    }

  protected:
    int invArg;
};
```

The calling function automatically handles the new `InvalidArgument Exception` because an `InvalidArgumentException` is an `Exception` and the `display()` member function is polymorphic.

Chapter 26

Inheriting Multiple Inheritance

. . . .

In This Chapter

▶ Introducing multiple inheritance

▶ Avoiding ambiguities with multiple inheritance

▶ Avoiding ambiguities with virtual inheritance

▶ Figuring out the ordering rules for multiple constructors

▶ Getting a handle on problems with multiple inheritance

. . . .

*I*n the class hierarchies discussed in other chapters, each class has inherited from a single parent. Such single inheritance is sufficient to describe most real-world relationships. Some classes, however, represent the blending of two classes into one. (Sounds sort of romantic, doesn't it.)

An example of such a class is the sleeper sofa. As the name implies, it is a sofa and a bed (although not a very comfortable bed). Thus, the sleeper sofa should be allowed to inherit bed-like properties. To address this situation, C++ allows a derived class to inherit from more than one base class. This is called *multiple inheritance*.

Describing the Multiple Inheritance Mechanism

To see how multiple inheritance works, look at the sleeper sofa example. Figure 26-1 shows the inheritance graph for class `SleeperSofa`. Notice how this class inherits from class `Sofa` and from class `Bed`. In this way, it inherits the properties of both.

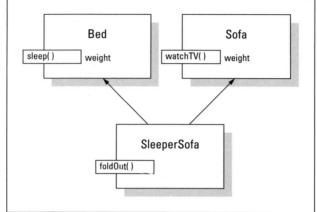

Figure 26-1:
Class
hierarchy of
a sleeper
sofa.

The code to implement class SleeperSofa looks like the following:

```
//
//  MultipleInheritance - a single class can inherit from
//                        more than one base class
//
#include <cstdio>
#include <cstdlib>
#include <iostream>
using namespace std;

class Bed
{
  public:
    Bed(){}
    void sleep(){ cout << "Sleep" << endl; }
    int weight;
};

class Sofa
{
  public:
    Sofa(){}
    void watchTV(){ cout << "Watch TV" << endl; }
    int weight;
};

// SleeperSofa - is both a Bed and a Sofa
class SleeperSofa : public Bed, public Sofa
{
  public:
    SleeperSofa(){}
    void foldOut(){ cout << "Fold out" << endl; }
};
```

```
int main(int nNumberofArgs, char* pszArgs[])
{
    SleeperSofa ss;

    // you can watch TV on a sleeper sofa like a sofa...
    ss.watchTV();      // Sofa::watchTV()

    //...and then you can fold it out...
    ss.foldOut();      // SleeperSofa::foldOut()

    // ...and sleep on it
    ss.sleep();

    // wait until user is ready before terminating program
    // to allow the user to see the program results
    system("PAUSE");
    return 0;
}
```

Here the class `SleeperSofa` inherits from both `Bed` and `Sofa`. This is apparent from the appearance of both classes in the class declaration. `SleeperSofa` inherits all the members of both base classes. Thus, both of the calls `ss.sleep()` and `ss.watchTV()` are legal. You can use a `SleeperSofa` as a `Bed` or a `Sofa`. Plus the class `SleeperSofa` can have members of its own, such as `foldOut()`. The output of this program appears as follows:

```
Watch TV
Fold out
Sleep
Press any key to continue . . .
```

Is this a great country or what?

Straightening Out Inheritance Ambiguities

Although multiple inheritance is a powerful feature, it introduces several possible problems. One is apparent in the preceding example. Notice that both `Bed` and `Sofa` contain a member `weight`. This is logical because both have a measurable weight. The question is, "Which `weight` does `SleeperSofa` inherit?"

The answer is "both." `SleeperSofa` inherits a member `Bed::weight` and a separate member `Sofa::weight`. Because they have the same name, unqualified references to `weight` are now ambiguous. This is demonstrated in the following snippet:

```
#include <iostream.h>

void fn()
{
    SleeperSofa ss;
    cout << "weight = "
         << ss.weight    // illegal - which weight?
         << "\n";
}
```

The program must now indicate one of the two weights by specifying the desired base class. The following code snippet is correct:

```
#include <iostream.h>
void fn()
{
    SleeperSofa ss;
    cout << "sofa weight = "
         << ss.Sofa::weight  // specify which weight
         << "\n";
}
```

Although this solution corrects the problem, specifying the base class in the application function isn't desirable because it forces class information to leak outside the class into application code. In this case, fn() has to know that SleeperSofa inherits from Sofa. These types of so-called name collisions weren't possible with single inheritance but are a constant danger with multiple inheritance.

Adding Virtual Inheritance

In the case of SleeperSofa, the name collision on weight was more than a mere accident. A SleeperSofa doesn't have a bed weight separate from its sofa weight. The collision occurred because this class hierarchy does not completely describe the real world. Specifically, the classes have not been completely factored.

Thinking about it a little more, it becomes clear that both beds and sofas are special cases of a more fundamental concept: furniture. (I suppose I could get even more fundamental and use something like object with mass, but furniture is fundamental enough.) Weight is a property of all furniture. This relationship is shown in Figure 26-2.

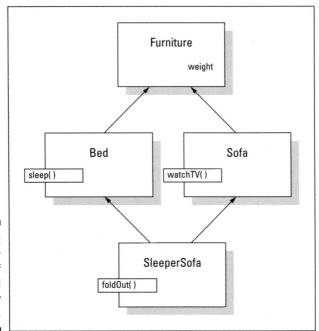

Figure 26-2:
Further
factoring of
beds and
sofas (by
weight).

Figure 26-2:
Further
factoring of
beds and
sofas (by
weight).

Factoring out the class Furniture should relieve the name collision. With much relief and great anticipation of success, I generate the C++ class hierarchy shown in the following program, MultipleInheritanceFactoring:

```
//
//   MultipleInheritanceFactoring - a single class can
//                    inherit from more than one base class
//
#include <cstdio>
#include <cstdlib>
#include <iostream>
using namespace std;

// Furniture - more fundamental concept; this class
//             has "weight" as a property
class Furniture
{
  public:
    Furniture(int w) : weight(w) {}
    int weight;
};

class Bed : public Furniture
```

```
{
  public:
    Bed(int weight) : Furniture(weight) {}
    void sleep(){ cout << "Sleep" << endl; }
};

class Sofa : public Furniture
{
  public:
    Sofa(int weight) : Furniture(weight) {}
    void watchTV(){ cout << "Watch TV" << endl; }
};

// SleeperSofa - is both a Bed and a Sofa
class SleeperSofa : public Bed, public Sofa
{
  public:
    SleeperSofa(int weight) : Sofa(weight), Bed(weight) {}
    void foldOut(){ cout << "Fold out" << endl; }
};

int main(int nNumberofArgs, char* pszArgs[])
{
    SleeperSofa ss(10);

    // Section 1 -
    // the following is ambiguous; is this a
    // Furniture::Sofa or a Furniture::Bed?
    /*
    cout << "Weight = "
         << ss.weight
         << endl;
     */

    // Section 2 -
    // the following specifies the inheritance path
    // unambiguously - sort of ruins the effect
    SleeperSofa* pSS = &ss;
    Sofa* pSofa = (Sofa*)pSS;
    Furniture* pFurniture = (Furniture*)pSofa;
    cout << "Weight = "
         << pFurniture->weight
         << endl;

    // wait until user is ready before terminating program
    // to allow the user to see the program results
    system("PAUSE");
    return 0;
}
```

Imagine my dismay when I find that this doesn't help at all — the reference to
weight in Section 1 of main() is still ambiguous. (I wish my weight were as
ambiguous!) "Okay," I say (not really understanding why weight is still ambiguous), "I'll try casting ss to a Furniture."

```
#include <iostream.h>

void fn()
{
  SleeperSofa ss;
  Furniture* pF;
  pF = (Furniture*)&ss; // use a Furniture pointer...
  cout << "weight = "    // ...to get at the weight
       << pF->weight
       << "\n";
};
```

Casting ss to a Furniture doesn't work either. Now, I get some strange message that the cast of SleeperSofa* to Furniture* is ambiguous. What's
going on?

The explanation is straightforward. SleeperSofa doesn't inherit from
Furniture directly. Both Bed and Sofa inherit from Furniture and then
SleeperSofa inherits from them. In memory, a SleeperSofa looks like
Figure 26-3.

You can see that a SleeperSofa consists of a complete Bed followed by a
complete Sofa followed by some SleeperSofa unique stuff. Each of these
subobjects in SleeperSofa has its own Furniture part, because each inherits from Furniture. Thus, a SleeperSofa contains two Furniture objects!

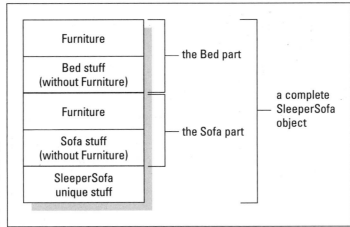

Figure 26-3:
Memory
layout of a
SleeperSofa.

I haven't created the hierarchy shown in Figure 26-2 after all. The inheritance hierarchy I have actually created is the one shown in Figure 26-4.

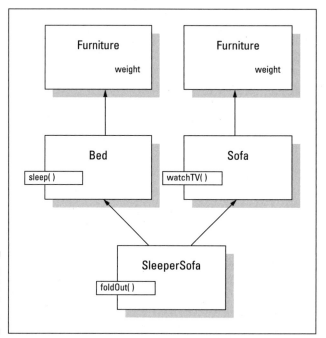

Figure 26-4:
Actual
result of my
first attempt.

The MultipleInheritanceFactoring program demonstrates this duplication of the base class. Section 2 specifies exactly which `weight` object by recasting the pointer `SleeperSofa` first to a `Sofa*` and then to a `Furniture*`.

But `SleeperSofa` containing two `Furniture` objects is nonsense. `SleeperSofa` needs only one copy of `Furniture`. I want `SleeperSofa` to inherit only one copy of `Furniture`, and I want `Bed` and `Sofa` to share that one copy. C++ calls this *virtual inheritance* because it uses the virtual keyword.

I hate this overloading of the term *virtual* because virtual inheritance has nothing to do with virtual functions.

Armed with this new knowledge, I return to class `SleeperSofa` and implement it as follows:

```
//
//  VirtualInheritance - using virtual inheritance the
//             Bed and Sofa classes can share a common base
//
#include <cstdio>
```

```
#include <cstdlib>
#include <iostream>
using namespace std;

// Furniture - more fundamental concept; this class
//             has "weight" as a property
class Furniture
{
  public:
    Furniture(int w = 0) : weight(w) {}
    int weight;
};

class Bed : virtual public Furniture
{
  public:
    Bed() {}
    void sleep(){ cout << "Sleep" << endl; }
};

class Sofa : virtual public Furniture
{
  public:
    Sofa(){}
    void watchTV(){ cout << "Watch TV" << endl; }
};

// SleeperSofa - is both a Bed and a Sofa
class SleeperSofa : public Bed, public Sofa
{
  public:
    SleeperSofa(int weight) : Furniture(weight) {}
    void foldOut(){ cout << "Fold out" << endl; }
};

int main(int nNumberofArgs, char* pszArgs[])
{
    SleeperSofa ss(10);

    // Section 1 -
    // the following is no longer ambiguous;
    // there's only one weight shared between Sofa and Bed
    // Furniture::Sofa or a Furniture::Bed?
    cout << "Weight = "
         << ss.weight
         << endl;

    // Section 2 -
    // the following specifies the inheritance path
    // unambiguously - sort of ruins the effect
    SleeperSofa* pSS = &ss;
    Sofa* pSofa = (Sofa*)pSS;
    Furniture* pFurniture = (Furniture*)pSofa;
```

```
        cout << "Weight = "
             << pFurniture->weight
             << endl;

        // wait until user is ready before terminating program
        // to allow the user to see the program results
        system("PAUSE");
        return 0;
}
```

Notice the addition of the keyword virtual in the inheritance of Furniture in Bed and Sofa. This says, "Give me a copy of Furniture unless you already have one somehow, in which case I'll just use that one." A SleeperSofa ends up looking like Figure 26-5 in memory.

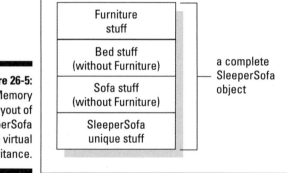

Figure 26-5:
Memory layout of SleeperSofa with virtual inheritance.

Here you can see that a SleeperSofa inherits Furniture, and then Bed minus the Furniture part, followed by Sofa minus the Furniture part. Bringing up the rear are the members unique to SleeperSofa. (Note that this may not be the order of the elements in memory, but that's not important for the purpose of this discussion.)

Now the reference in fn() to weight is not ambiguous because a SleeperSofa contains only one copy of Furniture. By inheriting Furniture virtually, you get the desired inheritance relationship as expressed in Figure 26-2.

If virtual inheritance solves this problem so nicely, why isn't it the norm? The first reason is that virtually inherited base classes are handled internally much differently than normally inherited base classes, and these differences involve extra overhead. The second reason is that sometimes you want two copies of the base class (although this is unusual).

As an example of the latter, consider a `TeacherAssistant` who is both a `Student` and a `Teacher`, both of which are subclasses of `Academician`. If the university gives its teaching assistants two IDs — a student ID and a separate teacher ID — the class `TeacherAssistant` will need to contain two copies of class `Academician`.

Constructing the Objects of Multiple Inheritance

The rules for constructing objects need to be expanded to handle multiple inheritance. The constructors are invoked in the following order:

1. First, the constructor for any virtual base classes is called in the order in which the classes are inherited.

2. Then the constructor for all nonvirtual base classes is called in the order in which the classes are inherited.

3. Next, the constructor for all member objects is called in the order in which the member objects appear in the class.

4. Finally, the constructor for the class itself is called.

Notice that base classes are constructed in the order in which they are inherited and not in the order in which they appear on the constructor line.

Voicing a Contrary Opinion

I should point out that not all object-oriented practitioners think that multiple inheritance is a good idea. In addition, many object-oriented languages don't support multiple inheritance.

Multiple inheritance is not an easy thing for the language to implement. This is mostly the compiler's problem (or the compiler writer's problem). But multiple inheritance adds overhead to the code when compared to single inheritance, and this overhead can become the programmer's problem.

More importantly, multiple inheritance opens the door to additional errors. First, ambiguities such as those mentioned in the earlier section "Straightening Out Inheritance Ambiguities" pop up. Second, in the presence of multiple inheritance, casting a pointer from a subclass to a base class often involves changing the value of the pointer in sophisticated and mysterious ways. Let me leave the details to the language lawyers and compiler writers.

I suggest that you avoid using multiple inheritance until you're comfortable with C++. Single inheritance provides enough expressive power to get used to. Later, you can study the manuals until you're sure that you understand exactly what's going on when you use multiple inheritance. One exception is the use of commercial libraries such as Microsoft's Foundation Classes (MFC), which use multiple inheritance quite a bit. These classes have been checked out and are safe.

Don't get me wrong. I'm not out and out against multiple inheritance. The fact that Microsoft and others use multiple inheritance effectively in their class libraries proves that it can be done. However, multiple inheritance is a feature that you want to hold off on using until you're ready for it.

Chapter 27

Tempting C++ Templates

● ●

In This Chapter

▶ Examining how templates can be applied to functions

▶ Combining common functions into a single template definition

▶ Defining a template or class

▶ Reviewing the advantages of a template over the more generic "void" approach

● ●

*T*he Standard C++ Library provides a set of basic functions. The C++ library presents a complete set of math, time, input/output, and DOS operations, to name just a few. Many of the earlier programs in this book use the so-called character string functions defined in the include file `strings.h`. The argument types for many of these functions are fixed. For example, both of the arguments to `strcpy(char*, char*)` must be a pointer to a null-terminated character string — nothing else makes sense.

There are functions that are applicable to multiple types. Consider the example of the lowly `max()` function, which returns the maximum of two arguments. The function declarations in Table 27-1 all make sense.

Table 27-1	Possible Variants of maximum() Function
Function Name	*Operation Performed*
`maximum(int, int):`	Returns the maximum of two integers.
`maximum (unsigned int, unsigned int)`	Returns the maximum of two unsigned values. Because there are no negative numbers, the expression (0 - 1) "rolls over" to become a very large unsigned value, rather than the "normal" or signed value –1.
`Maximum (double, double)`	Performs the same comparison operation but on floating numbers.
`Maximum (char, char)`	Returns the character that occurs later in the alphabet (including all special characters).

I would like to implement `maximum()` for all four cases. Of course, C++ can promote all of the types specified into `double`. Thus, you could argue that the
`maximum(double, double)` version is all that is actually needed. Consider,
however, what that would mean to the following expression:

```cpp
// prototype a max() function
double maximum(double, double);

// user function
void fn(int nArg1, int nArg2)
{
    int nLarger = (int)maximum((double)nArg1, (double)nArg2);

    // ...continue...
}
```

In this case, both `nArg1` and `nArg2` must be promoted to `double` with the
accompanying loss of accuracy. This `maximum()` function returns a `double`.
This value must be demoted from `double` back to an `int` via the cast before
it can be assigned to `nLarger`. The function might work without loss of accuracy, but the numerous conversions take much more computer time than a
silly `maximum()` function should. In any case, the function doesn't work the
way the user would expect or hope.

Of course, you could overload `maximum()` with all the possible versions:

```cpp
double maximum(double d1, double d2)
{
    if (d1 > d2)
    {
        return d1;
    }
    return d2;
}
int maximum(int n1, int n2)
{
    if (n1 > n2)
    {
        return n1;
    }
    return n2;
}
char maximum(char c1, char c2)
{
    if (c1 > c2)
    {
        return c1;
    }
    return c2;
}

// ...repeat for all other numeric types...
```

This approach works. Now C++ selects the best match, `maximum(int, int)`, for a reference such as `maximum(1, 2)`. However, creating the same function for each type of variable is a gross waste of time.

The source code for all the `maximum(T, T)` functions follows the same pattern, where `T` is one of the numeric types. It would be so convenient if you could write the function once and let C++ supply the type `T` as needed when the function is used. In fact, C++ lets you write the `maximum()` function in exactly this way and provides an actual type for `T` as needed.

Generalizing a Function into a Template

A template function enables you to write what looks like a function but that uses one or more type holders that C++ converts into a true type at compile time.

The following MaxTemple program defines a template for a generic `maximum()` function:

```
// MaxTemplate - create a template max() function
//                that returns the greater of two types
#include <cstdio>
#include <cstdlib>
#include <iostream>

using namespace std;

// simplistic exception class for this example only
template <class T>
T maximum(T t1, T t2)
{
    if (t1 > t2)
    {
        return t1;
    }
    return t2;
};

int main(int argc, char* pArgs[])
{
    // find the maximum of two int's
    cout << "The maximum of 1 and 2 is "
         << maximum(1, 2)
         << endl;

    // repeat for two doubles
    cout << "The maximum of 1.5 and 2.5 is "
```

```
            << maximum(1.5, 2.5)
            << endl;

    system("PAUSE");
    return 0;
}
```

The keyword `template` is followed by angle brackets containing one or more type holders, each preceded by the keyword class, a constant, or both. In this case, the definition of `maximum<T>(T, T)` will call the "unknown type" T. Following the angle brackets is what looks like a normal function definition. In this case, the template function `T maximum<T>(T t1, T t2)` returns the larger of two objects `t1` and `t2`, each of which is of type T, where T is a class to be defined later.

A template function is useless until it is converted into a real function. C++ replaces T with an actual type. The `main()` function implicitly causes C++ to create two versions of `maximum()` in the MaxTemplate program example.

Creating a function from a template is called *instantiating* the template.

The first call `maximum(1, 2)` causes C++ to create a version of the function where T is replaced by `int`. The second call creates a separate function `maximum(double, double)`. The output from this program appears as follows:

```
The maximum of 1 and 2 is 2
The maximum of 1.5 and 2.5 is 2.5
Press any key to continue . . .
```

Be very careful about terminology. For example, I'm a hip, bad bicyclist, which is not the same thing as a bad hip bicyclist. Here's another example: A template function is not a function. The prototype for a template function is `maximum<T>(T, T)`. The function that this template creates when T is `int` is the function (not template function) `maximum(int, int)`. Your life will be easier if you remember to keep the terms straight.

Notice that the following won't work:

```
double d = max(1, 2.0);
```

The problem is that the type of the first argument and that of the second don't match. The type of the arguments must match the template function `maximum<T>(T, T)` declaration exactly. The example expression would match a template function `maximum<T1, T2>(T1, T2)`. C++ could replace type T1 with int and T2 with double.

You can force the instantiation of a template by providing a prototype declaration. In general, this is safer anyway:

```
float maximum(float, float);   // creates an instance of
                               // maximum<T>(T, T) where T =
           float
```

C++ can't compile a template function until the template is expanded into a real function. If your template function has compile errors, you probably won't know it until you instantiate the template function.

Template Classes

C++ also allows the programmer to define template classes. A template class follows the same principle of using a conventional class definition with a placeholder for some unknown support classes. For example, the following TemplateVector program creates a vector for any class that the user provides (a *vector* is a type of container in which the objects are stored in a row; an *array* is the classic vector example).

```cpp
// TemplateVector - implement a vector that uses a template
//                  type
#include <cstdlib>
#include <cstdio>
#include <iostream>
#include <sstream>
#include <string>
using namespace std;

// TemplateVector - a simple templatized array
template <class T>
class TemplateVector
{
  public:
    TemplateVector(int nArraySize)
    {
        // store off the number of elements
        nSize = nArraySize;
        array = new T[nArraySize];
            reset();
    }
    int size() { return nWriteIndex; }
    void reset() { nWriteIndex = 0; nReadIndex = 0; }
    void add(T object)
    {
        if (nWriteIndex < nSize)
        {
            array[nWriteIndex++] = object;
        }
    }
    T get()
    {
```

```
            return array[nReadIndex++];
    }

  protected:
    int nSize;
    int nWriteIndex;
    int nReadIndex;
    T* array;
};

// exercise two vectors, one of integers and another of names
void intFn();
void nameFn();

int main(int argc, char* pArgs[])
{
    intFn();
    nameFn();

    system("PAUSE");
    return 0;
}

// Integers - manipulate a collection of integers
void intFn()
{
    // create a vector
    TemplateVector<int> integers(10);

    // add values to the vector
    cout << "Give me a series integer values to add to a
            vector\n"
        << "(Enter a negative number to terminate):" <<
            endl;
    for(;;)
    {
        int n;
        cin  >> n;

        if (n < 0) { break; }
        integers.add(n);
    }

    cout << "\nHere are the numbers you entered" << endl;
    for(int i = 0; i < integers.size(); i++)
    {
        cout << i << ":" << integers.get() << endl;
    }
}

// Names - create and manipulate a vector of names
class Name
{
```

```
  public:
    Name(char* n = "") : name(n) {}
    string display() { return name; }
  protected:
    string name;
};

void nameFn()
{
    // create a vector
    TemplateVector<Name> names(10);

    // add values to the vector
    cout << "Enter names\n"
         << "(Enter an 'x' to quit):" << endl;
    for(;;)
    {
        char buffer[80];
        do
        {
            cin.getline(buffer, 80);
        } while(strlen(buffer) == 0);
        if (stricmp(buffer, "x") == 0)
        {
            break;
        }
        names.add(Name(buffer));
    }

    cout << "\nHere are the names you entered" << endl;
    for(int i = 0; i < names.size(); i++)
    {
        Name name = names.get();
        cout << i << ":" << name.display() << endl;
    }
}
```

The template class `TemplateVector<T>` contains an array of objects of class T. The template class presents two member functions: `add()` and `get()`. The `add()` function adds an object of class T into the next empty spot in the array. The corresponding function `get()` returns the next object in the array.

The TemplateVector program instantiates this vector class once for simple `int`s and a second time for the user-defined class `Name`.

The `intFn()` function creates a vector of integers with room for 10. The program reads integer values from the keyboard, saves them off and then spits the values back out using the functions provided by `TemplateVector`.

The second function, `nameFn()`, creates a vector of `Name` objects. Again, the function reads in names and then displays them back to the user.

Notice that the `TemplateVector` handles both `int` values and `Name` objects with equal ease. Notice also how similar the `nameFn()` and `intFn()` functions are, even though integers and names have nothing to do with each other.

A sample session appears as follows:

```
Give me a series integer values to add to a vector
(Enter a negative number to terminate):
5
10
15
-1

Here are the numbers you entered
0:5
1:10
2:15
Enter names
(Enter an 'x' to quit):
Chester
Fox
Penny
x

Here are the names you entered
0:Chester
1:Fox
2:Penny
Press any key to continue . . .
```

Do I Really Need Template Classes?

"But," you say, "can't I just create a simple `Array` class? Why mess with templates?"

Sure you can, if you know *a priori* what types of things you need arrays for. For example, if all you ever need is arrays of integers, you have no reason to create a template `Vector<T>`; you could just create the class `IntArray` and be finished.

The only other alternative is to use `void*`, which can point to any type of object. The following VoidVector program is based upon the use of `void` pointers:

```
// VoidVector - implement a vector that relies on void*
//              as the storage element
#include <cstdlib>
#include <cstdio>
#include <iostream>
```

```
using namespace std;

typedef void* VoidPtr;

class VoidVector
{
  public:
    VoidVector(int nArraySize)
    {
        // store off the number of elements
        nSize = nArraySize;
        ptr = new VoidPtr[nArraySize];
        reset();
    }
    int size() { return nWriteIndex; }
    void reset() { nWriteIndex = 0; nReadIndex = 0; }
    void add(void* pValue)
    {
        if (nWriteIndex < nSize)
        {
            ptr[nWriteIndex++] = pValue;
        }
    }
    VoidPtr get(){ return ptr[nReadIndex++]; }

  protected:
    int nSize;
    int nWriteIndex;
    int nReadIndex;
    VoidPtr* ptr;
};

int main(int argc, char* pArgs[])
{
    // create a vector
    VoidVector vv(10);

    // add values to the vector
    cout << "Give me a series integer values to add to a
            vector\n"
         << "(Enter a negative number to terminate):" <<
            endl;
    for(;;)
    {
        int* p = new int;
        cin  >> *p;

        if (*p < 0)
        {
            delete p;
            break;
        }
```

```
        vv.add((void*)p);
    }

    cout << "\nHere are the numbers you entered" << endl;
    for(int i = 0; i < vv.size(); i++)
    {
        int* p = (int*)vv.get();
        cout << i << ":" << *p << endl;
    }

    system("PAUSE");
    return 0;
}
```

This program defines a type `VoidPtr` to be equivalent to a `void*`.

The `typedef` keyword does nothing more than create a new name for an existing class. You can mentally insert `void*` everywhere you see `VoidPtr`. `typedefs` can make reading a function easier, and they also improve the syntax of a statement. It is sometimes not possible to get an existing template class to work properly when the type is a pointer. Wrapping a complex type like a pointer in a `typedef` solves the problem.

`VoidVector` provides the same `add()` and `get()` methods provided by the `TemplateVector` template class in the previous program.

This solution has (at least) three problems. First, it is somewhat clumsy to use, as demonstrated in `main()`. It is not possible to store a value, such as 10; you can pass only the address of an object. This means that you must allocate an `int*` off the heap to use as a storage place for the value read from the keyboard.

The second problem is the serious opportunity for screw up. You may have been tempted to simply add an `int` to the collection as follows:

```
int n;
cin >> n;
vv.add((void*)&n);
```

That would not work. The variable n has local scope. Its address will "go away" once control exits the `for` loop. At that point, the addresses in the vector will make no sense.

Actually, the problem is slightly worse — the address of n is the same for every iteration through the `for` loop.

The third problem is more serious. In order to retrieve a value from a `VoidVector`, you must know the type of object stored there. C++ cannot check the types to make sure that your assumption is correct. Suppose, for example, you thought that `double` variables were stored in `vv` instead of `int` values. The following code would have stored garbage into `dValue`:

```
double dValue = *(double*)get();
```

The program would certainly go astray; the casts to and from `void*` defeat the strong typing built into C++.

Tips for Using Templates

You should remember a few things when using templates. First, no code is generated for a template. (Code is generated after the template is converted into a concrete class or function.) This implies that a `.cpp` source file is almost never associated with a template class. The entire template class definition, including all the member functions, is contained in the `include` file so that it can be available for the compiler to expand.

Second, a template class does not consume memory. Therefore, there is no penalty for creating template classes if they are never instanced. On the other hand, a template class uses memory every time it is instanced. Thus, the code for `Array<Student>` consumes memory even if `Array<int>` already exists.

Finally, a template class cannot be compiled and checked for errors until it is converted into a real class. Thus, a program that references the template class `Array<T>` might compile even though `Array<T>` contains obvious syntax errors. The errors won't appear until a class such as `Array<int>` or `Array<Student>` is created.

Chapter 28

Standardizing on the Standard Template Library

Some programs can deal with data as it arrives and dispense with it. Most programs, however, must store data for later processing. A structure that is used to store data is known generically as a container or a collection (I use the terms interchangeably). This book has relied heavily on the array for data storage so far. The array container has a couple of very nice properties: It stores and retrieves things very quickly. In addition, the array can be declared to hold any type of object in a type-safe way. Weighed against that, however, are two very large negatives.

First, you must know the size of the array at the time it is created. This requirement is generally not achievable, although you will sometimes know that the number of elements cannot exceed some "large value." Viruses, however, commonly exploit this type of "it can't be larger than this" assumption, which turns out to be incorrect. There is no real way to "grow" an array except to declare a new array and copy the contents of the old array into the newer, larger version.

Second, inserting elements anywhere within the array involves copying elements within the array. This is costly in terms of both memory and computing time. Sorting the elements within an array is even more expensive.

C++ now comes with the Standard Template Library or STL, which includes many different types of containers, each with its own set of advantages (and disadvantages).

The C++ Standard Template Library is a very large library of sometimes-complex containers. This session is considered just an overview of the power of the STL.

The string Container

The most common form of array is the zero-terminated character string used to display text, which clearly shows both the advantages and disadvantages of the array. Consider how easy the following appears:

```
cout << "This is a string";
```

But things go sour quickly when you try to perform an operation even as simple as concatenating two strings:

```
char* concatCharString(char* s1, char* s2)
{
    int length = strlen(s1) + strlen(s2) + 1;
    char* s = new char[length];
    strcpy(s, s1);
    strcat(s, s2);
    return s;
}
```

The STL provides a string container to handle display strings. The string class provides a number of operations (including overloaded operators) to simplify the manipulation of character strings. The same concat() operation is performed as follows using string objects:

```
string concat(string s1, string s2)
{
    return s1 + s2;
}
```

I tried to avoid using string class in other chapters in this book because I don't explain it until here. However, most programmers use the string class more often than they use null terminated character arrays.

The following STLString program demonstrates just a few of the capabilities of the string class:

```
// STLString - demonstrates just a few of the features
//             of the string class which is part of the
//             Standard Template Library
#include <string>
#include <cstdlib>
#include <iostream>
using namespace std;

// concat - return the concatenation of two strings
string concat(string s1, string s2)
{
    return s1 + s2;
}
```

```
// removeSpaces - remove any spaces within a string
string removeSpaces(string s)
{
    // find the offset of the first space;
    // keep searching the string until no more spaces found
    size_t offset;
    while((offset = s.find(" ")) != -1)
    {
        // remove the space just discovered
        s.erase(offset, 1);
    }
    return s;
}

// insertPhrase - insert a phrase in the position of
//                <ip> for insertion point
string insertPhrase(string source)
{
    size_t offset = source.find("<ip>");
    if (offset != -1)
    {
        source.erase(offset, 4);
        source.insert(offset, "Randall");
    }
    return source;
}


int main(int argc, char* pArgs[])
{
    // create a string that is the sum of two smaller strings
    cout << "string1 + string2 = "
         << concat("string1 ", "string2")
         << endl;

    // create a test string and then remove all spaces from
    // it using simple string methods
    string s2("The phrase");
    cout << "<" << s2 << "> minus spaces = <"
         << removeSpaces(s2) << ">" << endl;

    // insert a phrase within the middle of an existing
    // sentence (at the location of "<ip>")
    string s3 = "Stephen <ip> Davis";
    cout << s3 + " -> " + insertPhrase(s3) << endl;

    system("PAUSE");
    return 0;
}
```

The operator+() operation performs the concatenation function that earlier sessions implemented using the concatCharacterString() method.

The `removeSpaces()` method removes any spaces found within the string provided. It does this by using the `string.find()` operation to return the offset of the first " " that it finds. Once found, `removeSpaces()` uses the `erase()` method to remove the space. The `find()` method returns an offset of –1 when no more spaces are left.

The type `size_t` is defined within the STL include files as an integer that can handle the largest array index possible on your machine. This is typically a long of some type; however, the `size_t` is used to further source code portability between computers. Visual Studio C++.NET will generate a warning if you use `int` instead.

The `insertPhrase()` method uses the `find()` method to find the insertion point. It then calls `erase` to remove the "`<ip>`" flag and the `string.insert()` to insert a new string within the middle of an existing string.

The resulting output is as follows:

```
string1 + string2 = string1 string2
<this is a test string> minus spaces = <thisisateststring>
Stephen <ip> Davis -> Stephen Randall Davis
Press any key to continue . . .
```

The list Containers

The Standard Template Library provides a large number of containers — many more than I can describe in a single session. However, I provide here a description of two of the more useful families of containers.

The STL `list` container retains objects by linking them together like Lego blocks. Objects can be snapped apart and snapped back together in any order. This makes the `list` ideal for inserting objects, sorting, merging, and otherwise rearranging objects. The following example STLList program uses the `list` container to sort a set of names:

```
// STLList - use the list container of the
//           Standard Template Library to input
//           and sort a string of names
#include <list>
#include <string>
#include <cstdio>
#include <cstdlib>
#include <iostream>

// declare a list of string objects
using namespace std;
list<string> names;
```

```
int main(int argc, char* pArgs[])
{
    // input a string of names
    cout << "Input a name (input a null to terminate list)"
         << endl;
    while(true)
    {
        string name;
        cin >> name;
        if ((name.compare("x") == 0) ||
            (name.compare("X") == 0))
        {
            break;
        }
        names.push_back(name);
    }

    // sort the list
    // (this works since String implements a comparison
            operator)
    names.sort();

    // display the sorted list
    // keep displaying names until the collection is empty
    cout << "\nSorted output:" << endl;
    while(!names.empty())
    {
        // get the first name in the list
        string name = names.front();
        cout << name << endl;

        // remove that name from the list
        names.pop_front();
    }

    system("PAUSE");
    return 0;
}
```

This example defines the variable `names` to be a `list` of `string` objects. The program starts by reading names from the keyboard. Each name is added to the end of the list names using the `push_back()` method. The program exits the loop when the user enters the name `"x"`. The list of names is sorted by invoking the single list method `sort()`.

The program displays the sorted list of names by removing objects from the front of the list until the list is empty.

The following is an example output from the program:

```
Input a name (input an x to terminate list)
Adams
Davis
Valentine
Smith
Wilson
x

Sorted output:
Adams
Davis
Smith
Valentine
Wilson
Press any key to continue . . .
```

The list container provides a large set of operators. Simple operations include insert, swap, and erase. This same container also gives the programmer the ability to automatically iterate through the list invoking the same user-defined function on each object.

The operation that the list cannot provide is random access. Because objects can be snapped together in any order, there is no quick way for the list class to return the *n*th object.

Iterators

The STLList sample program presented in the prior section uses a destructive approach to iterating through the list. The pop_front() method moves the user through the list by removing the first object in each case.

The programmer iterates through an array by providing the index of each element. However, this technique doesn't work for containers like list that don't allow for random access. One could imagine a solution based upon methods such as getFirst() and getNext(); however, the designers of the STL wanted to provide a common method for traversing any type of container. For this, the STL defines the iterator.

An iterator is an object that points to the members of a container. In general, every iterator supports the following functions:

- ✔ A class can return an iterator that points to the first member of the collection.
- ✔ The iterator can be moved from one member to the next.
- ✔ The program can retrieve the element pointed to by the iterator.

The code necessary to iterate through a `list` is different from that necessary to traverse a `vector` (to name just two examples). However, the iterator hides these details.

The following STLListUserClass program uses an iterator to traverse an STL list in a non-destructive way:

```
// STLListUserClass - use a list to contain and sort a
//                    user defined class
#include <list>
#include <string>
#include <cstdio>
#include <cstdlib>
#include <iostream>

using namespace std;

// Student - some example user defined class
class Student
{
  public:
    Student(char* pszName, int id)
    {
        name = new string(pszName);
        ssID = id;
    }
    string* name;
    int ssID;
};

// the following function is required to support the
// sort operation
bool operator<(Student& s1, Student& s2)
{
    return s1.ssID < s2.ssID;
}

// define the collection of students
list<Student> students;

int main(int argc, char* pArgs[])
{
    // add three student objects to the list
    students.push_back(*new Student("Marion Haste", 10));
    students.push_back(*new Student("Dewie Cheatum", 5));
    students.push_back(*new Student("Stew Dent, Sr.", 15));

    // now sort the list
    students.sort();

    // and iterate through the list:
    // 1) allocate an iterator that points to the first
    //    element in the list
```

```
    list<Student>::iterator iter = students.begin();

    // 2) continue to loop through the list until the
    //      iterator
    //    hits the end of the list
    while(iter != students.end())
    {
        // 3) retrieve the Student that the iterator points at
        Student& s = *iter;
        cout << s.ssID << " - " << *s.name << endl;

        // 4) now move the iterator over to the next element
        //    int the list
        iter++;
    }

    system("PAUSE");
    return 0;
}
```

This program defines a list of user-defined Student objects (rather than simple names). Three calls to push_back() add elements to the list (hard-coding these calls keeps the program smaller). The call to sort() is the same as that used in the STLList program.

The sort() function within the Standard Template Library classes requires the user to overload the "less than" operator. (This is one of the few places where a user-defined operator other than assignment is required.) operator<(Student&, Student&) is invoked by the expression s1 < s2 when both s1 and s2 are of type Student.

The program allocates an iterator iter to navigate its way through the list. Look carefully at the iterator declaration: list<Student>::iterator is an iterator to a list container of Student objects. The strong typing is demonstrated clearly by the assignment (see Step 3 in preceding code): *iter returns a reference to a Student object.

The output of this program appears as follows:

```
5 - Dewie Cheatum
10 - Marion Haste
15 - Stew Dent, Sr.
Press any key to continue . . .
```

How a sort() sorts

I have glossed over an interesting point: How does the `sort()` method know which of two elements in the list is "bigger"? In other words, what determines the sort order? C++ defines its own sorting order for some types. For example, C++ knows which of two `int`s is larger. In addition, the STL sorted the collection of ASCII strings contained in the `name` collection using the same rules that a dictionary uses.

The STLList program did not need to take any special measures when sorting names. C++ does not know which of two `Student` objects

is larger — the global function `::operator <(Student&, Student&)` serves this purpose. The `sort()` method invokes this function as it makes its way through the list to determine the proper sort order.

As an experiment, reverse the sense of the `operator<()` function as follows:

```
    return s1.ssID > s2.ssID;
```

The result is a list sorted in the exact opposite direction.

Using Maps

Maps are one other class of collection. There are a number of different types of maps, but they all share a common property: Maps are designed to allow elements to be stored and retrieved quickly according to some key or index. The following next program demonstrates the principle.

For example, a school may register students by a unique identification number. This ID is used in every facet of school life. This ID is used to retrieve student information, check out books from the library, and assign grades in courses. It is important that any program be able to retrieve a student by his or her student ID quickly and efficiently.

The following STLMap program creates and uses a collection of `Student` objects, which are keyed by ID:

```
// STLMap - use a map container to retain a collection of
//          objects ordered by a key
#include <cstdio>
#include <cstdlib>
#include <iostream>
#include <sstream>
#include <string>
#include <map>
```

```
using namespace std;

// SC - Student comparison function; designed to determine
//      the sorting order of the students
struct SC
{
    bool operator()(const int id1, const int id2) const
    {
        return id1 < id2;
    }
};
// the map actually contains a Pair; the left element
// being the key while the right element is the data (in
// this case Student)
class Student;
typedef Student* SP;
typedef pair<const int, Student*>  Pair;
typedef map<int, SP, SC> Map;
typedef map<int, SP, SC>::iterator MapIterator;

// collection of Students
Map students;

// Student - define the important properties of a student
//           including the key use when looking him/her up
//           from the student rolls(student id)
class Student
{
  public:
    Student(char* pszName, int id)
              : studentIDKey(id), name(pszName) {}

    // getKey - the key is used as an index into the map
    const int getKey() { return studentIDKey; }

    // display - create a meaningful output
    //           for a Student object
    string display()
    {
        ostringstream out;
        out << studentIDKey << " - " << name;
        return out.str();
    }

  protected:
    // Student elements are keyed by student id
    const int studentIDKey;

    // the name of the student (plus any other data)
    string name;
};

int main(int argc, char* pArgs[])
```

```
{
    // add a few of students to the students collection -
    // a map actually stores objects as "pairs" with the
    // left member being the key and the right the actual
            object
    Student* pS;
    pS = new Student("Sean Yours", 3456);
    Pair* ptr = new Pair(pS->getKey(), pS);
    students.insert(*ptr);

    // a map overloads the index operator to create the Pair
    // and insert it into the map for us
    students[1234] = new Student("Fresch Man", 1234);
    students[5678] = new Student("Student, Jr.", 5678);

    // iterate through the collection of students;
    // a map is always retained in the sorted order
    // determined by the SC class
    cout << "Sorted list of students:" << endl;
    MapIterator iter = students.begin();
    while(iter != students.end())
    {
        Pair p = *iter;
        Student* s = p.second;
        cout << s->display() << endl;
        iter++;
    }

    // the increment and decrement operator can also be used
    // to find the successor and predecessor
    cout << "\nLook up student 3456" << endl;
    MapIterator p = students.find(3456);
    cout << "Found student " << p->second->display() << endl;

    MapIterator p1 = p;
    MapIterator prior = --p1;       // <- predecessor
    cout << "Predecessor = "
         << prior->second->display() << endl;

    MapIterator p2 = p;
    MapIterator successor = ++p2; // <-successor
    cout << "Successor = "
         << successor->second->display() << endl;

    // find() returns the end iterator when it can't find the
    // object in question; operator[] returns a NULL
    if (students.find(0123) == students.end())
    {
        cout << "The call students.find(0123) returns "
             << "students.end() since student 0123 doesn't
        exist"
             << endl;
    }
```

```
    // output using index
    cout << "To test index: students[3456] = "
         << students[3456]->display() << endl;

    if (students[0123] == NULL)
    {
        cout << "but students[0123] returns a NULL"
             << endl;
    }

    system("PAUSE");
    return 0;
}
```

The key to the program (if you can pardon the pun) is found in the initial three typedefs. A map contains a set of Pair objects, each of which contains a first and second element. The first element is the student ID key, and the second is the Student object. The Map class adds an object of class SC. This class contains a single method that compares two Student objects to determine which is larger. (This is slightly more complicated than the global function used with the list collection, but the effect is the same.)

The STLMap program begins by creating three Student Pair objects and adding them to the list. The iteration through the container displays the Student objects in order by student ID. There is no need to invoke a sort() method because map classes already retain objects sorted by key.

The second section of the STLMap program looks up a student by ID using the find() method. The program also demonstrates how easy it is to retrieve the prior and next objects in the list using the decrement and increment operators.

The output from the program appears as follows:

```
Sorted list of students:
1234 - Fresch Man
3456 - Sean Yours
5678 - Student, Jr.

Look up student 3456
Found student 3456 - Sean Yours
Predecessor = 1234 - Fresch Man
Successor = 5678 - Student, Jr.
The call students.find(0123) returns students.end() since
          student 0123 doesn't exist
To test index: students[3456] = 3456 - Sean Yours
but students[0123] returns a NULL
Press any key to continue . . .
```

Part VI
The Part of Tens

The 5th Wave   By Rich Tennant

@RICHTENNANT

"We're here to clean the code."

In this part . . .

*W*hat *For Dummies* book would be complete without a Part of Tens? In Chapter 29, I cover ten ways to avoid adding bugs to your C++ program. (Most of these suggestions work for C programs too, at no extra charge.) Chapter 30 lists the ten most important compiler options available in the Dev-C++ compiler, which is available to the reader on the enclosed CD-ROM.

Chapter 29

Ten Ways to Avoid Adding Bugs to Your Program

*I*n this chapter, I look at several ways to minimize errors, as well as ways to make debugging the errors that are introduced easier.

Enabling All Warnings and Error Messages

The syntax of C++ allows for a lot of error checking. When the compiler encounters a construct that it cannot decipher, it has no choice but to generate an error message. Although the compiler attempts to sync back up with the next statement, it does not attempt to generate an executable program.

Disabling warning and error messages is a bit like unplugging the Check Engine light on your car dashboard because it bothers you: Ignoring the problem doesn't make it go away. If your compiler has a Syntax Check from Hell mode, enable it. Both Visual Studio.NET and Dev-C++ have an Enable All Messages option — set it. You save time in the end.

During all its digging around in your source code, a good C++ compiler also looks for suspicious-looking syntactical constructs, such as the following code snippet:

```
#include "student.h"
#include "MyClass.h"
Student* addNewStudent(MyClass myObject,
                       char *pName,
                       SSNumber ss)
{
    Student* pS;
    if (pName != 0)
    {
        pS = new Student(pName, ss);
        myObject.addStudent(pS);
    }
    return pS;
}
```

Here you see that the function first creates a new Student object that it then adds to the MyClass object provided. (Presumably addStudent() is a member function of MyClass.)

If a name is provided (that is, pName is not 0), a new Student object is created and added to the class. With that done, the function returns the Student created to the caller. The problem is that if pName is 0, pS is never initialized to anything. A good C++ compiler can detect this path and generate a warning that "pS might not be initialized when it's returned to the caller and maybe you should look into the problem," or words to that effect.

Insisting on Clean Compiles

Don't start debugging your code until you remove or at least understand all the warnings generated during compilation. Enabling all the warning messages if you then ignore them does you no good. If you don't understand the warning, look it up. What you don't know *will* hurt you.

Adopting a Clear and Consistent Coding Style

Coding in a clear and consistent style not only enhances the readability of the program but also results in fewer coding mistakes. Remember, the less brain power you have to spend deciphering C++ syntax, the more you have left over for thinking about the logic of the program at hand. A good coding style enables you to do the following with ease:

- Differentiate class names, object names, and function names
- Know something about the object based on its name
- Differentiate preprocessor symbols from C++ symbols (that is, #defined objects should stand out)
- Identify blocks of C++ code at the same level (this is the result of consistent indentation)

In addition, you need to establish a standard module header that provides information about the functions or classes in the module, the author (presumably, that's you), the date, the version of the compiler you're using, and a modification history.

Finally, all programmers involved in a single project should use the same style. Trying to decipher a program with a patchwork of different coding styles is confusing.

Limiting the Visibility

Limiting the visibility of class internals to the outside world is a cornerstone of object-oriented programming. The class is responsible for its own internals; the application is responsible for using the class to solve the problem at hand.

Specifically, limited visibility means that data members should not be accessible outside the class — that is, they should be marked as protected. (There is another storage class, private, that is not discussed in this book.) In addition, member functions that the application software does not need to know about should also be marked protected. Don't expose any more of the class internals than necessary.

A related rule is that public member functions should trust application code as little as possible. Any argument passed to a public member function should be treated as though it might cause bugs until it has been proven safe. A function such as the following is an accident waiting to happen:

```
class Array
{
   public:
      Array(int s)
      {
          size = 0;
          pData = new int[s];
          if (pData)
          {
              size = s;
          }
      }
   ~Array()
      {
          delete pData;
          size = 0;
          pData = 0;
      }
      //either return or set the array data
      int data(int index)
      {
          return pData[index];
      }
      int data(int index, int newValue)
      {
          int oldValue = pData[index];
          pData[index] = newValue;
          return oldValue;
      }
   protected:
      int size;
      int *pData;
};
```

The function data(int) allows the application software to read data out of Array. This function is too trusting; it assumes that the index provided is within the data range. What if the index is not? The function data(int, int) is even worse because it overwrites an unknown location.

What's needed is a check to make sure that the index is in range. In the following, only the data(int) function is shown for brevity:

```
int data(unsigned int index)
{
    if (index >= size)
    {
        throw Exception("Array index out of range");
    }
    return pData[index];
}
```

Now an out-of-range `index` will be caught by the check. (Making `index` unsigned precludes the necessity of adding a check for negative `index` values.)

Commenting Your Code While You Write It

You can avoid errors if you comment your code as you write it rather than waiting until everything works and then go back and add comments. I can understand not taking the time to write voluminous headers and function descriptions until later, but you always have time to add short comments while writing the code.

Short comments should be enlightening. If they're not, they aren't worth much. You need all the enlightenment you can get while you're trying to make your program work. When you look at a piece of code you wrote a few days ago, comments that are short, descriptive, and to the point can make a dramatic contribution to helping you figure out exactly what it was you were trying to do.

In addition, consistent code indentation and naming conventions make the code easier to understand. It's all very nice when the code is easy to read after you're finished with it, but it's just as important that the code be easy to read while you're writing it. That's when you need the help.

Single-Stepping Every Path at Least Once

It may seem like an obvious statement, but I'll say it anyway: As a programmer, it's important for you to understand what your program is doing. Nothing gives you a better feel for what's going on under the hood than single-stepping the program with a good debugger. (The debugger in both Dev-C++ and Visual Studio.NET work just fine.)

Beyond that, as you write a program, you sometimes need raw material in order to figure out some bizarre behavior. Nothing gives you that material better than single-stepping new functions as they come into service.

Finally, when a function is finished and ready to be added to the program, every logical path needs to be traveled at least once. Bugs are much easier to find when the function is examined by itself rather than after it has been thrown into the pot with the rest of the functions — and your attention has gone on to new programming challenges.

Avoid Overloading Operators

Other than using the assignment operator `operator=()`, you should hold off overloading operators until you feel comfortable with C++. Overloading operators other than assignment is almost never necessary and can significantly add to your debugging woes as a new programmer. You can get the same effect by defining and using the proper public member functions instead.

After you've been C-plus-plussing for a few months, feel free to return and start overloading operators to your heart's content.

Heap Handling

As a general rule, programmers should allocate and release heap memory at the same "level." If a member function `MyClass::create()` allocates a block of heap memory and returns it to the caller, there should be a member function `MyClass::release()` that returns the memory to the heap. Specifically, `MyClass::create()` should not require the parent function to release the memory. This certainly doesn't avoid all memory problems — the parent function may forget to call `MyClass::release()` — but it does reduce the possibility somewhat.

Using Exceptions to Handle Errors

The exception mechanism in C++ is designed to handle errors conveniently and efficiently. In general, you should throw an error indicator rather than return an error flag. The resulting code is easier to write, read, and maintain. Besides, other programmers have come to expect it — you wouldn't want to disappoint them, would you?

It is not necessary to throw an exception from a function that returns a "didn't work" indicator if this is a part of everyday life for that function. Consider a function `lcd()` that returns the least common denominators of a number passed to it as an argument. That function will not return any values when presented a prime number (a prime number cannot be evenly divided by any other number). This is not an error — the `lcd()` function has nothing to say when given a prime.

Avoiding Multiple Inheritance

Multiple inheritance, like operator overloading, adds another level of complexity that you don't need to deal with when you're just starting out. Fortunately, most real-world relationships can be described with single inheritance. (Some people claim that multiple inheritance is not necessary at all — I'm not sure that I'm not one of them.)

Feel free to use multiple-inherited classes from commercial libraries. For example, the Microsoft MFC classes that are key to Visual Studio 6 make heavy use of multiple inheritance. Microsoft has spent a considerable amount of time setting up its classes, and it knows what it's doing.

After you feel comfortable with your level of understanding of C++, experiment with setting up some multiple inheritance hierarchies. That way, you'll be ready when the unusual situation that requires multiple inheritance to describe it accurately arises.

Chapter 30

The Ten Most Important Optional Features of Dev-C++

*T*his chapter reviews some of the settings within the Dev-C++ environment that might affect you on a normal day of C++ programming. This chapter also touches on the Dev-C++ profiler.

Customize Editor Settings to Your Taste

Programming should be a pleasant experience. C++ has enough unpleasant things to deal with, so you don't need an editor that doesn't think like you do. Fortunately, Dev-C++ allows you to "have it your way." Choose Tools⇨Editor Options to change editor settings.

Let me start with a few settings that don't make much difference. For example, I prefer four spaces for a tab — you might prefer another amount. In addition, I have the editor draw a line down column 60 on the display to keep a single line of code from extending so far that I can't see the rest of my program.

Checking Use Syntax Highlighting tells the editor to color words within your program to indicate their type. The editor flags comment lines with one color, keywords such as `switch` another, variable names yet another, and so on. The myriad of colors is a little nauseating at first, but it's very useful once you get used to it. You can change the colors used, but I don't see much point in doing so.

The Auto Indent feature is intended to be a labor saving device: The editor tabs the cursor over the "appropriate" column when you press Return. Normally, the appropriate column is the same as the previous line that isn't a comment or blank. The cursor automatically indents after an open brace. Unfortunately, it doesn't unindent upon seeing a close brace (nothing's perfect). Backspace Unindents is a related and corresponding setting.

I deselected Use Tab Character. This forces the editor to use spaces, and spaces only, to position the cursor. I did this primarily because I cut and pasted programs from Dev-C++ into my word processor when writing this book.

The Highlight matching braces/parenthesis setting has a serious implication that gets its own Top 10 listing.

Highlight Matching Braces/Parentheses

The Highlight matching braces/parenthesis setting appears in the Editor Options window that is accessible from the Tools menu. When set, the Dev-C++ editor looks for the corresponding opening brace whenever you enter a closed brace. In addition, when you select either an open or closed brace, Dev-C++ changes the corresponding brace to Bold. The same rules apply for parentheses.

This feature helps you keep your braces matched. You can easily forget a closed brace when you're entering your program. It's just as easy to get the braces screwed up when editing your program.

There is, however, a serious downside when using Dev-C++ Version 4.9.8.0: You can't open a module in which there are more open braces than closed braces. It seems that the editor scans your `.cpp` file when you open it to figure out which closed brace goes with which open brace. The editor hangs up if it runs out of program before it finds enough closed braces.

Thus, if Dev-C++ appears to just go away when you open your C++ source code module, try the following:

1. **Kill Dev-C++ — it's not going to return anyway. Press Control-Alt-Delete. Select the Task Manager option. Select Dev-C++ from the list of active programs that appear. Finally, select End Task.**

2. **Start Dev-C++ from the Start menu without a file.**

3. **Uncheck the Highlight matching flag.**

4. **Open your file.**

If that doesn't work, punt and download the most recent version from the `www.bloodshed.net` Web site, because something is wrong.

Enable Exception Handling

Exception handling is the flexible error handling mechanism discussed in Chapter 25. Choose Tools⇨Compiler Options. Select the Settings tab. Work your way through the tree of compiler options in the left window until you find Code Generation. Make sure that the Enable exception handling flag is set to Yes — the default for this setting is No.

Adding exception handling code makes your program slightly larger and slightly slower. However, that's a small price to pay for the exception error handling mechanism. See Chapter 25 if you don't believe me.

Include Debugging Information (Sometimes)

The Generate debugging information flag is also one of the compiler options. Choose Tools⇨Compiler Options. Select the Settings tab. Click Linker in the options tree. The Generate debugging information flag should be set to Yes during the debug process. The debugger doesn't work if this flag isn't set. In addition, Dev-C++ has only limited information to fall back on if your program crashes.

When the debugging flag is set to Yes, Dev-C++ includes the location within the program of every label and every line of code. (That's how the debugger knows where to set breakpoints.) Even lines of code from library routines, code that you didn't write, are included. All this location information can add up. This information adds to the executable file.

I compiled one of my programs first with the debug flag turned on and a second time with it turned off. The executable was a whopping 1.2MB. The same program generated a 440K executable file.

The moral is: Be sure that the Generate debugging information flag is activated during the entire development period, but clear the flag for the final release version.

Create a Project File

You can generate a program from a single .cpp file without using a project file. This is fine for small programs. However, you should break larger programs into smaller modules that can be understood more easily. Building multiple .cpp modules into a single program requires a Project file. I describe this in Chapter 22.

Customize the Help Menu

Dev-C++'s help default topics are limited to the compiler, and don't include the C++ language or any of its libraries. Fortunately, Dev-C++ allows you customize the Help options. You can add files in Microsoft Help (.hlp) and Compiled HTML (.chm) formats to Help. (***Note:*** You'll have to find extra .hlp and .chm files. You can find these on the Web if you look hard enough. Neither Dev-C++ nor www.bloodshed.net provide an extra Help file.)

As an example, I downloaded the freely available Help file Win32.hlp. This file lists the Windows operating system Application Program Interface (API) calls. Choose Help⇨Customize Help Menu to access the Help Menu Editor.

Click the Add button along the top of the window. Dev-C++ opens a browse window. Navigate to the help file that you want to add. Select the file and click OK. Finally, check the appropriate boxes at the bottom of the window. Here I included the Win32.hlp file in the Help search. Click OK. The contents of the new help file are now available from the Help menu.

You can add as many help files as you like.

Reset Breakpoints after Editing the File

Dev-C++ sets breakpoints based on line number. Unfortunately, it does not move the breakpoint when a line is inserted or removed from the source file. For example, suppose that I set a breakpoint on line 10 within my program. If I then add a comment between lines 9 and 10, the breakpoint now points to the comment. Obviously, comments are not executed, so the breakpoint becomes meaningless.

Remember to recheck your breakpoints to be sure they still make sense after you edit the .cpp source file.

Avoid Illegal Filenames

Dev-C++ isn't very good at identifying illegal filenames. Rather than generating a meaningful message (such as maybe, "Illegal Filename"), the compiler generates a string of misleading error messages.

Dev-C++ can't handle filenames that contain spaces. The filename `My Program.cpp` is not allowed. Nor can it handle folder names containing spaces. The filename `C:\My Folder\MyProgram.cpp` is not legal either.

Dev-C++ can handle network files, but the Console window cannot. Thus, you can compile the program `\\Randy\MyFolder\MyProgram.cpp`, but you can't debug resulting executable. In addition, the program executes normally at first but generates some obscure operating system error message before it completes.

Include #include Files in Your Project

C++ allows you to collect statements into separate files that you can `#include` in multiple source files. C++ puts no restrictions on the type of things that you can put in an include file. However, you should put only the following types of statements in an include file:

- ✔ Function prototypes
- ✔ Class definitions
- ✔ Template definitions of all types
- ✔ Definition of all global variables

You should not include executable statements (except for functions within the class definition itself) in an include file. Remember to add the include filename to the project list, even though it contains no source code. Doing so tells Dev-C++ to rebuild the C++ source whenever an include file changes.

Executing the Profiler

You shouldn't be overly concerned with how fast your program will run when you're writing. (By this, I'm not suggesting that you do really stupid things that take up lots of computer time.) It's hard enough to write a working program without worrying about writing tricky "efficient" C++ code statements. In addition, it's an odd fact that, if you ask a programmer where she spends most of her programming time, she's almost always wrong!

But what if your program is too slow and you want to spiff it up? Fortunately, Dev-C++ (and most other C++ environments) offers something known as a *profiler.* This nifty little tool watches your program to determine where it's spending its time. Once you know that, you can decide where to spend your valuable coding time.

To enable Profiling, I chose Tools⇨Compiler Options. Then I selected Settings and Code profiling to set Generate Profiling Info for Analysis.

I then added the following edited version of the DeepCopy program from Chapter 18:

```cpp
//
//  DeepCopy  - provide a program to profile
//
#include <cstdio>
#include <cstdlib>
#include <iostream>
#include <strings.h>

#include <profile.h>
using namespace std;

class Person
{
  public:
    Person(char *pN)
    {
        pName = new char[strlen(pN) + 1];
        if (pName != 0)
        {
            strcpy(pName, pN);
        }
    }

    Person(Person& p)
    {
        pName = new char[strlen(p.pName) + 1];
        if (pName != 0)
        {
            strcpy(pName, p.pName);
        }
    }

    ~Person()
    {
        if (pName != 0)
        {
            delete pName;
            pName = 0;
        }
    }
```

```
      char *pName;
};

void fn1(Person& p)
{
    // create a new object
    // Person* p1 = new Person(p.pName);
    Person p1(p);
}
void fn2(Person p)
{
    // create a new object
    Person* p1 = new Person(p);
    delete p1;
}

int main(int nNumberofArgs, char* pszArgs[])
{
    Person p("This_is_a_very_long_name");

    for(int i = 0; i < 1000000; i++)
    {
        fn1(p);
        fn2(p);
    }
    return 0;
}
```

This program does nothing more than call `fn1()` and `fn2()` millions of times — you can't get an accurate picture of a program that executes in less than one second. That's okay because you don't need to worry about making a program that executes in a second or two any faster anyway. Adding the loop causes the program to take a few seconds to complete.

In addition, I removed the output statements. You quickly discover that output is a very slow process. The time spent outputting information to the screen would have swamped everything else.

When executed, the program opened a Console window for a few minutes and then closed the window. Not very exciting so far. I then selected Execute⇨Profile Analysis. The window shown in Figure 30-1 appeared.

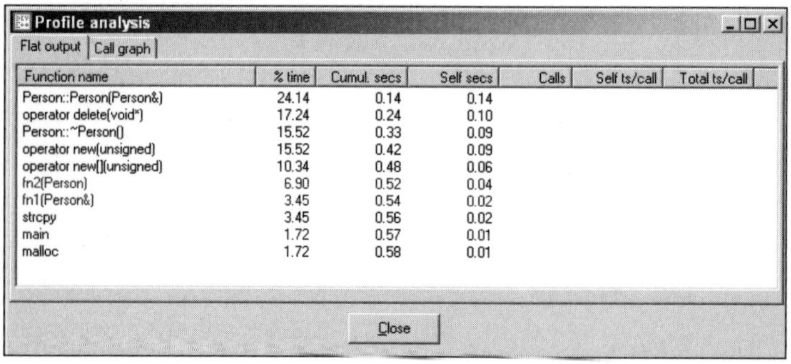

Figure 30-1:
A profile
analysis
shows you
where a
program is
spending
its time.

Function name	% time	Cumul. secs	Self secs	Calls	Self ts/call	Total ts/call
Person::Person(Person&)	24.14	0.14	0.14			
operator delete(void*)	17.24	0.24	0.10			
Person::~Person()	15.52	0.33	0.09			
operator new(unsigned)	15.52	0.42	0.09			
operator new[](unsigned)	10.34	0.48	0.06			
fn2(Person)	6.90	0.52	0.04			
fn1(Person&)	3.45	0.54	0.02			
strcpy	3.45	0.56	0.02			
main	1.72	0.57	0.01			
malloc	1.72	0.58	0.01			

Interpreting a profile takes a certain amount of practice. This window shows the functions invoked during the execution of the program (there may be other functions in the program, but they were never called). The first column lists the names of the function followed by the percentage of time spent in that function in the second column. In this case, just more than 24 percent of the program's execution time was spent in the copy constructor `Person::Person(Person&)`. The Self Secs column refers to the total amount of time spent within the function — an entire 0.14 second was spent in the copy constructor (almost one-fifth of a second — shocking!).

Does this mean that the copy constructor is the slowest function in the program? Not necessarily. In reality, the program spent more time in this function because it was called more often than any other — the copy constructor is invoked from both `fn1()` and `fn2()`.

Skipping down to these two functions, you can see that `fn2()` took more time than `fn1()`. In fact, `fn2()` took twice as much time as `fn1()` — 0.04 second versus 0.02 second. `fn1()` creates a new copy of the `Person` object passed to it. However, `fn1()` receives its argument by reference from `main()`.

By comparison, `main()` passes the `Person` object to `fn2()` by value. This causes C++ to invoke the copy constructor. The `fn2()` function then makes a copy of the copy. Finally, `fn2()` creates the copy from heap memory using the `new` keyword. Allocating memory off the heap takes a certain amount of time.

Appendix

About the CD

On the CD-ROM

▶ Dev-C++, a full featured, integrated C++ compiler and editor

▶ The source code for the programs in this book (your typing fingers will thank you)

▶ Example programs too large for the book

▶ Online C++ help files

System Requirements

Be sure that your computer meets the minimum system requirements in the following list. If your computer doesn't match up to most of these requirements, you may have problems using the contents of the CD.

✔ PC with a Pentium or faster processor

✔ Microsoft Windows Me, NT4, 2000, or later; or Linux

✔ At least 64MB of RAM installed on your computer

✔ At least 30MB of available hard disk space

✔ CD-ROM drive

Additional requirements apply if you will be using Visual Studio.NET or Visual C++.NET rather than the Dev-C++ development environment included on the enclosed CD-ROM. See the Visual Studio installation documentation for details.

If you need more information on the basics, check out these books published by Wiley: *PCs For Dummies,* by Dan Gookin; *Windows 98 For Dummies, Windows 2000 Professional For Dummies,* and *Microsoft Windows Me Millennium Edition For Dummies,* all by Andy Rathbone.

Using the CD with Microsoft Windows

To install the items from the CD to your hard drive, follow these steps:

1. **Insert the CD into your computer's CD-ROM drive.**

2. **Click the Start button and choose Run from the menu.**

3. **Type** D:\, **where** *D* **is the letter for your CD-ROM drive, and click OK.**

4. **Double-click the file License.txt.**

   This file contains the end-user license that you agree to by using the CD. When you finish reading the license, close the program, most likely NotePad, that displayed the file.

5. **Double-click the file Readme.txt.**

   This file contains instructions about installing the software from this CD. It might be helpful to leave this text file open while you are using the CD.

   To install Dev-C++ from the CD to your computer, continue with these steps:

6. **Double-click the folder devcpp.**

7. **Find the file named devcpp*dddd*.exe, where *dddd* are digits (for example, devcpp4980.exe).**

   This is the setup file for the Dev-C++ environment. Follow the installation instructions in Chapter 1.

   To copy the source code from the book onto your hard disk, continue with these steps:

8. **Double-click the My Computer icon located on your desktop.**

   The My Computer window opens.

9. **Drag the folder CPP_Programs from the CD-ROM to your computer's C drive.**

   This step copies the source files to your hard drive where you can edit them as described in Chapter 1. The source files are grouped by chapter. Each program is described within the book.

   You will find five folders, Budget1 through Budget5. These folders contain example programs too large to fit in the book. Bonus Chapter 1, in Adobe Acrobat format, describes the program.

10. **Double-click the file STL_doc\index.html to start the Standard Template Library documentation.**

    The Standard Template Library documentation is a hierarchical and descriptive, but highly technical, description of the STL.

11. **Drag the STL_doc folder to your computer's hard drive (optional).**

    You may prefer to copy the STL_doc to your hard drive so that it is available even when you're catching a few tunes from your newest Willie Nelson CD.

Using the CD with Linux

To install the items from the CD to your hard drive, follow these steps:

1. **Log in as root.**

2. **Insert the CD into your computer's CD-ROM drive.**

3. **If your computer has Auto-Mount enabled, wait for the CD to mount; otherwise, follow these steps:**

    a. Command line instructions:

       At the command prompt type

       mount /dev/cdrom /mnt/cdrom

       (This mounts the *cdrom* device to the `mnt/cdrom` directory. If your device has a different name, change *cdrom* to that device name — for example, *cdrom1*.)

    b. Graphical:

       Right-click the CD-ROM icon on the desktop and choose Mount CD-ROM. This mounts your CD-ROM.

4. **Copy the CPP_Program directory to /src. Refer to Chapter 1 for instructions on how best to use these source files.**

    The version of Dev-C++ contained on the CD-ROM is not compatible with Linux; however, you can download a version for your operating system at `www.bloodshed.net`. Installation instructions are included at that site.

5. **To remove the CD from your CD-ROM drive, follow these steps:**

    a. Command line instructions:

       At the command prompt type

       umount /mnt/cdrom

    b. Graphical:

       Right-click the CD-ROM icon on the desktop and choose UMount CD-ROM. This unmounts your CD-ROM.

After you have installed the programs you want, you can eject the CD. Carefully place it back in the plastic jacket of the book for safekeeping.

What You'll Find

This section provides a summary of the software on this CD.

Shareware programs are fully functional, free trial versions of copyrighted programs. If you like particular programs, register with their authors for a nominal fee and receive licenses, enhanced versions, and technical support. *Freeware programs* are free copyrighted games, applications, and utilities. You can copy them to as many PCs as you like — free — but they have no technical support. *GNU software* is governed by its own license, which is included in the folder of the GNU software. There are no restrictions on distribution of this software. See the GNU license for more details. *Trial, demo,* or *evaluation* versions are usually limited either by time or functionality (such as no capability for saving projects).

Development tools

Here are the development tools included on the accompanying CD-ROM:

- ✔ **Dev-C++, from Bloodshed Software:** For Windows 98, Me, NT 4 or later, 2000 or XP. GNU software. This integrated development environment includes C++ compiler, editor, and debugger. All the programs in this book have been tested with the version of Dev-C++ found on the CD-ROM.

   Bloodshed Software works on Dev-C++ constantly. You can download the most recent version of Dev-C++ from www.bloodshed.net; however, it is possible, though unlikely, that some inconsistency will result in an error when compiling one or more of the .CPP program files.

   Dev-C++ is not compatible with the older 8.3 filenames. Dev-C++ requires support for extended filenames.

- ✔ **Documentation for the Standard Template Library (STL_doc), Copyright the Hewlett-Packard Company, 1994, and Silicon Graphics Computer Systems, Inc., 1996-1999:** The following conditions govern its use:

   Permission to use, copy, modify, distribute and sell this software and its documentation for any purpose is hereby granted without fee, provided that the above copyright notice appears in all copies and that both that copyright notice and this permission notice appear in supporting documentation. Silicon Graphics makes no representations about the suitability of this software for any purpose. It is provided "as is" without express or implied warranty.

   The STL docs are an HTML-based set of documentation to the Standard Template Library. An ISO-compliant implementation of the STL is already present in the Dev-C++ package.

Program source code

Source code for the following programs are included on the CD-ROM:

- ✔ **CPP_Programs, copyright Wiley:** The CPP_Programs folder contains the .CPP programs that appear in this book. The programs are further organized into chapter subfolders within the main CPP_Programs folder.

- ✔ **BUDGET, copyright Wiley Publications:** The BUDGET folder contains a set of programs that demonstrate some of the principles of C++ programming but that are too large to include within the book's pages. All the BUDGET programs implement a set of simple checking and savings accounts. BUDGET1, which is meant to be read at the end of Part II, uses basic programming techniques. BUDGET2 implements some of the object-based programming techniques presented in Part III. BUDGET3 is a fully object-oriented program that you expect to find at the end of Part IV. BUDGET4 and BUDGET5 implement features common to the Standard Template Library as described in Chapters 27 and 28. These programs are further described in Bonus Chapter 1, which can be found on this CD-ROM.

If You've Got Problems (Of the CD Kind)

I tried my best to compile programs that work on most computers with the minimum system requirements. Alas, your computer may differ, and some programs may not work properly for some reason.

The two likeliest problems are that you don't have enough memory (RAM) for the programs you want to use or that you have other programs running that are affecting installation or the running of a program. If you receive error messages like `Not enough memory` or `Setup cannot continue`, try one or more of these methods and then try using the software again:

- ✔ **Turn off any anti-virus software that you have on your computer.** Installers sometimes mimic virus activity and may make your computer incorrectly believe that it is being infected by a virus.

- ✔ **Close all running programs.** The more programs running, the less memory available to other programs. Installers also typically update files and programs. So, if you keep other programs running, installation may not work properly.

If you still have trouble with the CD-ROM, please call the Wiley Product Technical Support phone number: 800-762-2974. Outside the United States, call 317-572-3994. You can also contact Wiley Product Technical Support through the Internet at www.wiley.com/techsupport. Wiley Publishing will provide technical support only for installation and other general quality control items; for technical support on the applications themselves, consult the program's vendor or author of this book at www.stephendavis.com.

To place additional orders or to request information about other Wiley products, please call 800-225-5945.

Wiley Publishing, Inc.
End-User License Agreement

5. Limited Warranty.

   (a) WPI warrants that the Software and Software Media are free from defects in materials and workmanship under normal use for a period of sixty (60) days from the date of purchase of this Book. If WPI receives notification within the warranty period of defects in materials or workmanship, WPI will replace the defective Software Media.

   (b) WPI AND THE AUTHOR(S) OF THE BOOK DISCLAIM ALL OTHER WARRANTIES, EXPRESS OR IMPLIED, INCLUDING WITHOUT LIMITATION IMPLIED WARRANTIES OF MERCHANTABILITY AND FITNESS FOR A PARTICULAR PURPOSE, WITH RESPECT TO THE SOFTWARE, THE PROGRAMS, THE SOURCE CODE CONTAINED THEREIN, AND/OR THE TECHNIQUES DESCRIBED IN THIS BOOK. WPI DOES NOT WARRANT THAT THE FUNCTIONS CONTAINED IN THE SOFTWARE WILL MEET YOUR REQUIREMENTS OR THAT THE OPERATION OF THE SOFTWARE WILL BE ERROR FREE.

   (c) This limited warranty gives you specific legal rights, and you may have other rights that vary from jurisdiction to jurisdiction.

6. Remedies.

   (a) WPI's entire liability and your exclusive remedy for defects in materials and workmanship shall be limited to replacement of the Software Media, which may be returned to WPI with a copy of your receipt at the following address: Software Media Fulfillment Department, Attn.: C++ For Dummies, 5th Edition, Wiley Publishing, Inc., 10475 Crosspoint Blvd., Indianapolis, IN 46256, or call 1-800-762-2974. Please allow four to six weeks for delivery. This Limited Warranty is void if failure of the Software Media has resulted from accident, abuse, or misapplication. Any replacement Software Media will be warranted for the remainder of the original warranty period or thirty (30) days, whichever is longer.

   (b) In no event shall WPI or the author be liable for any damages whatsoever (including without limitation damages for loss of business profits, business interruption, loss of business information, or any other pecuniary loss) arising from the use of or inability to use the Book or the Software, even if WPI has been advised of the possibility of such damages.

   (c) Because some jurisdictions do not allow the exclusion or limitation of liability for consequential or incidental damages, the above limitation or exclusion may not apply to you.

7. U.S. Government Restricted Rights. Use, duplication, or disclosure of the Software for or on behalf of the United States of America, its agencies and/or instrumentalities "U.S. Government" is subject to restrictions as stated in paragraph (c)(1)(ii) of the Rights in Technical Data and Computer Software clause of DFARS 252.227-7013, or subparagraphs (c) (1) and (2) of the Commercial Computer Software - Restricted Rights clause at FAR 52.227-19, and in similar clauses in the NASA FAR supplement, as applicable.

8. General. This Agreement constitutes the entire understanding of the parties and revokes and supersedes all prior agreements, oral or written, between them and may not be modified or amended except in a writing signed by both parties hereto that specifically refers to this Agreement. This Agreement shall take precedence over any other documents that may be in conflict herewith. If any one or more provisions contained in this Agreement are held by any court or tribunal to be invalid, illegal, or otherwise unenforceable, each and every other provision shall remain in full force and effect.

GNU General Public License

Version 2, June 1991

Copyright (C) 1989, 1991 Free Software Foundation, Inc.

59 Temple Place - Suite 330, Boston, MA 02111-1307, USA

Preamble

The licenses for most software are designed to take away your freedom to share and change it. By contrast, the GNU General Public License is intended to guarantee your freedom to share and change free software—to make sure the software is free for all its users. This General Public License applies to most of the Free Software Foundation's software and to any other program whose authors commit to using it. (Some other Free Software Foundation software is covered by the GNU Library General Public License instead.) You can apply it to your programs, too.

When we speak of free software, we are referring to freedom, not price. Our General Public Licenses are designed to make sure that you have the freedom to distribute copies of free software (and charge for this service if you wish), that you receive source code or can get it if you want it, that you can change the software or use pieces of it in new free programs; and that you know you can do these things.

To protect your rights, we need to make restrictions that forbid anyone to deny you these rights or to ask you to surrender the rights. These restrictions translate to certain responsibilities for you if you distribute copies of the software, or if you modify it.

For example, if you distribute copies of such a program, whether gratis or for a fee, you must give the recipients all the rights that you have. You must make sure that they, too, receive or can get the source code. And you must show them these terms so they know their rights.

We protect your rights with two steps: (1) copyright the software, and (2) offer you this license which gives you legal permission to copy, distribute and/or modify the software.

Also, for each author's protection and ours, we want to make certain that everyone understands that there is no warranty for this free software. If the software is modified by someone else and passed on, we want its recipients to know that what they have is not the original, so that any problems introduced by others will not reflect on the original authors' reputations.

Finally, any free program is threatened constantly by software patents. We wish to avoid the danger that redistributors of a free program will individually obtain patent licenses, in effect making the program proprietary. To prevent this, we have made it clear that any patent must be licensed for everyone's free use or not licensed at all.

The precise terms and conditions for copying, distribution and modification follow.

TERMS AND CONDITIONS FOR COPYING, DISTRIBUTION AND MODIFICATION

0. This License applies to any program or other work which contains a notice placed by the copyright holder saying it may be distributed under the terms of this General Public License. The "Program", below, refers to any such program or work, and a "work based on the Program" means either the Program or any derivative work under copyright law: that is to say, a work containing the Program or a portion of it, either verbatim or with modifications and/or translated into another language. (Hereinafter, translation is included without limitation in the term "modification".) Each licensee is addressed as "you".

    Activities other than copying, distribution and modification are not covered by this License; they are outside its scope. The act of running the Program is not restricted, and the output from the Program is covered only if its contents constitute a work based on the Program (independent of having been made by running the Program). Whether that is true depends on what the Program does.

1. You may copy and distribute verbatim copies of the Program's source code as you receive it, in any medium, provided that you conspicuously and appropriately publish on each copy an appropriate copyright notice and disclaimer of warranty; keep intact all the notices that refer to this License and to the absence of any warranty; and give any other recipients of the Program a copy of this License along with the Program.

    You may charge a fee for the physical act of transferring a copy, and you may at your option offer warranty protection in exchange for a fee.

2. You may modify your copy or copies of the Program or any portion of it, thus forming a work based on the Program, and copy and distribute such modifications or work under the terms of Section 1 above, provided that you also meet all of these conditions:

    a) You must cause the modified files to carry prominent notices stating that you changed the files and the date of any change.

    b) You must cause any work that you distribute or publish, that in whole or in part contains or is derived from the Program or any part thereof, to be licensed as a whole at no charge to all third parties under the terms of this License.

    c) If the modified program normally reads commands interactively when run, you must cause it, when started running for such interactive use in the most ordinary way, to print or display an announcement including an appropriate copyright notice and a notice that there is no warranty (or else, saying that you provide a warranty) and that users may redistribute the program under these conditions, and telling the user how to view a copy of this License. (Exception: if the Program itself is interactive but does not normally print such an announcement, your work based on the Program is not required to print an announcement.)

    These requirements apply to the modified work as a whole. If identifiable sections of that work are not derived from the Program, and can be reasonably considered independent and separate works in themselves, then this License, and its terms, do not apply to those sections when you distribute them as separate works. But when you distribute the same sections as part of a whole which is a work based on the Program, the distribution of the whole must be on the terms of this License, whose permissions for other licensees extend to the entire whole, and thus to each and every part regardless of who wrote it.

Thus, it is not the intent of this section to claim rights or contest your rights to work written entirely by you; rather, the intent is to exercise the right to control the distribution of derivative or collective works based on the Program.

In addition, mere aggregation of another work not based on the Program with the Program (or with a work based on the Program) on a volume of a storage or distribution medium does not bring the other work under the scope of this License.

3. You may copy and distribute the Program (or a work based on it, under Section 2) in object code or executable form under the terms of Sections 1 and 2 above provided that you also do one of the following:

   a) Accompany it with the complete corresponding machine-readable source code, which must be distributed under the terms of Sections 1 and 2 above on a medium customarily used for software interchange; or,

   b) Accompany it with a written offer, valid for at least three years, to give any third party, for a charge no more than your cost of physically performing source distribution, a complete machine-readable copy of the corresponding source code, to be distributed under the terms of Sections 1 and 2 above on a medium customarily used for software interchange; or,

   c) Accompany it with the information you received as to the offer to distribute corresponding source code. (This alternative is allowed only for noncommercial distribution and only if you received the program in object code or executable form with such an offer, in accord with Subsection b above.)

The source code for a work means the preferred form of the work for making modifications to it. For an executable work, complete source code means all the source code for all modules it contains, plus any associated interface definition files, plus the scripts used to control compilation and installation of the executable. However, as a special exception, the source code distributed need not include anything that is normally distributed (in either source or binary form) with the major components (compiler, kernel, and so on) of the operating system on which the executable runs, unless that component itself accompanies the executable.

If distribution of executable or object code is made by offering access to copy from a designated place, then offering equivalent access to copy the source code from the same place counts as distribution of the source code, even though third parties are not compelled to copy the source along with the object code.

4. You may not copy, modify, sublicense, or distribute the Program except as expressly provided under this License. Any attempt otherwise to copy, modify, sublicense or distribute the Program is void, and will automatically terminate your rights under this License. However, parties who have received copies, or rights, from you under this License will not have their licenses terminated so long as such parties remain in full compliance.

5. You are not required to accept this License, since you have not signed it. However, nothing else grants you permission to modify or distribute the Program or its derivative works. These actions are prohibited by law if you do not accept this License. Therefore, by modifying or distributing the Program (or any work based on the Program), you indicate your acceptance of this License to do so, and all its terms and conditions for copying, distributing or modifying the Program or works based on it.

6. Each time you redistribute the Program (or any work based on the Program), the recipient automatically receives a license from the original licensor to copy, distribute or modify the Program subject to these terms and conditions. You may not impose any further restrictions on the recipients' exercise of the rights granted herein. You are not responsible for enforcing compliance by third parties to this License.

7. If, as a consequence of a court judgment or allegation of patent infringement or for any other reason (not limited to patent issues), conditions are imposed on you (whether by court order, agreement or otherwise) that contradict the conditions of this License, they do not excuse you from the conditions of this License. If you cannot distribute so as to satisfy simultaneously your obligations under this License and any other pertinent obligations, then as a consequence you may not distribute the Program at all. For example, if a patent license would not permit royalty-free redistribution of the Program by all those who receive copies directly or indirectly through you, then the only way you could satisfy both it and this License would be to refrain entirely from distribution of the Program.

   If any portion of this section is held invalid or unenforceable under any particular circumstance, the balance of the section is intended to apply and the section as a whole is intended to apply in other circumstances.

   It is not the purpose of this section to induce you to infringe any patents or other property right claims or to contest validity of any such claims; this section has the sole purpose of protecting the integrity of the free software distribution system, which is implemented by public license practices. Many people have made generous contributions to the wide range of software distributed through that system in reliance on consistent application of that system; it is up to the author/donor to decide if he or she is willing to distribute software through any other system and a licensee cannot impose that choice.

   This section is intended to make thoroughly clear what is believed to be a consequence of the rest of this License.

8. If the distribution and/or use of the Program is restricted in certain countries either by patents or by copyrighted interfaces, the original copyright holder who places the Program under this License may add an explicit geographical distribution limitation excluding those countries, so that distribution is permitted only in or among countries not thus excluded. In such case, this License incorporates the limitation as if written in the body of this License.

9. The Free Software Foundation may publish revised and/or new versions of the General Public License from time to time. Such new versions will be similar in spirit to the present version, but may differ in detail to address new problems or concerns.

   Each version is given a distinguishing version number. If the Program specifies a version number of this License which applies to it and "any later version", you have the option of following the terms and conditions either of that version or of any later version published by the Free Software Foundation. If the Program does not specify a version number of this License, you may choose any version ever published by the Free Software Foundation.

10. If you wish to incorporate parts of the Program into other free programs whose distribution conditions are different, write to the author to ask for permission. For software which is copyrighted by the Free Software Foundation, write to the Free Software Foundation; we sometimes make exceptions for this. Our decision will be guided by the two goals of preserving the free status of all derivatives of our free software and of promoting the sharing and reuse of software generally.

Index